The Britannica Guide to
Sound and Light

PHYSICS EXPLAINED

The Britannica Guide to
Sound and Light

EDITED BY ERIK GREGERSEN, ASSOCIATE EDITOR,
SCIENCE AND TECHNOLOGY

Britannica
Educational Publishing

IN ASSOCIATION WITH

ROSEN
EDUCATIONAL SERVICES

Published in 2011 by Britannica Educational Publishing
(a trademark of Encyclopædia Britannica, Inc.)
in association with Rosen Educational Services, LLC
29 East 21st Street, New York, NY 10010.

First Edition

Britannica Educational Publishing
Michael I. Levy: Executive Editor
J.E. Luebering: Senior Manager
Marilyn L. Barton: Senior Coordinator, Production Control
Steven Bosco: Director, Editorial Technologies
Lisa S. Braucher: Senior Producer and Data Editor
Yvette Charboneau: Senior Copy Editor
Kathy Nakamura: Manager, Media Acquisition
Erik Gregersen: Associate Editor, Science and Technology

Rosen Educational Services
Nicholas Croce: Editor
Nelson Sá: Art Director
Cindy Reiman: Photography Manager
Matthew Cauli: Designer, Cover Design
Introduction by Jennifer Capuzzo

Library of Congress Cataloging-in-Publication Data

The Britannica guide to sound and light / edited by Erik Gregersen.
    p. cm. — (Physics explained)
"In association with Britannica Educational Publishing, Rosen Educational Services."
Includes bibliographical references and index.
ISBN 978-1-61530-300-7 (lib. bdg.)
1. Sound—Popular works. 2. Light—Popular works. I. Gregersen, Erik. II. Title: Guide to sound and light. III. Title: Sound and light.
QC225.3.G85 2011
534—dc22

2010013444

Manufactured in the United States of America

On the cover, p. iii: This graphic shows sound waves displayed on an oscilloscope. © *www.istockphoto.com/Clearview images*

On page x: Prisms are able to break up white light into its component colors. *Shutterstock.com*

On page xviii: This graphic shows sound waves displayed on an oscilloscope. *Shutterstock.com*

On pages 1, 57, 69, 81, 147, 199, 223, 287, 332, 334, 336, 340: Shown here are sound waves represented on the screen of a device that measures the output of sound. *Shutterstock.com*

CONTENTS

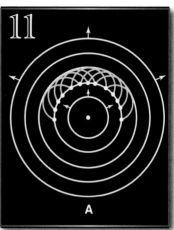

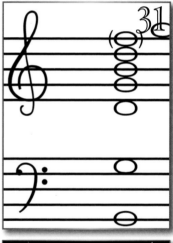

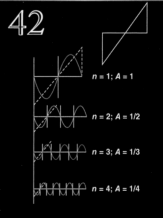

object

θ_1

θ_2

89

95

102

dark

bright

dark

bright

dark

bright

dark

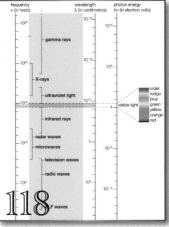

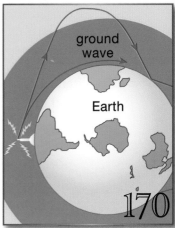

INTRODUCTION

The complex fields of light and sound may be rooted in complicated scientific theory, but their applications are felt in everyday activities. The simple acts of watching television and grocery shopping have changed tremendously due to advancements in optics and acoustics. Attending a concert can be more than just an entertaining experience when one considers the architectural, visual, and acoustical feats that all employ light and sound technology. The degree to which these branches of physics have impacted modern life is difficult to estimate, and the scientific exploration of their concepts continues to alter the world around us.

Understanding sound waves is critical to anyone beginning to study sound. Plane waves spread through space as a plane rather than as a sphere of increasing radius. Plane waves, for their simplicity, are good models for clarifying the behaviour of sound waves in general and understanding terms such as *wavelength*, *period*, and *frequency*. While a plane wave travels through space in a linear fashion, more typically sound waves travel spherically, increasing in radius as they disseminate. These circular waves travel forward, creating new wave fronts.

Not every waveform travels through the air as sound does. Two identical waves traveling on the same line in opposite directions form a standing wave. Both its shape and frequency match those of its two comprising waves. The bounded setting that helps produce a standing wave can be found in string and wind instruments. In a string instrument, for example, a string is stretched by fastening each end to a fixed point, and when the string is plucked, it vibrates and sends identical waves in opposite directions. Wind instruments act as bounded mediums for standing waves in a slightly different way. Instead of two separate waves composing the standing wave, it is the original wave driven into one end of the instrument that reflects off the other end and travels in the opposite direction of its original route that produces the standing wave.

By applying the same principles to the human voice, it is easy to understand how different vowel sounds are formed. The vocal column is similar to a wind instrument in both structure and function. It is a closed-tube resonator, where one end, the vocal folds, is closed and the other end, the mouth, is open. The throat, mouth, and lips change shape, impacting the frequencies of the formants, determined by the tension in the vocal folds. The resulting variations in amplitude create different vowel sounds.

Understanding how sound works is only part of the study of sound. Like the proverbial tree in the woods, there must be a receptor. As such, the ear's range of response is huge. The ear canal acts as a closed tube, and the threshold of hearing varies depending on sound frequencies. For a low frequency, such as that of a heartbeat, the threshold for hearing rises, which explains why the human ear cannot continually detect such sounds without outside devices. For the same reason, audio components contain a feature that increases the intensity of low frequencies when the volume or loudness intensifies. The musical result equalizes the proportion of treble and bass to the ear, even as the loudness increases.

The relationship between sound and hearing is analogous to the one between light and vision. Just as understanding how sound is created and disseminated is futile without the understanding of how the ear receives that information, a discussion of light behaviour needs to include some consideration of eye behaviour. It is that very relationship between the perception of light and the nature of light that perplexed the ancient world.

The ancient Greek philosophers made the first documented theories about the nature of light. Pythagoras, Empedocles, Epicurus, Euclid, and Ptolemy all proposed theories and conducted studies on how light and vision behaved. The nature of their studies differed in how each philosopher perceived the role of vision in the study of light. As a result, the human perception of light encumbered the study of the early theories of light.

The Islamic world furthered scientific progress after the decline of Greek philosophy. Leading theories on light shifted away from the Pythagorean model, and by the 11th century, mathematician and astronomer Ibn al-Haytham correctly reversed the Greek belief that light originated in the eye and found its way toward an object. While Ptolemy was one of the first to study the behaviour of light in terms of refraction and transmission, Ibn al-Haytham advanced those concepts by providing mathematical exploration of light reflection from spherical and parabolic mirrors. He also furthered the early Greek optical studies by providing advanced sketches of the human eye. The impact of these advances can be seen in Roger Bacon's work on the dissemination of light through simple lenses in the 13th century.

By the 17th century the focus of the scientific world returned to Europe. Dutch inventors introduced the world to compound microscopes and to the telescope. The advances in light study continued with Galileo's astronomical discoveries of Jupiter's moons and Saturn's rings, Johannes Kepler's mathematical work in the focusing properties of lenses, and Willebrord Snell and Pierre de Fermat's work on the path of light rays between two mediums. By the end of the century, Danish astronomer Ole Rømer estimated the value for the speed of light, discovering that its speed was finite. As these empirical studies took place, other leaders in scientific thought advanced the understanding of the physical behaviour of light. René Descartes understood light as a pressure wave, while English physicist Robert Hooke described light as a "rapid vibration of any medium through which it" passes and spreads.

By the advent of the 18th century Christiaan Huygens founded the first wave theory of light. Isaac Newton became the leading expert on the particle theory of light and discovered that white light consisted of different colours. The debate between the wave models of light and the particle models of light pervades the history of optical study. The field of geometrical optics focuses on the paths of light rays as they propagate through mediums and reflect, disperse, or come into focus. Electromagnetism studies light as a wave of electric and magnetic fields. The introduction of scientific work on the subatomic level in the 20th century further fueled the debate between wave and particle theories and led to the emergence of the quantum theory of light. This paradoxical study of light provides evidence that white light consists of particles with wavelike properties.

The study of the production, control, transmission, reception, and effects of sound is called acoustics. By studying the mechanical vibrations in the field of acoustics, physicists have contributed to developments in architecture, geology, and medicine. Architectural acoustics explores the concept of reverberation time. By studying the absorbers and reflectors in a room, an ideal construction can be reached for achieving optimal acoustic performances. If a room's purpose is to host a speaking engagement, for example, the clarity of that sound is improved by short reverberation time and the room is constructed to that end. On the other hand, longer reverberation time is ideal in a room hosting a music performance.

Of course, not all sounds are audible to human beings. Vibrations of frequencies greater than 20 kilohertz, or ultrasonics, are greater than the upper limit of the audible range for humans. Some animals and insects can hear sounds in the human ultrasonic frequency range, a discovery that has led to practical applications such as roach and rodent repellent. These devices utilize loud sounds in a high frequency range as a form of pest control.

Ultrasonics also plays a role in sonar applications as well. The term *sonar* comes from the combination of "sound navigation and ranging." By measuring the time it takes for transmitted pulses of sound or ultrasound to bounce off an object and return to the source, scientists and oceanographers have located lost ships, tracked submarines, uncovered explosive mines, and discovered optimal fishing spots for trade fishermen. Many burglar alarms also use ultrasonic technology.

The medical world has embraced ultrasonic technology as the nondestructive alternative to X-rays. Here again pulses of ultrasound are transmitted into the body, and the amount of time it takes for the ultrasound to reflect off the objects or organs it encounters reveals possible tumours or problems with blood flow. Heart valve defects and arterial diseases can be detected using ultrasonic techniques. In addition to diagnosis, doctors have also used ultrasound technology to treat ailments such as transmitting shock waves to destroy kidney stones and emitting heat from ultrasonic waves onto the area surrounding some cancerous tumours.

Just as some wave frequencies are greater than the range of human hearing, other wave frequencies fall below that range. These waves, known as infrasonics, occur in natural phenomena such as earthquakes, waterfalls, and volcanoes. Atmospheric infrasonics include wind and thunder. Some animals such as elephants are sensitive to infrasonics.

The flow of energy at the speed of light in the form of electric and magnetic fields that comprise electromagnetic waves is known as electromagnetic radiation.

Electromagnetic radiation frequencies range from the low values of radio waves, television waves, and microwaves to the higher values of ultraviolet light, X-rays, and gamma rays. The various forms of radiation travel in different patterns at different speeds and lend themselves to various modern applications. Radio waves, for example, travel as frequency bands and reflect back to Earth by the ionosphere. Doctors use radio waves in conjunction with magnetic fields to produce MRI pictures of the human body. Microwaves, on the other hand, travel between parabolic dish antennas. In addition to their well-known function of heating food, microwave radar can guide airplanes and ships. At the highest end of the electromagnetic radiation spectrum, gamma rays are between 10,000 and 10,000,000 times more energetic than visible light. Their highly penetrating power makes gamma rays simultaneously hazardous and beneficial. Careful modern applications include the sterilization of medical supplies and the destruction of organisms that cause food spoilage.

A laser stimulates atoms or molecules to emit light at specific wavelengths. The result is usually a narrow beam of radiation. Lasers were invented in 1960 and have gradually developed varied and useful applications. In construction, a laser's visible red beam can project straight lines for alignment and surveying. Doctors use lasers for eye surgeries as the favourable and less invasive alternative to cutting into the eye. Other innovations credited to laser technology include compact disc players, supermarket checkout scanners, and military target designators. The types of lasers vary depending on the medium that generates the beam. Crystals, glasses, gases, and liquids can all serve as laser media.

Optics is the comprehensive study of light, including its genesis, propagation, behaviour, and effects. Physical optics focuses on light's nature and properties, while geometrical optics deals with the laws and principles that direct and explain the properties of light media. An optical image occurs when a lens or mirror system reflects, refracts, or diffracts light waves to form a reproduction of an object. Images are described as either real or virtual, depending on where they are formed. A real image is formed outside of the instrument, such as on a video screen. A virtual image is formed inside the instrument and is seen by looking into an eyepiece, such as with a microscope.

Optical systems comprise various components such as lenses, mirrors, light sources, and fibre-optic bundles, to name a few. Each element of the system serves a specific function. Plane mirrors, for example, may be needed to reverse an image. Nonclassical imaging systems include bifocal and trifocal spectacle lenses. Modern innovations in optics have led to the application of holography in the nondestructive testing of materials, such as analyzing auto tires for structural flaws.

Advancements in the study of sound and light have impacted modern life. The fields of entertainment and communication have seen improvement in the way information is delivered. Progress in acoustics and optics has also improved military, maritime, and architectural functions. This volume will trace those developments and explore the laws and concepts that govern the fields of sound and light, providing biographical sketches of those who have impacted these two branches of physics.

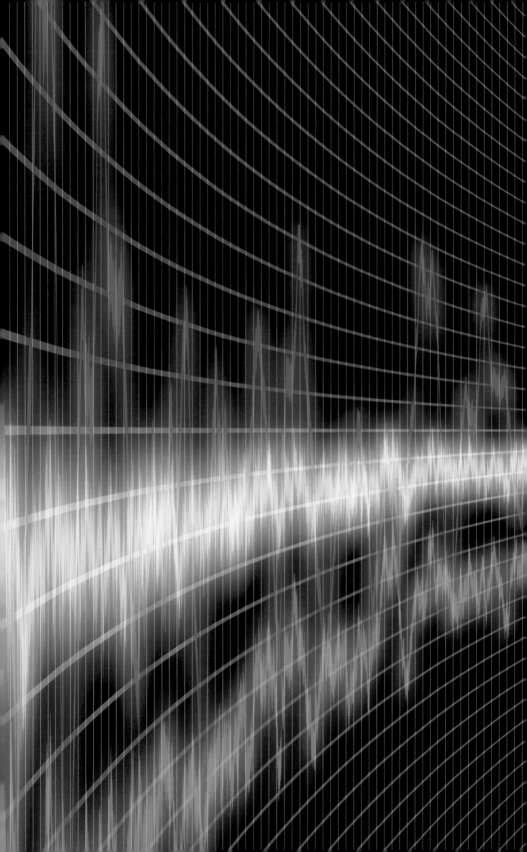

The strict physical definition of sound is a mechanical disturbance from a state of equilibrium that propagates through an elastic material medium. A purely subjective definition of sound is also possible, as that which is perceived by the ear, but such a definition is not particularly illuminating and is unduly restrictive, for it is useful to speak of sounds that cannot be heard by the human ear, such as those that are produced by dog whistles or by sonar equipment.

The study of sound should begin with the properties of sound waves. There are two basic types of wave, transverse and longitudinal, differentiated by the way in which the wave is propagated. In a transverse wave, such as the wave generated in a stretched rope when one end is wiggled back and forth, the motion that constitutes the wave is perpendicular, or transverse, to the direction (along the rope) in which the wave is moving. An important family of transverse waves is generated by electromagnetic sources such as light or radio, in which the electric and magnetic fields constituting the wave oscillate perpendicular to the direction of propagation.

Sound propagates through air or other mediums as a longitudinal wave, in which the mechanical vibration constituting the wave occurs along the direction of propagation of the wave. A longitudinal wave can be created in a coiled spring by squeezing several of the turns together to form a compression and then releasing them, allowing the compression to travel the length of the spring. Air can be viewed as being composed of layers analogous to such

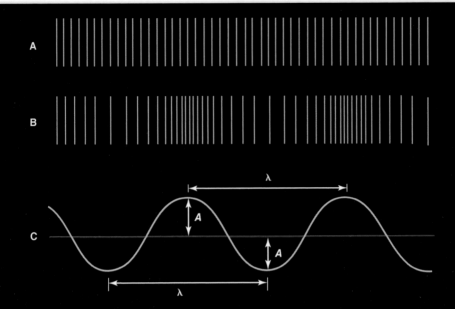

Graphic representations of a sound wave. (A) Air at equilibrium, in the absence of a sound wave; (B) compressions and rarefactions that constitute a sound wave; (C) transverse representation of the wave, showing amplitude (A) and wavelength (λ). Encyclopædia Britannica, Inc.

coils, with a sound wave propagating as layers of air "push" and "pull" at one another much like the compression moving down the spring.

A sound wave thus consists of alternating compressions and rarefactions, or regions of high pressure and low pressure, moving at a certain speed. Put another way, it consists of a periodic (that is, oscillating or vibrating) variation of pressure occurring around the equilibrium pressure prevailing at a particular time and place.

PLANE WAVES

A discussion of sound waves and their propagation can begin with an examination of a plane wave of a single frequency passing through the air. A plane wave is a wave that propagates through space as a plane, rather than as a sphere of increasing radius. As such, it is not perfectly representative of sound. A wave of single frequency would be heard as a pure sound such as that generated by a tuning fork that has been lightly struck. As a theoretical model, it helps to elucidate many of the properties of a sound wave.

WAVELENGTH, PERIOD, AND FREQUENCY

If represented by a sinusoidal curve, the pressure variation in a sound wave repeats itself in space over a specific distance. This distance is known as the wavelength of the sound, usually measured in metres and represented by λ. As the wave propagates through the air, one full wavelength takes a certain time period to pass a specific point in space; this period, represented by T, is usually measured in fractions of a second. In addition, during each one-second time interval, a certain number of wavelengths pass a point in space. Known as the frequency of the sound wave, the number of wavelengths passing per second is traditionally measured in hertz or kilohertz and is represented by f.

There is an inverse relation between a wave's frequency and its period, such that

$$fT = 1 \text{ or } f = \frac{1}{T}.$$ (1)

This means that sound waves with high frequencies have short periods, while those with low frequencies have long periods. For example, a sound wave with a frequency of 20 hertz would have a period of 0.05 second (i.e., 20 wavelengths/second × 0.05 second/wavelength = 1), while a sound wave of 20 kilohertz would have a period of 0.00005 second (20,000 wavelengths/second × 0.00005 second/wavelength = 1). Between 20 hertz and 20 kilohertz lies the frequency range of hearing for humans. The physical property of frequency is perceived physiologically as pitch, so that the higher the frequency, the higher the perceived pitch. There is also a relation between the wavelength of a sound wave, its frequency or period, and the speed of the wave (S), such that

$$S = f\lambda = \frac{\lambda}{T}.$$
(2)

AMPLITUDE AND INTENSITY

The equilibrium value of pressure is equal to the atmospheric pressure that would prevail in the absence of the sound wave. With passage of the compressions and rarefactions that constitute the sound wave, there would occur a fluctuation above and below atmospheric pressure. The magnitude of this fluctuation from equilibrium is known as the amplitude of the sound wave; measured in pascals, or newtons per square metre, it is represented by the letter A. The displacement or disturbance of a plane sound wave can be described mathematically by the general equation for wave motion, which is written in simplified form as

$$y(x, t) = A \sin 2\pi(ft - x/\lambda).$$
(3)

This equation describes a sinusoidal wave that repeats itself after a distance λ moving to the right $(+ x)$ with a velocity given by equation (2).

The amplitude of a sound wave determines its intensity, which in turn is perceived by the ear as loudness. Acoustic intensity is defined as the average rate of energy transmission per unit area perpendicular to the direction of propagation of the wave. Its relation with amplitude can be written as

$$I = \frac{A^2}{2\rho S},$$

(4)

where ρ is the equilibrium density of the air (measured in kilograms per cubic metre) and S is the speed of sound (in metres per second). Intensity (I) is measured in watts per square metre, the watt being the standard unit of power in electrical or mechanical usage.

The value of atmospheric pressure under "standard atmospheric conditions" is generally given as about 10^5 pascals, or 10^5 newtons per square metre. The minimum amplitude of pressure variation that can be sensed by the human ear is about 10^{-5} pascal, and the pressure amplitude at the threshold of pain is about 10 pascals, so the pressure variation in sound waves is very small compared with the pressure of the atmosphere. Under these conditions a sound wave propagates in a linear manner—that is, it continues to propagate through the air with very little loss, dispersion, or change of shape. However, when the amplitude of the wave reaches about 100 pascals (approximately one one-thousandth the pressure of the atmosphere), significant nonlinearities develop in the propagation of the wave.

Nonlinearity arises from the peculiar effects on air pressure caused by a sinusoidal displacement of air molecules. When the vibratory motion constituting a wave is small, the increase and decrease in pressure are also small and are very nearly equal. But when the motion of the wave is large, each compression generates an excess pressure of greater amplitude than the decrease in pressure caused by each rarefaction. This can be predicted by the ideal gas law, which states that increasing the volume of a gas by one-half decreases its pressure by only one-third, while decreasing its volume by one-half increases the pressure by a factor of two. The result is a net excess in pressure—a phenomenon that is significant only for waves with amplitudes above about 100 pascals.

The Decibel Scale

The ear mechanism is able to respond to both very small and very large pressure waves by virtue of being nonlinear; that is, it responds much more efficiently to sounds of very small amplitude than to sounds of very large amplitude. Because of the enormous nonlinearity of the ear in sensing pressure waves, a nonlinear scale is convenient in describing the intensity of sound waves. Such a scale is provided by the sound intensity level, or decibel level, of a sound wave, which is defined by the equation

$$L = 10 \log\left(\frac{I}{I_0}\right). \tag{5}$$

Here L represents decibels, which correspond to an arbitrary sound wave of intensity I, measured in watts per square metre. The reference intensity I_o, corresponding to a level of 0 decibels, is approximately the intensity of a wave of 1,000 hertz frequency at the threshold of hearing—about 10^{-12} watt per square metre. Because the decibel scale mirrors the function of the ear more accurately than a linear scale, it has several advantages in practical use.

A fundamental feature of this type of logarithmic scale is that each unit of increase in the decibel scale corresponds to an increase in absolute intensity by a constant multiplicative factor.

Thus, an increase in absolute intensity from 10^{-12} to 10^{-11} watt per square metre corresponds to an increase of 10 decibels, as does an increase from 10^{-1} to 1 watt per square metre. The correlation between the absolute intensity of a sound wave and its decibel level is interesting.

When the defining level of 0 decibel (10^{-12} watt per square metre) is taken to be at the threshold of hearing for a sound wave with a frequency of 1,000 hertz, then 130 decibels (10 watts per square metre) corresponds to the threshold of feeling, or the threshold of pain. (Sometimes the threshold of pain is given as 120 decibels, or 1 watt per square metre.)

Although the decibel scale is nonlinear, it is directly measurable, and sound-level metres are available for that purpose. Sound levels for audio systems, architectural acoustics, and other industrial applications are most often quoted in decibels.

THE SPEED OF SOUND

For longitudinal waves such as sound, wave velocity is in general given as the square root of the ratio of the elastic modulus of the medium (that is, the ability of the medium to be compressed by an external force) to its density:

$$S = \sqrt{\frac{B}{\rho}} .$$

(6)

Here ρ is the density and B the bulk modulus (the ratio of the applied pressure to the change in volume per unit volume of the medium).

IN GASES

In gas mediums this equation is modified to

$$S = \sqrt{\frac{1}{\rho K}} ,$$

(7)

where K is the compressibility of the gas. Compressibility (K) is the reciprocal of the bulk modulus (B), as in

$$K = \frac{1}{B} .$$

(8)

Using the appropriate gas laws, wave velocity can be calculated in two ways, in relation to pressure or in relation to temperature:

$$S = \sqrt{\frac{\gamma p}{\rho}} ;$$

(9)

or

$$S = \sqrt{\frac{\gamma R \theta}{M}} \ .$$

(10)

Here p is the equilibrium pressure of the gas in pascals, ρ is its equilibrium density in kilograms per cubic metre at pressure p, θ is absolute temperature in kelvins, R is the gas constant per mole, M is the molecular weight of the gas, and γ is the ratio of the specific heat at a constant pressure to the specific heat at a constant volume,

$$\gamma = \sqrt{\frac{C_p}{C_v}} \ .$$

(11)

Values for γ for various gases are given in many physics textbooks and reference works.

Equation (10) states that the speed of sound depends only on absolute temperature and not on pressure, since, if the gas behaves as an ideal gas, then its pressure and density, as shown in equation (9), will be proportional.

This means that the speed of sound does not change between locations at sea level and high in the mountains and that the pitch of wind instruments at the same temperature is the same anywhere. In addition, both equations (9) and (10) are independent of frequency, indicating that the speed of sound is in fact the same at all frequencies—that is, there is no dispersion of a sound wave as it propagates through air. One assumption here is that the gas behaves as an ideal gas. However, gases at very high pressures no longer behave like an ideal gas, and this results in some absorption and dispersion. In such cases equations (9) and (10) must be modified, as they are in advanced books on the subject.

In Liquids

For a liquid medium, the appropriate modulus is the bulk modulus, so that the speed of sound is equal to the square root of the ratio of the bulk modulus (B) to the equilibrium density (ρ), as shown in equation (6). The speed of sound in liquids varies slightly with temperature—a variation that is accounted for by empirical corrections to equation (6), as is indicated in the values given for water.

In Solids

For a long, thin solid the appropriate modulus is the Young's, or stretching, modulus (the ratio of the applied stretching force per unit area of the solid to the resulting change in length per unit length; named for the English physicist and physician Thomas Young). The speed of sound, therefore, is

$$S = \sqrt{\frac{Y}{\rho}} \,, \tag{12}$$

where Y is the Young's modulus and ρ is the density. There are various different speeds of sound in different types of solids.

In the case of a three-dimensional solid, in which the wave is traveling outward in spherical waves, the above expression becomes more complicated. Both the shear modulus, represented by η, and the bulk modulus B play a role in the elasticity of the medium:

$$S = \sqrt{\frac{(B + 4\eta/3)}{\rho}} \, .$$

(13)

CIRCULAR AND SPHERICAL WAVES

The above discussion of the propagation of sound waves begins with a simplifying assumption that the wave exists as a plane wave. In most real cases, however, a wave originating at some source does not move in a straight line but expands in a series of spherical wavefronts. The

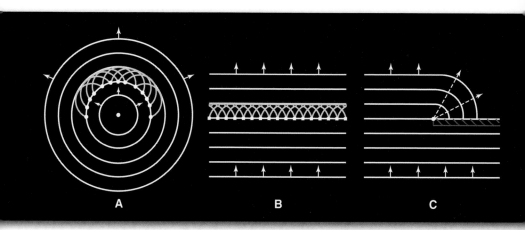

Huygens' wavelets. Originating along the fronts of (A) circular waves and (B) plane waves, wavelets recombine to produce the propagating wave front. (C) The diffraction of sound around a corner arising from Huygens' wavelets. Encyclopædia Britannica, Inc.

fundamental mechanism for this propagation is known as Huygens' principle, according to which every point on a wave is a source of spherical waves in its own right. The result is a Huygens' wavelet construction. The insightful point suggested by the Dutch physicist Christiaan Huygens is that all such wavelets form a new coherent wave that moves along at the speed of sound to form the next wave in the sequence. In addition, just as the wavelets add up in the forward direction to create a new wavefront, they also cancel one another, or interfere destructively, in the backward direction, so that the waves continue to propagate only in the forward direction.

The principle behind the adding up of Huygens' wavelets, involving a fundamental difference between matter and waves, is known as the principle of superposition. The old saying that no two things can occupy the same space at the same time is correct when applied to matter, but it does not apply to waves. Indeed, an infinite number of waves can occupy the same space at the same time; furthermore, they do this without affecting one another, so that each wave retains its own character independent of how many other waves are present at the same point and time. A radio or television antenna can receive the signal of any single frequency to which it is tuned, unaffected by the existence of any others. Likewise, the sound waves of two people talking may cross each other, but the sound of each voice is unaffected by the waves' having been simultaneously at the same point.

Superposition plays a key role in many of the wave properties of sound discussed in this section. It is also fundamental to the addition of Fourier components of a wave in order to obtain a complex wave shape.

Attenuation

A plane wave of a single frequency in theory will propagate forever with no change or loss. This is not the case with a circular or spherical wave, however. One of the most important properties of this type of wave is a decrease in intensity as the wave propagates. The mathematical explanation of this principle, which derives as much from geometry as from physics, is known as the inverse square law.

The Inverse Square Law

As a circular wave front (such as that created by dropping a stone onto a water surface) expands, its energy is distributed over an increasingly larger circumference. The intensity, or energy per unit of length along the circumference of the circle, will therefore decrease in an inverse relationship with the growing radius of the circle, or distance from the source of the wave. In the same way, as a spherical wave front expands, its energy is distributed over a larger and larger surface area. Because the surface area of a sphere is proportional to the square of its radius, the intensity of the wave is inversely proportional to the square of the radius. This geometric relation between the growing radius of a wave and its decreasing intensity is what gives rise to the inverse square law.

The decrease in intensity of a spherical wave as it propagates outward can also be expressed in decibels. Each factor of two in distance from the source leads to a decrease in intensity by a factor of four. For example, a factor of four decrease in a wave's intensity is equivalent to a decrease of six decibels, so that a spherical wave attenuates at a rate of six decibels for each factor of two increase in distance from the source. If a wave is propagating as a hemispherical wave above an absorbing surface, the intensity will be further reduced by a factor of two near the surface because of the lack of contributions of Huygens' wavelets from the missing hemisphere. Thus, the intensity of a wave propagating along a level, perfectly absorbent floor falls off at the rate of 12 decibels for each factor of two in distance from the source. This additional attenuation leads to the necessity of sloping the seats of an auditorium in order to retain a good sound level in the rear.

SOUND ABSORPTION

In addition to the geometric decrease in intensity caused by the inverse square law, a small part of a sound wave is lost to the air or other medium through various physical processes. One important process is the direct conduction of the vibration into the medium as heat, caused by the conversion of the coherent molecular motion of the sound wave into incoherent molecular motion in the air or other absorptive material. Another cause is the viscosity of a fluid medium (i.e., a gas or liquid). These two physical causes combine to produce the classical attenuation of a sound wave. This type of attenuation is proportional to the square of the sound wave's frequency, as expressed in the formula α/f^2, where α is the attenuation coefficient of the medium and f is the wave frequency. The amplitude of an attenuated wave is then given by

$$A(x) = A_0 e^{-\alpha x}, \tag{14}$$

where A_0 is the original amplitude of the wave and $A(x)$ is the amplitude after it has propagated a distance x through the medium.

There are different sound-absorption coefficients for different gases. The magnitudes of the coefficients indicate that, although attenuation is rather small for audible frequencies, it can become extremely large for high-frequency ultrasonic waves. Attenuation of sound in air also varies with temperature and humidity.

Because less sound is absorbed in solids and liquids than in gases, sounds can propagate over much greater distances in these mediums. For instance, the great range over which certain sea mammals can communicate is made possible partially by the low attenuation of sound in water. In addition, because absorption increases with frequency, it becomes very difficult for ultrasonic waves to penetrate a dense medium. This is a persistent limitation on the development of high-frequency ultrasonic applications.

Most sound-absorbing materials are nonlinear, in that they do not absorb the same fraction of acoustic waves of all frequencies. In architectural acoustics, an enormous effort is expended to use construction materials that absorb undesirable frequencies but reflect desired frequencies. Absorption of undesirable sound, such as that from machines in factories, is critical to the health of workers, and noise control in architectural and industrial acoustics has expanded to become an important field of environmental engineering.

DIFFRACTION

A direct result of Huygens' wavelets is the property of diffraction, the capacity of sound waves to bend around corners and to spread out after passing through a small hole or slit. If a barrier is placed in the path of half of a plane wave, the part of the wave passing just by the barrier will propagate in a series of Huygens' wavelets, causing the wave to spread into the shadow region behind the barrier. In light waves, wavelengths are very small compared with the size of everyday objects, so that very little diffraction occurs and a relatively clear shadow can be formed. The wavelengths of sound waves, on the other hand, are more nearly equal to the size of everyday objects, so that they readily diffract.

Diffraction of sound is helpful in the case of audio systems, in which sound emanating from loudspeakers spreads out and reflects off of walls to fill a room. It is also the reason why "sound beams" cannot generally be produced like light beams. On the other hand, the ability of a sound wave to diffract decreases as frequency rises and wavelength shrinks. This means that the lower frequencies of a voice bend around a corner more readily than the higher frequencies, giving the diffracted voice a "muffled" sound. Also, because the wavelengths of ultrasonic waves become extremely small at high frequencies, it is possible to create a beam of ultrasound. Ultrasonic beams have become very useful in modern medicine.

The scattering of a sound wave is a reflection of some part of the wave off of an obstacle around which the rest of the wave propagates and diffracts. The way in which the scattering occurs depends upon the relative size of the obstacle and the wavelength of the scattering wave. If the wavelength is large in relation to the obstacle, then the wave will pass by the obstacle virtually unaffected. In this case, the only part of the wave to be scattered will be the tiny part that strikes the obstacle; the rest of the wave, owing to its large wavelength, will diffract around the obstacle in a series of Huygens' wavelets and remain unaffected. If the wavelength is small in relation to the obstacle, the wave will not diffract strongly, and a shadow will be formed similar to the optical shadow produced by a small light source. In extreme cases, arising primarily with high-frequency ultrasound, the formalism of ray optics often used in lenses and mirrors can be conveniently employed.

If the size of the obstacle is the same order of magnitude as the wavelength, diffraction may occur, and this may result in interference among the diffracted waves. This would create regions of greater and lesser sound intensity, called acoustic shadows, after the wave has propagated past the obstacle. Control of such acoustic shadows becomes important in the acoustics of auditoriums.

REFRACTION

Diffraction involves the bending or spreading out of a sound wave in a single medium, in which the speed of sound is constant. Another important case in which sound waves bend or spread out is called refraction. This phenomenon involves the bending of a sound wave owing to changes in the wave's speed. Refraction is the reason why ocean waves approach a shore parallel to the beach and why glass lenses can be used to focus light waves. An important refraction of sound is caused by the natural temperature gradient of the atmosphere. Under normal conditions the Sun heats the ground and the ground heats the adjacent air. The heated air then cools as it rises, creating a gradient in which atmospheric temperature decreases with elevation by an amount known as the adiabatic lapse rate. Because sound waves propagate faster in warm air, they travel faster closer to the ground. This greater speed of sound in warmed air near the ground creates Huygens' wavelets that also spread faster near the ground. Because a sound wave propagates in a direction perpendicular to the wave front formed by all the Huygens' wavelets, sound under these conditions tends to refract upward and become "lost." The sound of thunder created by lightning may be refracted upward so strongly that a shadow region is created in which the lightning can be seen but the thunder cannot be heard. This typically occurs at a horizontal distance of about 22.5 km (14 miles) from a lightning bolt about 4 km (2.5 miles) high.

At night or during periods of dense cloud cover, a temperature inversion occurs; the temperature of the air increases with elevation, and sound waves are refracted back down to the ground. Temperature inversion is the reason why sounds can be heard much more clearly over longer distances at night than during the day—an effect often incorrectly attributed to the psychological result of nighttime quiet. The effect is enhanced if the sound is propagated over water, allowing sound to be heard remarkably clearly over great distances.

Refraction is also observable on windy days. Wind, moving faster at greater heights, causes a change in the effective speed of sound with distance above ground. When one speaks with the wind, the sound wave is refracted back down to the ground, and one's voice is able to "carry" farther than on a still day. When one speaks into the wind, however, the sound wave is refracted upward, away from the ground, and the voice is "lost."

Another example of sound refraction occurs in the ocean. Under normal circumstances the temperature of the ocean decreases with depth, resulting in the downward refraction of a sound wave originating under water—just the opposite of the shadow effect in air described above. Many marine biologists believe that this refraction enhances the propagation of the sounds of marine mammals such as dolphins and whales, allowing them to communicate with one another over enormous distances.

For ships such as submarines located near the surface of the water, this refraction creates shadow regions, limiting their ability to locate distant vessels.

REFLECTION

A property of waves and sound quite familiar in the phenomenon of echoes is reflection. This plays a critical role in room and auditorium acoustics, in large part determining the adequacy of a concert hall for musical performance or other functions. In the case of light waves passing from air through a glass plate, close inspection shows that some of the light is reflected at each of the air-glass interfaces while the rest passes through the glass. This same phenomenon occurs whenever a sound wave passes from one medium into another—that is, whenever the speed of sound changes or the way in which the sound propagates is substantially modified.

The direction of propagation of a wave is perpendicular to the front formed by all the Huygens' wavelets. As a plane wave reflects off some reflector, the reflector directs the wave fronts formed by the Huygens' wavelets just as a light reflector directs light "rays." The same law of reflection is followed for both sound and light, so that focusing a sound wave is equivalent to focusing a light ray.

Reflectors of appropriate shape are used for a variety of purposes or effects. For example, a parabolic reflector will focus a parallel wave of sound onto a specific point, allowing a very weak sound to be more easily heard. Such reflectors are used in parabolic microphones to collect sound from a distant source or to choose a location from which sound is to be observed and then focus it onto a microphone. An elliptical shape, on the other hand, can be used to focus sound from one point onto another—an arrangement called a whispering chamber. Domes in cathedrals and capitols closely approximate the shape of an ellipse, so that such buildings often possess focal points and function as a type of whispering chamber. Concert halls must avoid the smooth, curved shape of ellipses and parabolas, because strong echoes or focusing of sound from one point to another are undesirable in an auditorium.

IMPEDANCE

One of the important physical characteristics relating to the propagation of sound is the acoustic impedance of the medium in which the sound wave travels. Acoustic impedance (Z) is given by the ratio of the wave's acoustic pressure (p) to its volume velocity (U):

$$Z = \frac{p}{U}.$$

(15)

Like its analogue, electrical impedance (or electrical resistance), acoustic impedance is a measure of the ease with which a sound wave propagates through a particular medium. Also like electrical impedance, acoustic impedance involves several different effects applying to different situations. For example, specific acoustic impedance (z), the ratio of acoustic pressure to particle speed, is an inherent property of the medium and of the nature of the wave. Acoustic impedance, the ratio of pressure to volume velocity, is equal to the specific acoustic impedance per unit area. Specific acoustic impedance is useful in discussing waves in confined mediums, such as tubes and horns. For the simplest case of a plane wave, specific acoustic impedance is the product of the equilibrium density (ρ) of the medium and the wave speed (S):

$$z = \rho S. \tag{16}$$

The unit of specific acoustic impedance is the pascal second per metre, often called the rayl, after Lord Rayleigh. The unit of acoustic impedance is the pascal second per cubic metre, called an acoustic ohm, by analogy to electrical impedance.

IMPEDANCE MISMATCH

Mediums in which the speed of sound is different generally have differing acoustic impedances, so that, when a sound wave strikes an interface between the two, it encounters an impedance mismatch. As a result, some of the wave reflects while some is transmitted into the second medium. In the case of the well-known bell-in-vacuum experiment, the impedance mismatches between the bell and the air and between the air and the jar result in very little transmission of sound when the air is at low pressure.

The efficiency with which a sound source radiates sound is enhanced by reducing the impedance mismatch between the source and the outside air. For example, if a tuning fork is struck and held in the air, it will be nearly inaudible because of the inability of the vibrations of the tuning fork to radiate efficiently to the air. Touching the tuning fork to a wooden plate such as a tabletop will enhance the sound by providing better coupling between the vibrating tuning fork and the air. This principle is used in the violin and the piano, in which the vibrations of the strings are transferred first to the back and belly of the violin or to the piano's sounding board, and then to the air.

Acoustic Filtration

Filtration of sound plays an important part in the design of air-handling systems. In order to attenuate the level of sound from blower motors and other sources of vibration, regions of larger or smaller cross-sectional area are inserted into air ducts. The impedance mismatch introduced into a duct by a change in the area of the duct or by the addition of a side branch reflects undesirable frequencies, as determined by the size and shape of the variation. A region of either larger or smaller area will function as a low-pass filter, reflecting high frequencies; an opening or series of openings will function as a high-pass filter, removing low frequencies. Some automobile mufflers make use of this type of filter.

A connected spherical cavity, forming what is called a band-pass filter, actually functions as a type of band

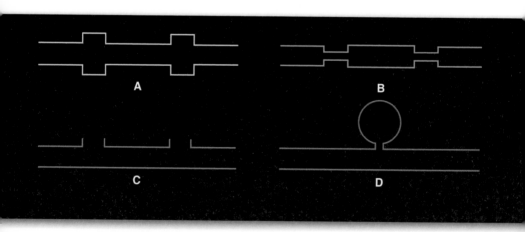

Acoustic filters typically used in air-handling systems. (A) and (B) Low-pass filters; (C) a high-pass filter; (D) a band-pass filter, which actually filters out vibrations within a narrow frequency range. Encyclopædia Britannica, Inc.

absorber or notch filter, removing a band of frequencies around the resonant frequency of the cavity.

Interference

Like waves in the ocean, sound waves can interact with other sound waves. The particular manner in which sound waves can combine is known as interference.

Constructive and Destructive

Two identical waves in the same place at the same time can interfere constructively if they are in phase or destructively if they are out of phase. "Phase" is a term that refers to the time relationship between two periodic signals. "In phase" means that they are vibrating together, while "out of phase" means that their vibrations are opposite. Opposite vibrations added together cancel each other.

Constructive interference leads to an increase in the amplitude of the sum wave, while destructive interference can lead to the total cancellation of the contributing waves. An interesting example of both interference and diffraction of sound, called the "speaker and baffle" experiment, involves a small loudspeaker and a large, square wooden sheet with a circular hole in it the size of the speaker. When music is played on the loudspeaker, sound waves from the front and back of the speaker, which are out of phase, diffract into the entire region around the speaker. The two waves interfere destructively and cancel each other, particularly at very low frequencies, where the wavelength is longest and the diffraction is thus greatest. When the speaker is held up behind the baffle, though, the sounds can no longer diffract and mix while they are out of phase, and as a consequence the intensity increases enormously. This experiment illustrates why loudspeakers are often mounted in boxes, so that the sound from the back cannot interfere with the sound from the front. In a home stereo system, when two speakers are wired properly, their sound waves are in phase along an antinodal line between the two speakers and in the area of best listening. If the two speakers are wired incorrectly—the wires being reversed on one of the speakers—their waves will be out of phase in the area of best listening and will interfere destructively—especially at low frequencies, so that the bass frequencies will be strongly attenuated.

A common application of destructive interference is the modern electronic automobile muffler. This device senses the sound propagating down the exhaust pipe and creates a matching sound with opposite phase. These two sounds interfere destructively, muffling the noise of the engine. Another application is in industrial noise control. This involves sensing the ambient sound in a workplace, electronically reproducing a sound with the opposite phase, and then introducing that sound into the environment so that it interferes destructively with the ambient sound to reduce the overall sound level.

BEATS

An important occurrence of the interference of waves is in the phenomenon of beats. In the simplest case, beats result when two sinusoidal sound waves of equal amplitude and very nearly equal frequencies mix. The frequency of the resulting sound (F) would be the average of the two original frequencies (f_1 and f_2):

$$F = \frac{f_1 + f_2}{2}.$$

(17)

The amplitude or intensity of the combined signal would rise and fall at a rate (f_b) equal to the difference between the two original frequencies,

$$f_b = f_1 - f_2,$$ (18)

where f_1 is greater than f_2.

Beats are useful in tuning musical instruments to each other: the farther the instruments are out of tune, the faster the beats. Other types of beats are also of interest. Second-order beats occur between the two notes of a mistuned octave, and binaural beats involve beating between tones presented separately to the two ears, so that they do not mix physically.

THE DOPPLER EFFECT

The Doppler effect is a change in the frequency of a tone that occurs by virtue of relative motion between the source of sound and the observer. When the source and the observer are moving closer together, the perceived frequency is higher than the normal frequency, or the frequency heard when the observer is at rest with respect to the source. When the source and the observer are moving farther apart, the perceived frequency is lower than the normal frequency. For the case of a moving source, one example is the falling frequency of a train whistle as the train passes a crossing. In the case of a moving observer, a passenger on the train would hear the warning bells at the crossing drop in frequency as the train speeds by.

For the case of motion along a line, where the source moves with speed v_s and the observer moves with speed v_o

through still air in which the speed of sound is S, the general equation describing the change in frequency heard by the observer is

$$f_o = f_s \frac{S + v_o}{S - v_s}.$$

(19)

In this equation the speeds of the source and the observer will be negative if the relative motion between the source and observer is moving them apart, and they will be positive if the source and observer are moving together.

From this equation, it can be deduced that a Doppler effect will always be heard as long as the relative speed between the source and observer is less than the speed of sound. The speed of sound is constant with respect to the air in which it is propagating, so that, if the observer moves away from the source at a speed greater than the speed of sound, nothing will be heard. If the source and the observer are moving with the same speed in the same direction, v_o and v_s will be equal in magnitude but with the opposite sign; the frequency of the sound will therefore remain unchanged, like the sound of a train whistle as heard by a passenger on the moving train.

SONIC BOOMS

If the speed of the source is greater than the speed of sound, another type of wave phenomenon will occur: the sonic boom. A sonic boom is a type of shock wave that occurs when waves generated by a source over a period of time add together coherently, creating an unusually strong sum wave. An analogue to a sonic boom is the V-shaped bow wave created in water by a motorboat when its speed is greater than the speed of the waves. In the case of an aircraft flying faster than the speed of sound (about 1,230 km [764 miles] per hour), the shock wave takes the form of a cone in three-dimensional space called the Mach cone. The Mach number is defined as the ratio of the speed of the aircraft to the speed of sound. The higher the Mach number—that is, the faster the aircraft—the smaller the angle of the Mach cone.

STANDING WAVES

This section focuses on waves in bounded mediums—in particular, standing waves in such systems as stretched strings, air columns, and stretched membranes. The principles discussed here are directly applicable to the operation of string and wind instruments.

When two identical waves move in opposite directions along a line, they form a standing wave—that is, a wave form that does not travel through space or along a string even though (or because) it is made up of two oppositely traveling waves. The resulting standing wave is sinusoidal, like its two component waves, and it oscillates at the same frequency. An easily visualized standing wave can be created by stretching a rubber band between two fixed points, displacing its centre slightly, and releasing it so that it vibrates back and forth between two extremes. In musical instruments, a standing wave can be generated by driving the oscillating medium (such as the reeds of a woodwind) at one end; the standing waves are then created not by two separate component waves but by the original wave and its reflections off the ends of the vibrating system.

IN STRETCHED STRINGS

For a stretched string of a given mass per unit length (μ) and under a given tension (F), the speed (v) of a wave in the string is given by the following equation:

$$v = \sqrt{\frac{F}{\mu}}\,.$$

(20)

When a string of a given length (L) is plucked gently in the middle, a vibration is produced with a wavelength (λ) that is twice the length of the string:

$$\lambda = 2L.$$

(21)

FUNDAMENTALS AND HARMONICS

The frequency (f_1) of this vibration can then be obtained by the following adaptation of equation (20):

$$f_1 = \frac{v}{\lambda} = \left(\frac{1}{2L}\right)\sqrt{\frac{F}{\mu}}\,.$$

(22)

As the vibration that has the lowest frequency for that particular type and length of string under a specific tension, this frequency is known as the fundamental, or first harmonic.

Additional standing waves can be created in a stretched string. The fundamental is labeled $n = 1$. Because

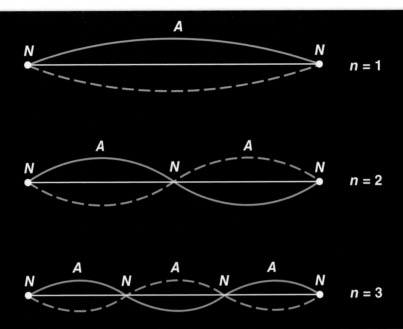

The first three harmonic standing waves in a stretched string. Nodes (N) and antinodes (A) are marked. The harmonic number (n) for each standing wave is given on the right. Encyclopædia Britannica, Inc.

a string must be stretched by holding it in place at its ends, each end is fixed, and there can be no motion of the string at these points. The ends are called nodal points, or nodes, and labeled *N*. In the centre of the string is the point at which the string vibrates with its greatest amplitude; this is called an antinodal point, or antinode, and labeled *A*.

For the next two vibrational modes, the string is divided into equal segments called loops. Each loop is one-half wavelength long, and the wavelength is related to the length of the string by the following equation:

$$\lambda_n = \frac{2L}{n}.$$ (23)

Here the integer n equals the number of loops in the standing wave. From equation (22) above, the frequencies of these vibrations (f_n) can be deduced as

$$f_n = \frac{v}{\lambda_n} = \left(\frac{n}{2L}\right)\sqrt{\frac{F}{\mu}} \; ; \tag{24}$$

or, in terms of the fundamental frequency f_1,

$$f_n = n f_1 . \tag{25}$$

Here n is called the harmonic number, because the sequence of frequencies existing as standing waves in the string are integral multiples, or harmonics, of the fundamental frequency.

In the second harmonic, which is labeled $n = 2$, the string vibrates in two sections, so that the string is one full wavelength long. Because the wavelength of the second harmonic is one-half that of the fundamental, its frequency is twice that of the fundamental. Similarly, the frequency of the third harmonic (labeled $n = 3$) is three times that of the fundamental.

OVERTONES

Another term sometimes applied to these standing waves is overtones. The second harmonic is the first overtone, the third harmonic is the second overtone, and so forth. *Overtone* is a term generally applied to any higher-frequency standing wave, whereas the term *harmonic* is reserved for those cases in which the frequencies of the

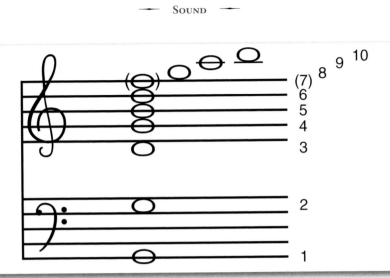

The first 10 notes in the overtone series of G$_2$. The harmonic number of each note is to the right. Encyclopædia Britannica, Inc.

overtones are integral multiples of the frequency of the fundamental. Overtones or harmonics are also called resonances. In the phenomenon of resonance, a system that vibrates at some natural frequency is subjected to external vibrations of the same frequency; as a result, the system resonates, or vibrates at a large amplitude.

The sequence of frequencies defined by equation (25), known as the overtone series, plays an important part in the analysis of musical instruments and musical tone quality. During the Middle Ages in Europe, keyboard instruments were sometimes tuned to a scale in which the primary chords were true frequencies of the overtone series. This tuning method, called just intonation, provided beatless chords, because the notes in the chord were members of a single overtone series.

MERSENNE'S LAWS

From equation (22) can be derived three "laws" detailing how the fundamental frequency of a stretched string depends on the length, tension, and mass per unit length of the string. Known as Mersenne's laws, these can be written as follows:

1. The fundamental frequency of a stretched string is inversely proportional to the length of the string, keeping the tension and the mass per unit length of the string constant:

$$f_1 \propto \frac{1}{L}. \qquad (26)$$

2. The fundamental frequency of a stretched string is directly proportional to the square root of the tension in the string, keeping the length and the mass per unit length of the string constant:

$$f_1 \propto \sqrt{F}. \qquad (27)$$

3. The fundamental frequency of a stretched string is inversely proportional to the mass per unit length of the string, keeping the length and the tension in the string constant:

$$f_1 \propto \frac{1}{\sqrt{\mu}}. \qquad (28)$$

Mersenne's laws help explain the construction and operation of string instruments. The lower strings of a guitar or violin are made with a greater mass per unit length, and the higher strings made thinner and lighter. This means that the tension in all the strings can be made more nearly the same, resulting in a more uniform sound. In a grand piano, the tension in each string is over 100 pounds, creating a total force on the frame of between 40,000 and 60,000 pounds. A large variation in tension between the lower and the higher strings could lead to warping of the piano frame, so that, in order to apply even tension throughout, the higher strings are shorter and smaller in diameter while the bass strings are constructed of heavy wire wound with additional thin wire. This construction makes the wires stiff, causing the overtones to be higher in frequency than the ideal harmonics and leading to the slight inharmonicity that plays an important part in the characteristic piano tone.

IN AIR COLUMNS

In a manner analogous to the treatment of standing waves in a stretched string, it is possible to carry out an analysis of the structure of standing waves in air columns. If two identical sinusoidal waves move in opposite directions in a column of air, a standing wave of the same frequency will be formed, just as it is in a string. The standing wave will consist of equally spaced nodes and antinodes with a loop length equal to one-half wavelength in air. Because the motion of the air forming this standing wave is rather complicated, the graphic representation is more abstract, but it can be drawn in a similar manner to that of the string.

Tubes are classified by whether both ends of the tube are open (an open tube) or whether one end is open and one end closed (a closed tube). The basic acoustic difference is that the open end of a tube allows motion of the air; this results in the occurrence there of a velocity or displacement

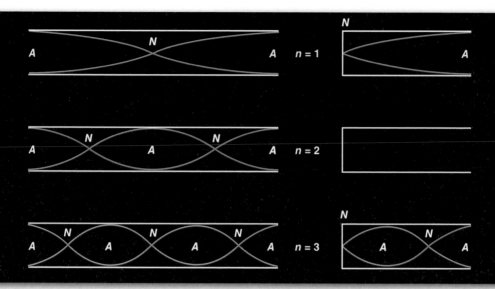

The first three harmonic standing waves in (left) *open and* (right) *closed tubes. Velocity nodes (N) and antinodes (A) are marked. The harmonic number (n) for each standing wave is given in the centre. The second harmonic does not exist in a closed tube.* Encyclopædia Britannica, Inc.

antinode similar to the centre of the fundamental mode of a stretched string. On the other hand, the air at the closed end of a tube cannot move, so that a closed end results in a velocity node similar to the ends of a stretched string.

OPEN TUBES

In an open tube, the standing wave of the lowest possible frequency for that particular length of tube (in other words, the fundamental) has antinodes at each end and a node in the centre. This means that an open tube is one-half wavelength long. The fundamental frequency (f_1) is thus

$$f_1 = \frac{S}{\lambda} = \frac{S}{2L_o},$$

(29)

where L_o is the length of the open tube. The standing wave of each successive harmonic has one additional loop. The wavelength (λ_n) of each successive standing wave is calculated as

$$\lambda_n = \frac{2L_o}{n},$$

(30)

and the frequency (f_n) as

$$f_n = \frac{nS}{2L_o} = n f_1,$$

(31)

just as in the case of the stretched string.

CLOSED TUBES

The end conditions of a closed tube create a node at the closed end and an antinode at the open end, so that the length of a closed tube (L_c) is one-quarter of a wavelength. For this reason, the length of the closed tubes is one-half that of the open tubes, so that both open and closed tubes produce the same fundamental frequency. In addition, the boundary conditions of a closed tube allow only an odd number of quarter-wavelengths to occupy any given length, so that

$$\lambda = \frac{4L_c}{n},$$

(32)

where only odd n are allowed. Thus, the frequencies of standing waves in a closed tube include only the odd harmonics,

$$f_n = \frac{nS}{4L_c} = nf_1,$$

(33)

where values for n are odd integers only.

MEASURING TECHNIQUES

A dramatic device used to "observe" the motion of air in a standing wave is the Kundt's tube. Cork dust is placed on the bottom of this tube, and a standing wave is created. A standing wave in a Kundt's tube consists of a complex series of small cell oscillations. The air is set in motion, and the vortex motion of the air cells blows the cork dust into small piles, forming a striation pattern. This pattern is very clear and strong at the velocity antinodes of the standing wave, but it disappears at the locations of nodal points. Alternating locations of nodes and antinodes are thus readily observed using this technique.

Under actual conditions, a node is located exactly at the closed end of a tube, but the antinode, owing to the way a wave reflects when it hits the open end, is actually out past the end of the tube by a small distance known as the end correction. The end correction depends primarily on the radius of the tube: it is approximately equal to 0.6 times the radius of an unflanged tube and 0.82 times the radius of a flanged tube. The effective length of the tube, which must be assumed for the value of L in the equations above, incorporates the end correction.

An important feature of this discussion of standing waves in air columns is that the terms *node* and *antinode* refer to the places in the vibrating medium where there is zero and maximum displacement or velocity. Many textbooks and reference works use illustrations in which the wave drawn in a tube represents pressure rather than velocity or displacement. In this case, a pressure node (corresponding to a displacement or velocity antinode) occurs at the open end of a tube, while a pressure antinode (corresponding to a displacement or velocity node) occurs at the closed end. Because most microphones respond to changes in pressure, this type of representation may be more useful when discussing experimental observations involving the use of microphones.

In Solid Rods

A thin metal rod can sustain longitudinal vibrations in much the same way as an air column. The ends of a rod, when free, act as antinodes, while any point at which the rod is held becomes a node, so that the representation of their standing waves is identical to that of an open tube. Such standing waves can be activated by sharply striking the end of the rod with a hard object or by scraping the rod with a cloth or with fingers coated with resin. The harmonic frequencies are then given by

$$f_n = \left(\frac{n}{2L}\right)\sqrt{\frac{Y}{\rho}} ,$$

(34)

where n is the harmonic number, Y is the Young's modulus, and ρ is the density of the material. This type of standing wave was used by German physicist Ernst Chladni in determining the speed of sound in metals.

IN NONHARMONIC SYSTEMS

The resonant systems described above have a series of standing-wave resonances that vibrate at the frequencies of the overtone series, but there are several systems whose resonances are not so simply related.

THE HELMHOLTZ RESONATOR

An important type of resonator with very different acoustic characteristics is the Helmholtz resonator, named after the German physicist Hermann von Helmholtz. Essentially a hollow sphere with a short, small-diameter neck, a Helmholtz resonator has a single isolated resonant frequency and no other resonances below about 10 times that frequency. The resonant frequency (f) of a classical Helmholtz resonator is determined by its volume (V) and by the length (L) and area (A) of its neck:

$$f = \left(\frac{S}{2\pi} \right) \sqrt{\frac{A}{LV}} \, , \tag{35}$$

where S is the speed of sound in air. As with the tubes discussed above, the value of the length of the neck should be given as the effective length, which depends on its radius.

The isolated resonance of a Helmholtz resonator made it useful for the study of musical tones in the mid-19th century, before electronic analyzers had been invented. When a resonator is held near the source of a sound, the air in it will begin to resonate if the tone being analyzed has a spectral component at the frequency of the resonator. By listening carefully to the tone of a musical instrument with such a resonator, it is possible to identify the spectral components of a complex sound wave such as those generated by musical instruments.

The air cavity of a string instrument, such as the violin or guitar, functions acoustically as a Helmholtz-type resonator, reinforcing frequencies near the bottom of the instrument's range and thereby giving the tone of the instrument more strength in its low range. The acoustic band-pass filter uses a Helmholtz resonator to absorb a

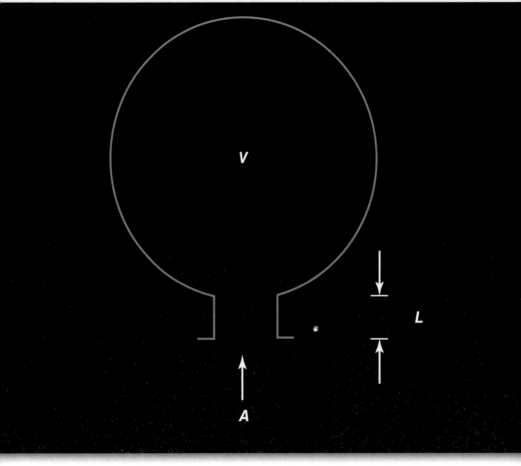

A classic Helmholtz resonator with volume V *and with a neck of length* L *and cross-sectional area* A. Encyclopædia Britannica, Inc.

band of frequencies from the sound wave passing down an air duct and then reemitting them with the opposite phase, so that they will interfere destructively with the incoming wave and cause it to attenuate. The large jugs used in a jug band also function as Helmholtz resonators, resonating at a single low frequency when air is blown across their openings. Tuning forks are often mounted on boxes, because the air cavity in a box oscillates like a Helmholtz resonator and provides coupling between the tuning fork and the outside air.

RECTANGULAR BOXES

An air cavity in the shape of a rectangular box has a sequence of nonharmonic resonances. In such a case the walls are nodal points, and there are standing waves between two parallel walls and mixed standing waves involving several walls. The frequencies of such standing waves are given by the relation

$$f = \left(\frac{S}{2}\right)\sqrt{\left(\frac{N_x}{x}\right)^2 + \left(\frac{N_y}{y}\right)^2 + \left(\frac{N_z}{z}\right)^2}, \qquad (36)$$

where x, y, and z are the dimensions of the box and N_x, N_y, and N_z are any integers. In the case where $N_y = N_z = 0$ and $N_x = 1$, the frequency is

$$f = \frac{S}{2x}, \qquad (37)$$

corresponding to a half-wavelength the length of the box. This type of resonance is found inside a loudspeaker box, and it must be avoided when tuning a bass reflex speaker port. Such resonances are also readily observed in shower stalls and small rooms such as music practice rooms with parallel walls. Because of these resonances, practice rooms are often made with oblique walls.

STRETCHED MEMBRANES

In a two-dimensional system—for instance, a vibrating plate or a stretched membrane such as a drumhead—the resonant frequencies are not related by integral multiples; that is, their resonances or overtones are inharmonic. Most tuned percussion instruments fall into this category, which is one reason why a tune played on bells or timpani is sometimes more difficult to follow than a tune played on a violin or trumpet. Part of the design goal for tuned bar instruments is to make the shape such that two or more of the resonant frequencies line up like those of wind or string instruments, rendering the pitch clearer. Some, such as the marimba and xylophone, use tubular resonators tuned to the desired frequency of the bar in order to reinforce any overtones that are harmonics of the tube. The South Asian tabla achieves its relatively clear pitch by using a nonuniform, or weighted, drumhead.

STEADY-STATE WAVES AND SPECTRAL ANALYSIS

Fundamental to the analysis of any musical tone is the spectral analysis, or Fourier analysis, of a steady-state wave. According to the Fourier theorem, a steady-state wave is composed of a series of sinusoidal components whose frequencies are those of the fundamental and its harmonics, each component having the proper amplitude and phase. The sequence of components that form this complex wave is called its spectrum.

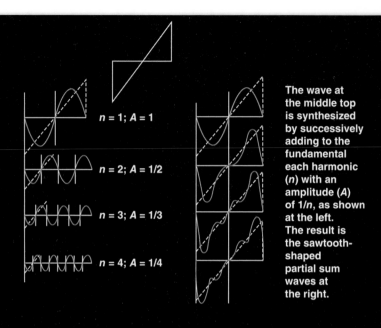

The wave at the middle top is synthesized by successively adding to the fundamental each harmonic (*n*) with an amplitude (*A*) of $1/n$, as shown at the left. The result is the sawtooth-shaped partial sum waves at the right.

$n = 1; A = 1$

$n = 2; A = 1/2$

$n = 3; A = 1/3$

$n = 4; A = 1/4$

Fourier synthesis of a complex wave. Encyclopædia Britannica, Inc.

THE SOUND SPECTROGRAPH

A sound that changes in time, such as a spoken word or a bird call, can be more completely described by examining how the Fourier spectrum changes with time. In a graph called the sound spectrograph, frequency of the complex sound is plotted versus time, with the more intense frequency components shown in the third dimension or more simply as a darker point on a two-dimensional graph. The so-called voiceprint is an example of a sound spectrograph. At one time it was believed that people have voiceprints that are as unique as their fingerprints, so that individuals could be identified by their voiceprints, but the technology of the voiceprint has never been developed. In certain bird atlases, sound spectrographs of bird calls are included with other information, allowing identification of each bird by its call.

Generation by Musical Instruments

The steady-state tone of any musical instrument can also be analyzed and its Fourier spectrum constructed. The amplitudes of the various spectral components partially determine the tone quality, or timbre, of the instrument.

Bore Configuration and Harmonicity

The bore shapes of musical instruments, which have developed over the centuries, have rather interesting effects. Cylindrical and conical bores can produce resonances that are harmonics of the fundamental frequencies, but bores that flare faster than a cone create nonharmonic overtones and thus produce raucous tones rather than good musical sounds. A fact discovered by early musical instrument builders, this is the reason why the musical instruments that have developed over the past millennium of Western history are limited to those with either cylindrical or conical bores. In general, a rapidly flaring bell is added to the end of the instrument to reduce the impedance mismatch as the sound emerges from the instrument, thus increasing the ability of the instrument to radiate sound.

The presence of any given harmonic in the spectrum of a particular musical instrument depends on the nature of the vibrating system. For example, if the system functions acoustically as an open tube or a vibrating string, all harmonics will likely be present in the wave. Examples of this are the flute, the recorder, and the violin. On the other hand, the clarinet functions acoustically as a closed tube, because it is cylindrical in shape and has a reed end. Therefore, as explained above, the odd harmonics are emphasized in the clarinet spectrum—particularly at low frequencies. Other wind instruments function acoustically as open tubes for a variety of reasons. The addition of a mouthpiece and a bell to a tube, either cylindrical or conical, results in all harmonics being possible, as in both the trumpet (cylindrical) and cornet (conical) family of brasses. Even after fixing a reed to one end of a conical tube—as in the oboe, bassoon, and saxophone families—the instruments still function acoustically as open tubes, producing all harmonics. The sawtooth wave, having all harmonics, therefore sounds more like a trumpet or a saxophone than like a clarinet.

Other Effects on Tone

Because many musical instrument families have similar spectra, there must be other factors that affect their tone quality and by which their tones can be distinguished. Attack transients, such as the way in which a string is bowed, a trumpet tongued, or a piano key struck, and decay transients, such as the way the sound of a plucked string dies away, are very important in many instruments, particularly those that are struck or plucked. Vibrato (a periodic slow change in pitch) and tremolo (a periodic slow change in amplitude) also aid the analysis of steady-state sounds.

Inharmonicities, or deviations of the frequencies of the harmonics from the exact multiples of the fundamental, are very important in tuned percussion instruments. For example, because of the inherent stiffness of piano strings, the overtones of the piano have slight inharmonicities. Indeed, the frequency of the 16th harmonic as played on the piano is about one-half step higher than the exact frequency of the harmonic.

VARIATIONS IN AIR PRESSURE

Basic to flutes and recorders, an edge tone is a stream of air that strikes a sharp edge, where it creates pressure changes in the air column that propagate down the tube. Reflections of these pressure variations then force the air stream back and forth across the edge, reinforcing the vibration at the resonant frequency of the tube. The time required to set up this steady-state oscillation is called the transient time of the instrument. The human ear is extremely sensitive to transients in musical tones, and such transients are crucial to the identification of various musical instruments whose spectra are similar.

In musical instruments the pressure variations generated by edge tones, a reed, or the lips set up standing waves in the air column that in turn drive the air stream, reed, or lips. Thus, contrary to common belief, the vibrations of the air column drive the reed or the lips open and closed; the reed or lips do not drive the air column. In the clarinet, for example, air is forced through the reed, creating a pulse of air that travels down the tube. Simultaneously, the reed is pulled closed by pressure of the lips and by rapid air flow out of the reed. After one reflection off the end of the tube, the pulse reflects as a rarefaction, holding the reed shut, but after the second reflection the pulse returns as a compression, forcing the reed open so that the process is repeated.

THE HUMAN VOICE

Groups of emphasized harmonics, known as formants, play a crucial role in the vowel sounds produced by the human voice. Vocal formants arise from resonances in the vocal column. The vocal column is about 17.5 cm (7 inches) long, on the average, with its lower end at the vocal folds and its upper end at the lips. Like a reed or like lips at the mouthpiece of a wind instrument, the vocal folds function acoustically as a closed end, so that the vocal column is a closed-tube resonator with resonant frequencies of about 500, 1,500, 2,500, and 3,500 hertz, and so on. The vibration frequency of the vocal folds, determined by the folds' tension, determines the frequency of the vocal sound. When a sound is produced, all harmonics are present in the spectrum, but those near the resonant frequencies of the vocal column are increased in amplitude. These emphasized frequency regions are the vocal formants. By changing the shape of the throat, mouth, and lips, the frequencies of the formants are varied, creating the different vowel sounds.

NOISE

The idea of noise is fundamental to the sound of many vibrating systems, and it is useful in describing the spectra of vocal sibilants as well. Just as white light is the combination of all the colours of the rainbow, so white noise can be defined as a combination of equally intense sound waves at all frequencies of the audio spectrum. A characteristic of noise is that it has no periodicity, and so it creates no recognizable musical pitch or tone quality, sounding rather like the static that is heard between stations of an FM radio.

Another type of noise, called pink noise, is a spectrum of frequencies that decrease in intensity at a rate of three decibels per octave. Pink noise is useful for applications of sound and audio systems because many musical and natural sounds have spectra that decrease in intensity at high frequencies by about three decibels per octave. Other forms of coloured noise occur when there is a wide noise spectrum but with an emphasis on some narrow band of frequencies—as in the case of wind whistling through trees or over wires. In another example, as water is poured into a tall cylinder, certain frequencies of the noise created by the gurgling water are resonated by the length of the tube, so that pitch rises as the tube is effectively shortened by the rising water.

HEARING

Hearing is the process by which the ear transforms sound vibrations in the external environment into nerve impulses that are conveyed to the brain, where they are interpreted as sounds. In order for a sound to be transmitted to the central nervous system, the energy of the sound undergoes three transformations. First, the air vibrations are converted to vibrations of the tympanic membrane and ossicles of the middle ear. These, in turn, become vibrations in the fluid within the cochlea. Finally, the fluid vibrations set up traveling waves along the basilar membrane that stimulate the hair cells of the organ of Corti. These cells convert the sound vibrations to nerve impulses in the fibres of the cochlear nerve, which transmits them to the brain stem, from which they are relayed, after extensive processing, to the primary auditory area of the cerebral cortex, the ultimate centre of the brain for hearing. Only when the nerve impulses reach this area does the listener become aware of the sound.

DYNAMIC RANGE OF THE EAR

The ear has an enormous range of response, both in frequency and in intensity. The frequency range of human hearing extends over three orders of magnitude, from about 20 hertz to about 20,000 hertz, or 20 kilohertz. The minimum audible pressure amplitude, at the threshold of hearing, is about 10^{-5} pascal, or about 10^{-10} standard atmosphere, corresponding to a minimum intensity of about 10^{-12} watt per square metre. The pressure fluctuation associated with the threshold of pain, meanwhile, is over 10 pascals—one million times the pressure or one trillion times the intensity of the threshold of hearing. In both cases, the enormous dynamic range of the ear dictates that its response to changes in frequency and intensity must be nonlinear.

American investigators Harvey Fletcher and W.A. Munson measured the response of the human ear to sounds of different intensity and frequency and found a set of equal-loudness curves that are named after them. The curves show the varying absolute intensities of a pure tone that has the same loudness to the ear at various frequencies. The determination of each curve, labeled by its loudness level in phons, involves the subjective judgment of a large number of people and is therefore an average statistical result. However, the curves are given a partially objective basis by defining the number of phons for each curve to be the same as the sound intensity level in decibels at 1,000 hertz—a physically measurable quantity. Fletcher and Munson placed the threshold of hearing at 0 phons, or 0 decibels at 1,000 hertz, but more accurate measurements now indicate that the threshold of hearing is slightly greater than that. For this reason, the curve for 0 phons is slightly lower than the intensity level of the threshold of hearing over the entire frequency range. The curve for 120 phons is sometimes called the threshold of pain, or the threshold of feeling.

Several interesting observations can be made regarding the Fletcher-Munson curves. The minimum intensity in the threshold of hearing occurs at about 4,000 hertz. This corresponds to the fundamental frequency at which the ear canal, acting as a closed tube about 2 cm (1 inch) long, has a specific resonance. The pressure variation corresponding to the threshold of hearing, roughly equivalent to placing the wing of a fly on the eardrum, causes a vibration of the eardrum of less than the radius of an atom. If the threshold of hearing did not rise for low frequencies, body sounds, such as heartbeat and blood pulsing, would be continually audible. Music is normally played at intensity levels between about 30 and 100 decibels. When it is played more softly, decreasing the sound level of all frequencies by the same amount, bass frequencies fall below the threshold of hearing. This is why the loudness control on an audio system raises the intensity of low frequencies — so that the music will have the same proportion of treble and bass to the ear as when it is played at a higher level.

As stated above, the ear has an enormous dynamic range, the threshold of pain corresponding to an intensity 12 orders of magnitude (10^{12} times) greater than the threshold of hearing. This leads to the necessity of a nonlinear intensity response. In order to be sensitive to intense waves and yet remain sensitive to very low intensities, the ear must respond proportionally less to higher intensity than to lower intensity. This response is logarithmic, because the ear responds to ratios rather than absolute pressure or intensity changes. At almost any region of the Fletcher-Munson diagram, the smallest change in intensity of a sinusoidal sound wave that can be observed, called the intensity just noticeable difference, is about one decibel (further reinforcing the value of the decibel intensity scale). One decibel corresponds to an absolute energy variation of a factor of about 1.25. Thus, the minimum observable change in the intensity of a sound wave is greater by a factor of nearly 10^{12} at high intensities than it is at low intensities.

The frequency response of the ear is likewise nonlinear. Relating frequency to pitch as perceived by the musician, two notes will "sound" similar if they are spaced apart in frequency by a factor of two, or octave. This means that the frequency interval between 100 and 200 hertz sounds the same as that between 1,000 and 2,000 hertz or between 5,000 and 10,000 hertz. In other words, the tuning of musical scales and musical intervals is associated with frequency ratios rather than absolute frequency differences in hertz. As a result of this empirical observation that all octaves sound the same to the ear, each frequency interval equivalent to an octave on the horizontal axis of the Fletcher-Munson scale is equal in length.

The audio frequency range encompasses nearly nine octaves. Over most of this range, the minimum change in the frequency of a sinusoidal tone that can be detected by the ear, called the frequency just noticeable difference, is about 0.5 percent of the frequency of the tone, or about one-tenth of a musical half-step. The ear is less sensitive near the upper and lower ends of the audible spectrum, so that the just noticeable difference becomes somewhat larger.

THE EAR AS SPECTRUM ANALYZER

The ear actually functions as a type of Fourier analysis device, with the mechanism of the inner ear converting mechanical waves into electrical impulses that describe the intensity of the sound as a function of frequency. Ohm's law of hearing is a statement of the fact that the perception of the tone of a sound is a function of the amplitudes of the harmonics and not of the phase relationships between them. This is consistent with the place theory of hearing, which correlates the observed pitch with the position along the basilar membrane of the inner ear that is stimulated by the corresponding frequency.

The intensity level at which a sound can be heard is affected by the existence of other stimuli. This effect, called masking, plays an important role in the psycho-physical response to sound. Low frequencies mask higher frequencies much more strongly than high frequencies mask lower ones; this is one reason why a complex wave is perceived as having a different tone quality or timbre from a pure wave of the same frequency, even though they have the same pitch. Noise of low frequencies can be used to mask unwanted distracting sounds, such as nearby conversation in an office, and to create greater privacy.

The ear is responsive to the periodicity of a wave, so that it will hear the frequency of a complex wave as that of the fundamental whether or not the fundamental is actually present as a component in the wave, although the wave will have a different timbre than it would were the fundamental actually present. This effect, known as the missing fundamental, subjective fundamental, or periodicity pitch, is used by the ear to create the fundamental in sound radiating from a small loudspeaker that is not capable of providing low frequencies.

If the intensity of a sound is sufficiently great, the wave shape will be distorted by the ear mechanism, owing to its nonlinearity. The spectral analysis of the sound will then include frequencies that are not present in the sound wave, causing a distorted perception of the sound. If two or more sounds of great intensity are presented to the ear, this effect will introduce what are called combination tones. Two pure tones of frequency f_1 and f_2 will create a series of new pure tones: the sum tones,

$$f_+ = nf_1 + mf_2;$$ (38)

and the difference tones,

$$f_- = |nf_1 - mf_2|.$$ (39)

(Here n and m are any two integers.) Sum tones are difficult to hear because they are masked by the higher-intensity tones creating them, but difference tones are often observed in musical performance. For example, if the two tones are adjacent members of the harmonic series, the fundamental of that series will be produced as a difference tone, enhancing the ability of the ear to identify the fundamental pitch.

BINAURAL PERCEPTION

The paths from the ears to the brain are separate; that is, each ear converts the sound reaching it into electrical impulses, so that sounds from the two ears mix in the brain not as physical vibrations but as electrical signals. This separation of pathways has the direct result that, if two pure tones are presented to each ear separately (i.e., binaurally) at low levels, it will be very difficult for the ears to compare the frequencies because with no direct mixing of the mechanical waves there will be no regular beats. This difference in pitch perception between the two ears, called diplacusis, is generally not a problem. A type of beating known as binaural beats can sometimes be observed when the two tones are presented binaurally.

Also, two tones very close to an octave apart produce another type of monaural beating as they change in phase. This effect, known as second-order beats or quality beats, is observed as a slight periodic change in the quality of the combined tone. It serves as a counterexample to Ohm's law of hearing, which suggests that the quality of a sound depends only on the amplitudes of the harmonics and not on their phases.

Although the two ears are not connected by mechanical means, the brain is sensitive to phase and is able to determine the phase relationship between stimuli presented to the two ears. Locating a sound source laterally in space makes use of fundamental properties of sound waves as well as the ability of the brain to identify the phase difference between signals from the two ears. At low frequencies, where the wavelength is large and the waves diffract strongly, the brain is able to perceive the phase difference between the same sound reaching both ears, and it can thus locate the direction from which the sound is coming. On the other hand, at high frequencies the wavelength may be so short that there may be more than one period of time delay between the signals arriving at the two ears, creating an ambiguity in the phase difference. Fortunately, at these high frequencies there is so much less diffraction of sound waves that the head actually shields one ear more than the other. In such cases the difference in intensity of the sound waves reaching the two ears, rather than their phase difference, is used by the ears in spatial localization. Spatial localization in the vertical direction is poor for most people.

Environmental Noise

Many forms of noise in the urban environment, including traffic and airplane noise, industrial noise, and noise from electronically amplified music performed at high audio levels in confined rooms, may contribute to hearing damage. Even when the noise level in a working environment may not be dangerous, it can be distracting for those who work in that environment and therefore lead to reduced work production. In addition to the sound level, the character of the noise may be important. Identifiable noises, such as talking or music, may be more distracting for many people than noise produced by air handlers, small motors, or traffic.

Low levels of noise may be overcome using additional absorbing material, such as heavy drapery or sound-absorbent tiles in enclosed rooms. Where low levels of identifiable noise may be distracting, or where privacy of conversations in adjacent offices and reception areas may be important, the undesirable sounds may be masked. A small white-noise source such as static or rushing air, placed in the room, can mask the sounds of conversation from adjacent rooms without being offensive or dangerous to the ears of people working nearby. This type of device is often used in offices of doctors and other professionals. Another technique for reducing personal noise level is through the use of hearing protectors, which are held over the ears in the same manner as an earmuff. By using commercially available earmuff-type hearing protectors, a decrease in sound level can be attained ranging typically from about 10 decibels at 100 hertz to over 30 decibels for frequencies above 1,000 hertz.

Environmental and industrial noise is regulated in the United States under the Occupational Safety and Health Act of 1970 and the Noise Control Act of 1972. Under these acts, the Occupational Safety and Health Administration has set up industrial noise criteria in order to provide limits on the intensity of sound exposure and on the time duration for which that intensity may be allowed. If an individual is exposed to various levels of noise for different time intervals during the day, the total exposure or dose (D) of noise is obtained from the relation $D = (C_1/T_1) + (C_2/T_2) + (C_3/T_3) + \ldots$, where C is the actual time of exposure and T is the allowable time of exposure at any level. Using this formula, the maximum allowable daily noise dose will be 1, and any daily exposure over 1 is unacceptable.

Criteria for indoor noise are summarized in three sets of specifications that have been derived by collecting subjective judgments from a large sampling of people in a variety of specific situations. These have developed into the noise criteria (NC) and preferred noise criteria (PNC) curves, which provide limits on the level of noise introduced into the environment. The NC curves, developed in 1957, aim to provide a comfortable working or living environment by specifying the maximum allowable level of noise in octave bands over the entire audio spectrum. The complete set of 11 curves specifies noise criteria for a broad range of situations. The PNC curves, developed in 1971, add limits on low-frequency rumble and high-frequency hiss; hence, they are preferred over the older NC standard. These criteria provide design goals for noise levels for a variety of different purposes. Part of the specification of a work or living environment is the appropriate PNC curve; in the event that the sound level exceeds PNC limits, sound-absorptive materials can be introduced into the environment as necessary to meet the appropriate standards.

Outdoor noise limits are also important for human comfort. Standard house construction will provide some shielding from external sounds if the house meets minimum standards of construction and if the outside noise level falls within acceptable limits. These limits are generally specified for particular periods of the day—for example, during daylight hours, during evening hours, and at night during sleeping hours. Because of refraction in the atmosphere owing to the nighttime temperature inversion, relatively loud sounds can be introduced into an area from a rather distant highway, airport, or railroad. One interesting technique for control of highway noise is the erection of noise barriers alongside the highway, separating the highway from adjacent residential areas. The effectiveness of such barriers is limited by the diffraction of sound, which is greater at the lower frequencies that often predominate in road noise, especially from large vehicles. In order to be effective, they must be as close as possible to either the source or the observer of the noise (preferably to the source), thus maximizing the diffraction that would be necessary for the sound to reach the observer. Another requirement for this type of barrier is that it must also limit the amount of transmitted sound in order to bring about significant noise reduction.

CHAPTER 2

ACOUSTICS

The science concerned with the production, control, transmission, reception, and effects of sound is called acoustics, a term derived from the Greek *akoustos*, meaning "hearing." Beginning with its origins in the study of mechanical vibrations and the radiation of these vibrations through mechanical waves, acoustics has had important applications in almost every area of life. It has been fundamental to many developments in the arts—some of which, especially in the area of musical scales and instruments, took place after long experimentation by artists and were only much later explained as theory by scientists. For example, much of what is now known about architectural acoustics was actually learned by trial and error over centuries of experience and was only recently formalized into a science.

Other applications of acoustic technology are in the study of geologic, atmospheric, and underwater phenomena. Psychoacoustics, the study of the physical effects of sound on biological systems, has been of interest since Pythagoras first heard the sounds of vibrating strings and of hammers hitting anvils in the 6th century BCE, but the application of modern ultrasonic technology has only recently provided some of the most exciting developments in medicine. Even today, research continues into many aspects of the fundamental physical processes involved in waves and sound and into possible applications of these processes in modern life.

EARLY EXPERIMENTATION

The origin of the science of acoustics is generally attributed to the Greek philosopher Pythagoras, whose experiments on the properties of vibrating strings that produce pleasing musical intervals were of such merit that they led to a tuning system that bears his name. Aristotle (4th century BCE) correctly suggested that a sound wave propagates in air through motion of the air—a hypothesis based more on philosophy than on experimental physics; however, he also incorrectly suggested that high frequencies propagate faster than low frequencies—an error that persisted for many centuries. Vitruvius, a Roman architectural engineer of the 1st century BCE, determined the correct mechanism for the transmission of sound waves, and he contributed substantially to the acoustic design of theatres. In the 6th century CE, the Roman philosopher Boethius documented several ideas relating science to music, including a suggestion that the human perception of pitch is related to the physical property of frequency.

The modern study of waves and acoustics is said to have originated with Galileo Galilei (1564–1642), who elevated to the level of science the study of vibrations and the correlation between pitch and frequency of the sound source. His interest in sound was inspired in part by his father, who was a mathematician, musician, and composer of some repute. Following Galileo's foundation work, progress in acoustics came relatively rapidly. The French mathematician Marin Mersenne studied the vibration of stretched strings; the results of these studies were summarized in the three Mersenne's laws. Mersenne's *Harmonicorum Libri* (1636) provided the basis for modern musical acoustics. Later in the century Robert Hooke, an English physicist, first produced a sound wave of known frequency, using a rotating cog wheel as a measuring device. Further developed in the 19th century by the French physicist Félix Savart, and now commonly called Savart's disk, this device is often used today for demonstrations during physics lectures. In the late 17th and early 18th centuries, detailed studies of the relationship between frequency and pitch and of waves in stretched strings were carried out by the French physicist Joseph Sauveur, who provided a legacy of acoustic terms used to this day and first suggested the name *acoustics* for the study of sound.

One of the most interesting controversies in the history of acoustics involves the famous and often misinterpreted "bell-in-vacuum" experiment, which has become a staple of contemporary physics lecture demonstrations. In this experiment the air is pumped out of a jar in which a ringing bell is located; as air is pumped out, the sound of the bell diminishes until it becomes inaudible. As late as the 17th century many philosophers and scientists believed that sound propagated via invisible particles originating at the source of the sound and moving through space to affect the ear of the observer. The concept of sound as a wave directly challenged this view, but it was not established experimentally until the first bell-in-vacuum experiment was performed by Athanasius Kircher, a German scholar, who described it in his book *Musurgia Universalis* (1650). Even after pumping the air out of the jar, Kircher could still hear the bell, so he concluded incorrectly that air was not required to transmit sound. In fact, Kircher's jar was not entirely free of air, probably because of inadequacy in his vacuum pump. By 1660 the Anglo-Irish scientist Robert Boyle had improved vacuum technology to the point where he could observe sound intensity decreasing virtually to zero as air was pumped out. Boyle then came to the correct conclusion that a medium such as air is required for transmission of sound waves. Although this conclusion is correct, as an explanation for the results of the bell-in-vacuum experiment it is misleading. Even with the mechanical pumps of today, the amount of air remaining in a vacuum jar is more than sufficient to transmit a sound wave. The real reason for a decrease in sound level upon pumping air out of the jar is that the bell is unable to transmit the sound vibrations efficiently to the less dense air remaining, and that air is likewise unable to transmit the sound efficiently to the glass jar. Thus, the real problem is one of an impedance mismatch between the air and the denser solid materials—and not the lack of a medium such as air, as is generally presented in textbooks. Nevertheless, despite the confusion regarding this experiment, it did aid in establishing sound as a wave rather than as particles.

MODERN ADVANCES

Simultaneous with these early studies in acoustics, theoreticians were developing the mathematical theory of waves required for the development of modern physics, including acoustics. In the early 18th century, the English mathematician Brook Taylor developed a mathematical theory of vibrating strings that agreed with previous experimental observations, but he was not able to deal with vibrating systems in general without the proper mathematical base. This was provided by Isaac Newton of England and Gottfried Wilhelm Leibniz of Germany, who, in pursuing other interests, independently developed the theory of calculus, which in turn allowed the derivation of the general wave equation by the French mathematician and scientist Jean Le Rond d'Alembert in the 1740s. The Swiss mathematicians Daniel Bernoulli and Leonhard Euler, as well as the Italian-French mathematician Joseph-Louis Lagrange, further applied the new equations of calculus to waves in strings and in the air. In the 19th century, Siméon-Denis Poisson of France extended these developments to stretched membranes, and the German mathematician

Rudolf Friedrich Alfred Clebsch completed Poisson's earlier studies. A German experimental physicist, August Kundt, developed a number of important techniques for investigating properties of sound waves. These included the Kundt's tube.

One of the most important developments in the 19th century involved the theory of vibrating plates. In addition to his work on the speed of sound in metals, Ernst Chladni had earlier introduced a technique of observing standing-wave patterns on vibrating plates by sprinkling sand onto the plates—a demonstration commonly used today. Perhaps the most significant step in the theoretical explanation of these vibrations was provided in 1816 by the French mathematician Sophie Germain, whose explanation was of such elegance and sophistication that errors in her treatment of the problem were not recognized until some 35 years later, by the German physicist Gustav Robert Kirchhoff.

The analysis of a complex periodic wave into its spectral components was theoretically established early in the 19th century by Jean-Baptiste-Joseph Fourier of France and is now commonly referred to as the Fourier theorem. The German physicist Georg Simon Ohm first suggested that the ear is sensitive to these spectral components; his idea that the ear is sensitive to the amplitudes but not the phases of the harmonics of a complex tone is known as Ohm's law of hearing (distinguishing it from the more famous Ohm's law of electrical resistance).

Hermann von Helmholtz made substantial contributions to understanding the mechanisms of hearing and to the psychophysics of sound and music. His book *On the Sensations of Tone As a Physiological Basis for the Theory of Music* (1863) is one of the classics of acoustics. In addition, he constructed a set of resonators, covering much of the audio spectrum, which were used in the spectral analysis of musical tones. The Prussian physicist Karl Rudolph Koenig, an extremely clever and creative experimenter, designed many of the instruments used for research in hearing and music, including a frequency standard and the manometric flame. The flame-tube device, used to render standing sound waves "visible," is still one of the most fascinating of physics classroom demonstrations. The English physical scientist John William Strutt, 3rd Lord Rayleigh, carried out an enormous variety of acoustic research; much of it was included in his two-volume treatise, *The Theory of Sound*, publication of which in 1877–78 is now thought to mark the beginning of modern acoustics. Much of Rayleigh's work is still directly quoted in contemporary physics textbooks.

The study of ultrasonics was initiated by the American scientist John LeConte, who in the 1850s developed a technique for observing the existence of ultrasonic waves with a gas flame. This technique was later used by the British physicist John Tyndall for the detailed study of the properties of sound waves. The piezoelectric effect, a primary means of producing and sensing ultrasonic waves, was discovered by the French physical chemist Pierre Curie and his brother Jacques in 1880. Applications of ultrasonics, however, were not possible until the development in the early 20th century of the electronic oscillator and amplifier, which were used to drive the piezoelectric element.

Among 20th-century innovators were the American physicist Wallace Sabine, considered to be the originator of modern architectural acoustics, and the Hungarian-born American physicist Georg von Békésy, who carried out experimentation on the ear and hearing and validated the commonly accepted place theory of hearing first suggested by Helmholtz. Békésy's book *Experiments in Hearing* (1960) is the magnum opus of the modern theory of the ear.

AMPLIFYING, RECORDING, AND REPRODUCING

The earliest known attempt to amplify a sound wave was made by Athanasius Kircher, of "bell-in-vacuum" fame; Kircher designed a parabolic horn that could be used either as a hearing aid or as a voice amplifier. The amplification of body sounds became an important goal, and the first stethoscope was invented by a French physician, René Laënnec, in the early 19th century.

Attempts to record and reproduce sound waves originated with the invention in 1857 of a mechanical sound-recording device called the phonautograph by Édouard-Léon Scott de Martinville. The first device that could actually record and play back sounds was developed by the American inventor Thomas Alva Edison in 1877. Edison's phonograph employed grooves of varying depth in a cylindrical sheet of foil, but a spiral groove on a flat rotating disk was introduced a decade later by the German-born American inventor Emil Berliner in an invention he called the gramophone. Much significant progress in recording and reproduction techniques was made during the first half of the 20th century, with the development of high-quality electromechanical transducers and linear electronic circuits. The most important improvement on the standard phonograph record in the second half of the century was the compact disc, which employed digital techniques developed in mid-century that substantially reduced noise and increased the fidelity and durability of the recording.

ARCHITECTURAL ACOUSTICS

Although architectural acoustics has been an integral part of the design of structures for at least 2,000 years, the subject was only placed on a firm scientific basis at the beginning of the 20th century by Wallace Sabine. Sabine pointed out that the most important quantity in determining the acoustic suitability of a room for a particular use is its reverberation time, and he provided a scientific basis by which the reverberation time can be determined or predicted.

REVERBERATION TIME

When a source creates a sound wave in a room or auditorium, observers hear not only the sound wave propagating directly from the source but also the myriad reflections from the walls, floor, and ceiling. These latter form the reflected wave, or reverberant sound. After the source ceases, the reverberant sound can be heard for some time as it grows softer. The time required, after the sound source ceases, for the absolute intensity to drop by a factor of 10^6 — or, equivalently, the time for the intensity level to drop by 60 decibels — is defined as the reverberation time (RT, sometimes referred to as RT_{60}). Sabine recognized that the reverberation time of an auditorium is related to the volume of the auditorium and to the ability of the walls, ceiling, floor, and contents of the room to absorb sound. Using these assumptions, he set forth the empirical relationship through which the reverberation time could be determined: $RT = 0.05V/A$, where RT is the reverberation time in seconds, V is the volume of the room in cubic feet, and A is the total sound absorption of the room, measured by the unit sabin. The sabin is the absorption equivalent to one square foot of perfectly absorbing surface — for example, a one-square-foot hole in a wall or five square feet of surface that absorbs 20 percent of the sound striking it.

Both the design and the analysis of room acoustics begin with this equation. Using the equation and the absorption coefficients of the materials from which the walls are to be constructed, an approximation can be obtained for the way in which the room will function acoustically. Absorbers and reflectors, or some combination of the two, can then be used to modify the reverberation time and its frequency dependence, thereby achieving the most desirable characteristics for specific uses. Representative absorption coefficients—showing the fraction of the wave, as a function of frequency, that is absorbed when a sound hits various materials—exist. The absorption from all the surfaces in the room are added together to obtain the total absorption (A).

While there is no exact value of reverberation time that can be called ideal, there is a range of values deemed to be appropriate for each application. These vary with the size of the room, but the averages can be calculated and indicated by lines on a graph. The need for clarity in understanding speech dictates that rooms used for talking must have a reasonably short reverberation time. On the other hand, the full sound desirable in the performance of music of the Romantic era, such as Wagner operas or Mahler symphonies, requires a long reverberation time. Obtaining a clarity suitable for the light, rapid passages of Bach or Mozart requires an intermediate value of reverberation time. For playing back recordings on an audio system, the reverberation time should be short, so as not to create confusion with the reverberation time of the music in the hall where it was recorded.

ACOUSTIC CRITERIA

Many of the acoustic characteristics of rooms and auditoriums can be directly attributed to specific physically measurable properties. Because the music critic or performing artist uses a different vocabulary to describe these characteristics than does the physicist, it is helpful to survey some of the more important features of acoustics and correlate the two sets of descriptions.

Liveness refers directly to reverberation time. A live room has a long reverberation time and a dead room a short reverberation time. *Intimacy* refers to the feeling that listeners have of being physically close to the performing group. A room is generally judged intimate when the first reverberant sound reaches the listener within about 20 milliseconds of the direct sound. This condition is met easily in a small room, but it can also be achieved in large halls by the use of orchestral shells that partially enclose the performers. Another example is a canopy placed above a speaker in a large room such as a cathedral: this leads to both a strong and a quick first reverberation and thus to a sense of intimacy with the person speaking.

The amplitude of the reverberant sound relative to the direct sound is referred to as *fullness*. *Clarity*, the opposite of fullness, is achieved by reducing the amplitude of the reverberant sound. Fullness generally implies a long reverberation time, while clarity implies a shorter reverberation time. A fuller sound is generally required of Romantic music or performances by larger groups, while more clarity would be desirable in the performance of rapid passages from Bach or Mozart or in speech.

Warmth and *brilliance* refer to the reverberation time at low frequencies relative to that at higher frequencies. Above about 500 hertz, the reverberation time should be the same for all frequencies. But at low frequencies an increase in the reverberation time creates a warm sound, while, if the reverberation time increased less at low frequencies, the room would be characterized as more brilliant.

Texture refers to the time interval between the arrival of the direct sound and the arrival of the first few reverberations. To obtain good texture, it is necessary that the first five reflections arrive at the observer within about 60 milliseconds of the direct sound. An important corollary to this requirement is that the intensity of the reverberations should decrease monotonically; there should be no unusually large late reflections.

Blend refers to the mixing of sounds from all the performers and their uniform distribution to the listeners. To achieve proper blend it is often necessary to place a collection of reflectors on the stage that distribute the sound randomly to all points in the audience.

Although the above features of auditorium acoustics apply to listeners, the idea of ensemble applies primarily to performers. In order to perform coherently, members of the ensemble must be able to hear one another. Reverberant sound cannot be heard by the members of an orchestra, for example, if the stage is too wide, has too high a ceiling, or has too much sound absorption on its sides.

ACOUSTIC PROBLEMS

Certain acoustic problems often result from improper design or from construction limitations. If large echoes are to be avoided, focusing of the sound wave must be avoided. Smooth, curved reflecting surfaces such as domes and curved walls act as focusing elements, creating large echoes and leading to bad texture. Improper blend results if sound from one part of the ensemble is focused to one section of the audience. In addition, parallel walls in an auditorium reflect sound back and forth, creating a rapid, repetitive pulsing of sound known as flutter echo and even leading to destructive interference of the sound wave. Resonances at certain frequencies should also be avoided by use of oblique walls.

Acoustic shadows, regions in which some frequency regions of sound are attenuated, can be caused by diffraction effects as the sound wave passes around large pillars and corners or underneath a low balcony. Large reflectors called clouds, suspended over the performers, can be of such a size as to reflect certain frequency regions while allowing others to pass, thus affecting the mixture of the sound.

External noise can be a serious problem for halls in urban areas or near airports or highways. One technique often used for avoiding external noise is to construct the auditorium as a smaller room within a larger room. Noise from air blowers or other mechanical vibrations can be reduced using techniques involving impedance and by isolating air handlers.

Good acoustic design must take account of all these possible problems while emphasizing the desired acoustic features. One of the problems in a large auditorium involves simply delivering an adequate amount of sound to the rear of the hall. The intensity of a spherical sound wave decreases in intensity at a rate of six decibels for each factor of two increase in distance from the source. If the auditorium is flat, a hemispherical wave will result. Absorption of the diffracted wave by the floor or audience near the bottom of the hemisphere will result in even greater absorption, so that the resulting intensity level will fall off at twice the theoretical rate, at about 12 decibels for each factor of two in distance. Because of this absorption, the floors of an auditorium are generally sloped upward toward the rear.

The human ear can hear sounds with frequencies between 20 hertz and 20 kilohertz. The vibrations of frequencies greater than the upper limit of the audible range for humans—that is, greater than about 20 kilohertz—are called ultrasonic.

The vibrations of frequencies less than the lower limit of the audible range for humans—that is, less than about 20 hertz—are called infrasonic. The range of infrasonic frequencies extends down to geologic vibrations that complete one cycle in 100 seconds or longer.

Many animals have the ability to hear sounds beyond the human frequency range. Some ranges of hearing for mammals and insects are interesting to compare with those of humans. A presumed sensitivity of roaches and rodents to frequencies in the 40 kilohertz region has led to the manufacture of "pest controllers" that emit loud sounds in that frequency range to drive the pests away, but they do not appear to work as advertised. Rhinoceroses and elephants communicate using infrasonic frequencies. Elephants can communicate over distances up to 4 km (2.5 miles) with 5- to 24-hertz calls.

ULTRASONICS

Within the domain of the ultrasonic, there are further gradations in frequency and amplitude. The term *sonic* is applied to ultrasound waves of very high amplitudes. Hypersound, sometimes called praetersound or microsound, is sound waves of frequencies greater than 10^{13} hertz. At such high frequencies it is very difficult for a sound wave to propagate efficiently; indeed, above a frequency of about 1.25×10^{13} hertz, it is impossible for longitudinal waves to propagate at all, even in a liquid or a solid, because the molecules of the material in which the waves are traveling cannot pass the vibration along rapidly enough.

TRANSDUCERS

An ultrasonic transducer is a device used to convert some other type of energy into an ultrasonic vibration. There are several basic types, classified by the energy source and by the medium into which the waves are being generated. Mechanical devices include gas-driven, or pneumatic, transducers such as whistles as well as liquid-driven transducers such as hydrodynamic oscillators and vibrating blades. These devices, limited to low ultrasonic frequencies, have a number of industrial applications, including drying, ultrasonic cleaning, and injection of fuel oil into burners. Electromechanical transducers are far more versatile and include piezoelectric and magnetostrictive devices. A magnetostrictive transducer makes use of a type of magnetic material in which an applied oscillating magnetic field squeezes the atoms of the material together, creating a periodic change in the length of the material and thus producing a high-frequency mechanical vibration. Magnetostrictive transducers are used primarily in the lower frequency ranges and are common in ultrasonic cleaners and ultrasonic machining applications.

By far the most popular and versatile type of ultrasonic transducer is the piezoelectric crystal, which converts an oscillating electric field applied to the crystal into a mechanical vibration. Piezoelectric crystals include quartz, Rochelle salt, and certain types of ceramic. Piezoelectric transducers are readily employed over the entire frequency range and at all output levels. Particular shapes can be chosen for particular applications. For example, a disk shape provides a plane ultrasonic wave, while curving the radiating surface in a slightly concave or bowl shape creates an ultrasonic wave that will focus at a specific point. Piezoelectric and magnetostrictive transducers also are employed as ultrasonic receivers, picking up an ultrasonic vibration and converting it into an electrical oscillation.

APPLICATIONS IN RESEARCH

One of the important areas of scientific study in which ultrasonics has had an enormous impact is cavitation. When water is boiled, bubbles form at the bottom of the container, rise in the water, and then collapse, leading to the sound of the boiling water. The boiling process and the resulting sounds have intrigued people since they were first observed, and they were the object of considerable research and calculation by the British physicists Osborne Reynolds and Lord Rayleigh, who applied the term *cavitation* to the process of formation of bubbles. Because an ultrasonic wave can be used carefully to control cavitation, ultrasound has been a useful tool in the investigation of the process. The study of cavitation has also provided important information on intermolecular forces.

Research is being carried out on aspects of the cavitation process and its applications. A contemporary subject of research involves emission of light as the cavity produced by a high-intensity ultrasonic wave collapses. This effect, called sonoluminescence, is believed to create instantaneous temperatures hotter than the surface of the Sun.

The speed of propagation of an ultrasonic wave is strongly dependent on the viscosity of the medium. This property can be a useful tool in investigating the viscosity of materials. Because the various parts of a living cell are distinguished by differing viscosities, acoustical microscopy can make use of this property of cells to "see" into living cells.

RANGING AND NAVIGATING

Sonar (sound navigation and ranging) has extensive marine applications. By sending out pulses of sound or ultrasound and measuring the time required for the pulses to reflect off a distant object and return to the source, the location of that object can be ascertained and its motion tracked. This technique is used extensively to locate and track submarines at sea and to locate explosive mines below the surface of the water. Two boats at known locations can also use triangulation to locate and track a third boat or submarine. The distance over which these techniques can be used is limited by temperature gradients in the water, which bend the beam away from the surface and create shadow regions. One of the advantages of ultrasonic waves over sound waves in underwater applications is that, because of their higher frequencies (or shorter wavelengths), the former will travel greater distances with less diffraction.

Ranging has also been used to map the bottom of the ocean, providing depth charts that are commonly used in navigation, particularly near coasts and in shallow waterways. Even small boats are now equipped with sonic ranging devices that determine and display the depth of the water so that the navigator can keep the boat from beaching on submerged sandbars or other shallow points. Modern fishing boats use ultrasonic ranging devices to locate schools of fish, substantially increasing their efficiency.

Even in the absence of visible light, bats can guide their flight and even locate flying insects (which they consume in flight) through the use of sonic ranging. Ultrasonic echolocation has also been used in traffic control applications and in counting and sorting items on an assembly line. Ultrasonic ranging provides the basis of the eye and vision systems for robots, and it has a number of important medical applications.

THE DOPPLER EFFECT

If an ultrasonic wave is reflected off a moving obstacle, the frequency of the resulting wave will be changed, or Doppler-shifted. The amount of the frequency shift can be used to determine the velocity of the moving obstacle. Just as the Doppler shift for radar, an electromagnetic wave, can be used to determine the speed of a moving car, so can the speed of a moving submarine be determined by the Doppler shift of a sonar beam. An important industrial application is the ultrasonic flow meter, in which reflecting ultrasound off a flowing liquid leads to a Doppler shift that is calibrated to provide the flow rate of the liquid. This technique also has been applied to blood flow in arteries.

MATERIALS TESTING

Nondestructive testing involves the use of ultrasonic echolocation to gather information on the integrity of mechanical structures. Since changes in the material present an impedance mismatch from which an ultrasonic wave is reflected, ultrasonic testing can be used to identify faults, holes, cracks, or corrosion in materials, to inspect welds, to determine the quality of poured concrete, and to monitor metal fatigue. Owing to the mechanism by which sound waves propagate in metals, ultrasound can be used to probe more deeply than any other form of radiation.

Ultrasonic procedures are used to perform in-service inspection of structures in nuclear reactors.

Structural flaws in materials can also be studied by subjecting the materials to stress and looking for acoustic emissions as the materials are stressed. Acoustic emission, the general name for this type of nondestructive study, has developed as a distinct field of acoustics.

High-Intensity Applications

High-intensity ultrasound has achieved a variety of important applications. Perhaps the most ubiquitous is ultrasonic cleaning, in which ultrasonic vibrations are set up in small liquid tanks in which objects are placed for cleaning. Cavitation of the liquid by the ultrasound, as well as the vibration, create turbulence in the liquid and result in the cleaning action. Ultrasonic cleaning is very popular for jewelry and has also been used with such items as dentures, surgical instruments, and small machinery. Degreasing is often enhanced by ultrasonic cleaning. Large-scale ultrasonic cleaners have also been developed for use in assembly lines.

Ultrasonic machining employs the high-intensity vibrations of a transducer to move a machine tool. If necessary, a slurry containing carborundum grit may be used; diamond tools can also be used. A variation of this technique is ultrasonic drilling, which makes use of pneumatic vibrations at ultrasonic frequencies in place of the standard rotary drill bit. Holes of virtually any shape can be drilled in hard or brittle materials such as glass, germanium, or ceramic.

Ultrasonic soldering has become important, especially for soldering unusual or difficult materials and for very clean applications. The ultrasonic vibrations perform the function of cleaning the surface, even removing the oxide layer on aluminum so that the material can be soldered. Because the surfaces can be made extremely clean and free from the normal thin oxide layer, soldering flux becomes unnecessary.

Chemical and Electrical Uses

The chemical effects of ultrasound arise from an electrical discharge that accompanies the cavitation process. This forms a basis for ultrasound's acting as a catalyst in certain chemical reactions, including oxidation, reduction, hydrolysis, polymerization and depolymerization, and molecular rearrangement. With ultrasound, some chemical processes can be carried out more rapidly, at lower temperatures, or more efficiently.

The ultrasonic delay line is a thin layer of piezoelectric material used to produce a short, precise delay in an electrical signal. The electrical signal creates a mechanical vibration in the piezoelectric crystal that passes through the crystal and is converted back to an electrical signal. A very precise time delay can be achieved by constructing a crystal with the proper thickness. These devices are employed in fast electronic timing circuits.

Medical Applications

Although ultrasound competes with other forms of medical imaging, such as X-ray techniques and magnetic resonance imaging, it has certain desirable features—for example, Doppler motion study—that the other techniques cannot provide. In addition, among the various modern techniques for the imaging of internal organs, ultrasonic devices are by far the least expensive. Ultrasound is also used for treating joint pains and for treating certain types of tumours for which it is desirable to produce localized heating. A very effective use of ultrasound deriving from its nature as a mechanical vibration is the elimination of kidney and bladder stones.

DIAGNOSIS

Much medical diagnostic imaging is carried out with X-rays. Because of the high photon energies of the X-ray, this type of radiation is highly ionizing—that is, X-rays are readily capable of destroying molecular bonds in the body tissue through which they pass. This destruction can lead to changes in the function of the tissue involved or, in extreme cases, its annihilation.

One of the important advantages of ultrasound is that it is a mechanical vibration and is therefore a nonionizing form of energy. Thus, it is usable in many sensitive circumstances where X-rays might be damaging. Also, the resolution of X-rays is limited owing to their great penetrating ability and the slight differences between soft tissues. Ultrasound, on the other hand, gives good contrast between various types of soft tissue.

Ultrasonic scanning in medical diagnosis uses the same principle as sonar. Pulses of high-frequency ultrasound, generally above one megahertz, are created by a piezoelectric transducer and directed into the body. As the ultrasound traverses various internal organs, it encounters changes in acoustic impedance, which cause reflections. The amount and time delay of the various reflections can be analyzed to obtain information regarding the internal organs. In the B-scan mode, a linear array of transducers is used to scan a plane in the body, and the resultant data is displayed on a television screen as a two-dimensional plot. The A-scan technique uses a single transducer to scan along a line in the body, and the echoes are plotted as a function of time. This technique is used for measuring the distances or sizes of internal organs. The M-scan mode is used to record the motion of internal organs, as in the study of heart dysfunction. Greater resolution is obtained in ultrasonic imaging by using higher frequencies—i.e., shorter wavelengths. A limitation of this property of waves is that higher frequencies tend to be much more strongly absorbed.

Because it is nonionizing, ultrasound has become one of the staples of obstetric diagnosis. During the process of drawing amniotic fluid in testing for birth defects, ultrasonic imaging is used to guide the needle and thus avoid damage to the fetus or surrounding tissue. Ultrasonic imaging of the fetus can be used to determine the date of conception, to identify multiple births, and to diagnose abnormalities in the development of the fetus.

Ultrasonic Doppler techniques have become very important in diagnosing problems in blood flow. In one technique, a three-megahertz ultrasonic beam is reflected off typical oncoming arterial blood with a Doppler shift of a few kilohertz—a frequency difference that can be heard directly by a physician. Using this technique, it is possible to monitor the heartbeat of a fetus long before a stethoscope can pick up the sound. Arterial diseases such as arteriosclerosis can also be diagnosed, and the healing of arteries can be monitored following surgery. A combination of B-scan imaging and Doppler imaging, known as duplex scanning, can identify arteries and immediately measure their blood flow; this has been extensively used to diagnose heart valve defects.

Using ultrasound with frequencies up to 2,000 megahertz, which has a wavelength of 0.75 micrometre in soft tissues (as compared with a wavelength of about 0.55 micrometre for light), ultrasonic microscopes have been developed that rival light microscopes in their resolution. The distinct advantage of ultrasonic microscopes lies in their ability to distinguish various parts of a cell by their viscosity. Also, because they require no artificial contrast mediums, which kill the cells, acoustic microscopy can study actual living cells.

THERAPY AND SURGERY

Because ultrasound is a mechanical vibration and can be well focused at high frequencies, it can be used to create internal heating of localized tissue without harmful effects on nearby tissue. This technique can be employed to relieve pains in joints, particularly in the back and shoulder. Also, research is now being carried out in the treatment of certain types of cancer by local heating, since focusing intense ultrasonic waves can heat the area of a tumour while not significantly affecting surrounding tissue.

Trackless surgery—that is, surgery that does not require an incision or track from the skin to the affected area—has been developed for several conditions. Focused ultrasound has been used for the treatment of Parkinson's disease by creating brain lesions in areas that are inaccessible to traditional surgery. A common application of this technique is the destruction of kidney stones with shock waves formed by bursts of focused ultrasound. In some cases, a device called an ultrasonic lithotripter focuses the ultrasound with the help of X-ray guidance, but a more common technique for destruction of kidney stones, known as endoscopic ultrasonic disintegration, uses a small metal rod inserted through the skin to deliver ultrasound in the 22- to 30-kilohertz frequency region.

INFRASONICS

The term *infrasonics* refers to waves of a frequency below the range of human hearing—i.e., below about 20 hertz. Such waves occur in nature in earthquakes, waterfalls, ocean waves, volcanoes, and a variety of atmospheric phenomena such as wind, thunder, and weather patterns. Calculating the motion of these waves and predicting the weather using these calculations, among other information, is one of the great challenges for modern high-speed computers.

Aircraft, automobiles, or other rapidly moving objects, as well as air handlers and blowers in buildings, also produce substantial amounts of infrasonic radiation. Studies have shown that many people experience adverse reactions to large intensities of infrasonic frequencies, developing headaches, nausea, blurred vision, and dizziness. On the other hand, a number of animals are sensitive to infrasonic frequencies. It is believed by many zoologists that this sensitivity in animals such as elephants may be helpful in providing them with early warning of earthquakes and weather disturbances. It has been suggested that the sensitivity of birds to infrasound aids their navigation and even affects their migration.

One of the most important examples of infrasonic waves in nature is in earthquakes. Three principal types of earthquake wave exist: the S-wave, a transverse body wave; the P-wave, a longitudinal body wave; and the L-wave, which propagates along the boundary of stratified mediums. L-waves, which are of great importance in earthquake engineering, propagate in a similar way to water waves, at low velocities that are dependent on frequency. S-waves are transverse body waves and thus can only be propagated within solid bodies such as rocks. P-waves are longitudinal waves similar to sound waves; they propagate at the speed of sound and have large ranges.

When P-waves propagating from the epicentre of an earthquake reach the surface of the Earth, they are converted into L-waves, which may then damage surface structures. The great range of P-waves makes them useful in identifying earthquakes from observation points a great distance from the epicentre. In many cases, the most severe shock from an earthquake is preceded by smaller shocks, which provide advance warning of the greater shock to come. Underground nuclear explosions also produce P-waves, allowing them to be monitored from any point in the world if they are of sufficient intensity.

The reflection of man-made seismic shocks has helped to identify possible locations of oil and natural-gas sources. Distinctive rock formations in which these minerals are likely to be found can be identified by sonic ranging, primarily at infrasonic frequencies.

CHAPTER 4
LIGHT

L ight is usually defined as electromagnetic radiation that can be detected by the human eye.
Electromagnetic radiation occurs over an extremely wide
range of wavelengths, from gamma rays, with wavelengths
less than about 1×10^{-11} metre, to radio waves measured
in metres. Within that broad spectrum the wavelengths
visible to humans occupy a very narrow band, from about
700 nanometres (nm; billionths of a metre) for red light
down to about 400 nm for violet light. The spectral
regions adjacent to the visible band are often referred to
as light also, infrared at the one end and ultraviolet at the
other. The speed of light in a vacuum is a fundamental
physical constant, the currently accepted value of which
is exactly 299,792,458 metres per second, or about 186,282
miles per second.

No single answer to the question "What is light?" sat-
isfies the many contexts in which light is experienced,
explored, and exploited. The physicist is interested in
the physical properties of light, the artist in an aesthetic
appreciation of the visual world. Through the sense
of sight, light is a primary tool for perceiving the world
and communicating within it. Light from the Sun warms
Earth, drives global weather patterns, and initiates the
life-sustaining process of photosynthesis. On the grandest
scale, light's interactions with matter have helped shape
the structure of the universe. Indeed, light provides a window on the universe, from cosmological to atomic scales.
Almost all of the information about the rest of the cosmos
reaches Earth in the form of electromagnetic radiation.
By interpreting that radiation, astronomers can glimpse

the earliest epochs of the universe, measure the general expansion of the universe, and determine the chemical composition of stars and the interstellar medium. Just as the invention of the telescope dramatically broadened exploration of the cosmos, so too the invention of the microscope opened the intricate world of the cell. The analysis of the frequencies of light emitted and absorbed by atoms was a principal impetus for the development of quantum mechanics. Atomic and molecular spectroscopies continue to be primary tools for probing the structure of matter, providing ultrasensitive tests of atomic and molecular models and contributing to studies of fundamental photochemical reactions.

Light transmits spatial and temporal information. This property forms the basis of the fields of optics and optical communications and myriad related technologies, both mature and emerging. Technological applications based on the manipulations of light include lasers, holography, and fibre-optic telecommunications systems.

In most everyday circumstances, the properties of light can be derived from the theory of classical electromagnetism, in which light is described as coupled electric and magnetic fields propagating through space as a traveling wave. However, this wave theory, developed in the mid-19th century, is not sufficient to explain the properties of light at very low intensities. At that level a quantum theory is needed to explain the characteristics of light and to explain the interactions of light with atoms and molecules. In its simplest form, quantum theory describes light as consisting of discrete packets of energy, called photons. However, neither a classical wave model nor a classical particle model correctly describes light; light has a dual nature that is revealed only in quantum mechanics. This surprising wave-particle duality is shared by all of the primary constituents of nature (e.g., electrons have both particle-like and wavelike aspects). Since the mid-20th century, a more comprehensive theory of light, known as quantum electrodynamics (QED), has been regarded by physicists as complete. QED combines the ideas of classical electromagnetism, quantum mechanics, and the special theory of relativity.

THEORIES OF LIGHT THROUGH HISTORY

While there is clear evidence that simple optical instruments such as plane and curved mirrors and convex lenses were used by a number of early civilizations, ancient Greek philosophers are generally credited with the first formal speculations about the nature of light. The conceptual hurdle of distinguishing the human perception of visual effects from the physical nature of light hampered the development of theories of light. Contemplation of the mechanism of vision dominated these early studies.

Ray Theories in the Ancient World

Pythagoras proposed that sight is caused by visual rays emanating from the eye and striking objects, whereas Empedocles (*c.* 450 BCE) seems to have developed a model of vision in which light was emitted both by objects and the eye. Epicurus (*c.* 300 BCE) believed that light is emitted by sources other than the eye and that vision is produced when light reflects off objects and enters the eye. Euclid (*c.* 300 BCE), in his *Optics*, presented a law of reflection and discussed the propagation of light rays in straight lines. Ptolemy (*c.* 100 CE) undertook one of the first quantitative studies of the refraction of light as it passes from one transparent medium to another, tabulating pairs of angles of incidence and transmission for combinations of several media.

With the decline of the Greco-Roman realm, scientific progress shifted to the Islamic world. In particular, al-Ma'mūn, the seventh ʿAbbāsid caliph of Baghdad, founded the House of Wisdom (Bayt al-Hikma) in 830 CE to translate, study, and improve upon Hellenistic works of science and philosophy. Among the initial scholars were al-Khwārizmī and al-Kindī. Known as the "philosopher of the Arabs," al-Kindī extended the concept of rectilinearly propagating light rays and discussed the mechanism of vision. By 1000, the Pythagorean model of light had been abandoned, and a ray model, containing the basic conceptual elements of what is now known as geometrical optics, had emerged. In particular, Ibn al-Haytham (Latinized as Alhazen), in *Kitab al-manazir* (*c.* 1038; "Optics"), correctly attributed vision to the passive reception of light rays reflected from objects rather than an active emanation of light rays from the eyes. He also studied the mathematical properties of the reflection of light from spherical and parabolic mirrors and drew detailed pictures of the optical components of the human eye. Ibn al-Haytham's work was translated into Latin in the 13th century and was a motivating influence on the Franciscan friar and natural philosopher Roger Bacon. Bacon studied the propagation of light through simple lenses and is credited as one of the first to have described the use of lenses to correct vision.

EARLY PARTICLE AND WAVE THEORIES

With the dawn of the 17th century, significant progress was reawakened in Europe. Compound microscopes were first constructed in the Netherlands between 1590 and 1608 (probably by Hans and Zacharias Jansen), and most sources credit another Dutchman, Hans Lippershey, with the invention of the telescope in 1608. The Italian astronomer Galileo quickly improved upon the design of the refracting telescope and used it in his discoveries of the moons of Jupiter and the rings of Saturn in 1610. (Refraction refers to the passage of light from one medium into another—in this case, from air into a glass lens.) The German astronomer Johannes Kepler presented an approximate mathematical analysis of the focusing properties of lenses in *Dioptrice* (1611). An empirical advance was made by the Dutch astronomer Willebrord Snell in 1621 with his discovery of the mathematical relation (Snell's law) between the angles of incidence and transmission for a light ray refracting through an interface between two media. In 1657 the French mathematician Pierre de Fermat presented an intriguing derivation of Snell's law based on his principle of least time, which asserted that light follows the path of minimum time in traveling from one point to another. The posthumous publication of the Jesuit mathematician Francesco Grimaldi's studies in 1665 first described what are now called diffraction effects, in which light passing an obstacle is seen to penetrate into the geometrical shadow. In 1676 the Danish astronomer Ole Rømer used his measurements of the changes in the apparent orbital periods of the moons of Jupiter over the course of a year to deduce an approximate value for the speed of light. The significance of Rømer's work was the realization that the speed of light is not infinite.

Seminal physical models of the nature of light were developed in parallel with the many empirical discoveries of the 17th century. Two competing models of light, as a collection of fast-moving particles and as a propagating wave, were advanced. In *La Dioptrique* (1637), French philosopher-mathematician René Descartes described light as a pressure wave transmitted at infinite speed through a pervasive elastic medium. The prominent English physicist Robert Hooke studied diffraction effects and thin-film interference and concluded in *Micrographia* (1665) that light is a rapid vibration of any medium through which it propagates. In his *Treatise on Light* (1690), the Dutch mathematician-astronomer Christiaan Huygens formulated the first detailed wave theory of light, in the context of which he was also able to derive the laws of reflection and refraction.

The most prominent advocate of a particle theory of light was Isaac Newton. Newton's careful investigations into the properties of light in the 1660s led to his discovery that white light consists of a mixture of colours. He struggled with a formulation of the nature of light, ultimately asserting in *Opticks* (1704) that light consists of a stream of corpuscles, or particles. To reconcile his particle model with the known law of refraction, Newton speculated that transparent objects (such as glass) exert attractive forces on the particles, with the consequence that the speed of light in a transparent medium is always greater than the speed of light in a vacuum. He also postulated that particles of different colours of light have slightly different masses, leading to different speeds in transparent media and hence different angles of refraction. Newton presented his speculations in *Opticks* in the form of a series of queries rather than as a set of postulates, possibly conveying an ambivalence regarding the ultimate nature of light. Because of his immense authority in the scientific community, there were few challenges to his particle model of light in the century after his death in 1727.

Newton's corpuscular model survived into the early years of the 19th century, at which time evidence for the wave nature of light became overwhelming. Theoretical and experimental work in the mid to late 19th century convincingly established light as an electromagnetic wave, and the issue seemed to be resolved by 1900. With the arrival of quantum mechanics in the early decades of the 20th century, however, the controversy over the nature of light resurfaced. As will be seen in the following sections, this scientific conflict between particle and wave models of light permeates the history of the subject.

GEOMETRICAL OPTICS: LIGHT AS RAYS

A detailed understanding of the nature of light was not needed for the development, beginning in the 1600s, of a practical science of optics and optical instrument design. Rather, a set of empirical rules describing the behaviour of light as it traverses transparent materials and reflects off smooth surfaces was adequate to support practical advances in optics. Known collectively today as geometrical optics, the rules constitute an extremely useful, though very approximate, model of light. Their primary applications are the analysis of optical systems—cameras, microscopes, telescopes—and the explanation of simple optical phenomena in nature.

LIGHT RAYS

The basic element in geometrical optics is the light ray, a hypothetical construct that indicates the direction of the propagation of light at any point in space. The origin of this concept dates back to early speculations regarding the nature of light. By the 17th century the Pythagorean notion of visual rays had long been abandoned, but the observation that light travels in straight lines led naturally to the development of the ray concept.

It is easy to imagine representing a narrow beam of light by a collection of parallel arrows—a bundle of rays. As the beam of light moves from one medium to another, reflects off surfaces, disperses, or comes to a focus, the bundle of rays traces the beam's progress in a simple geometrical manner.

Geometrical optics consists of a set of rules that determine the paths followed by light rays. In any uniform medium the rays travel in straight lines. The light emitted by a small localized source is represented by a collection of rays pointing radially outward from an idealized "point source." A collection of parallel rays is used to represent light flowing with uniform intensity through space; examples include the light from a distant star and the light from a laser. The formation of a sharp shadow when an object is illuminated by a parallel beam of light is easily explained by tracing the paths of the rays that are not blocked by the object.

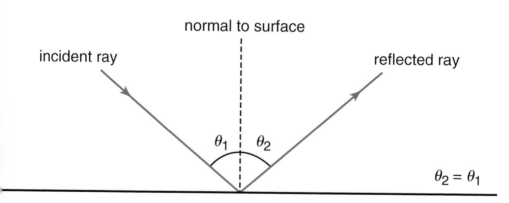

For a smooth surface, the angle of incidence (θ_1) equals the angle of reflection (θ_2), as measured with reference to the normal (perpendicular line) to the surface. Encyclopædia Britannica, Inc.

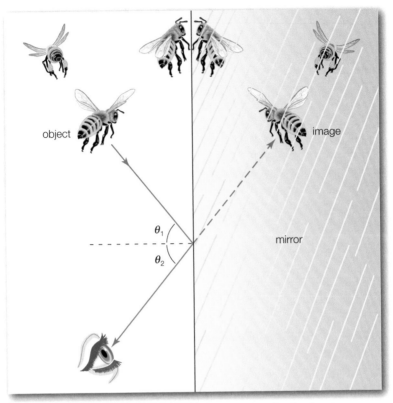

Reflection of light in a mirror. According to the law of reflection, images are reflected from a smooth surface, such as a mirror, at the same angle (θ_2) as the incidence angle (θ_1). When the eye "sees" an object in three-dimensional space in a mirror, it is actually viewing an image along sight lines created by the reflection of light from the surface of the mirror. Encyclopædia Britannica, Inc.

REFLECTION AND REFRACTION

Light rays change direction when they reflect off a surface, move from one transparent medium into another, or travel through a medium whose composition is continuously changing. The law of reflection states that, on reflection from a smooth surface, the angle of the reflected ray is equal to the angle of the incident ray. (By convention, all angles in geometrical optics are measured

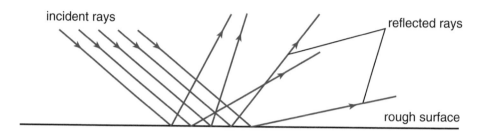

incident rays

reflected rays

rough surface

When light strikes rough surfaces, it reflects at many angles. This diffuse reflection enables illuminated objects to be seen from almost any line-of-sight location. Encyclopædia Britannica, Inc.

with respect to the normal to the surface—that is, to a line perpendicular to the surface.) The reflected ray is always in the plane defined by the incident ray and the normal to the surface. The law of reflection can be used to understand the images produced by plane and curved mirrors. Unlike mirrors, most natural surfaces are rough on the scale of the wavelength of light, and, as a consequence, parallel incident light rays are reflected in many different directions, or diffusely. Diffuse reflection is responsible for the ability to see most illuminated surfaces from any position—rays reach the eyes after reflecting off every portion of the surface.

When light traveling in one transparent medium encounters a boundary with a second transparent medium (e.g., air and glass), a portion of the light is reflected and a portion is transmitted into the second medium. As the transmitted light moves into the second medium, it changes its direction of travel; that is, it is refracted. The law of refraction, also known as Snell's law, describes the relationship between the angle of incidence (θ_I) and the angle of refraction (θ_2), measured with respect to the normal ("perpendicular line") to the surface, in mathematical terms: $n_I \sin \theta_I = n_2 \sin \theta_2$, where n_I and n_2

are the index of refraction of the first and second media, respectively. The index of refraction for any medium is a dimensionless constant equal to the ratio of the speed of light in a vacuum to its speed in that medium.

By definition, the index of refraction for a vacuum is exactly 1. Because the speed of light in any transparent medium is always less than the speed of light in a vacuum, the indices of refraction of all media are greater than 1, with indices for typical transparent materials between 1 and 2. For example, the index of refraction of air at standard conditions is 1.0003, water is 1.33, and glass is about 1.5.

The basic features of refraction are easily derived from Snell's law. The amount of bending of a light ray as it crosses a boundary between two media is dictated by the difference in the two indices of refraction. When

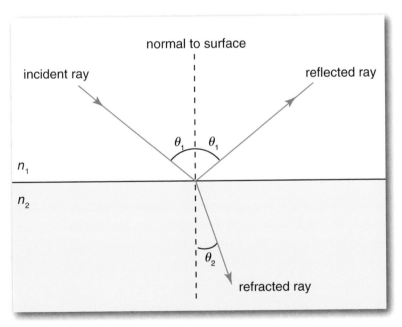

The law of refraction, or Snell's law, predicts the angle at which a light ray will bend, or refract, as it passes from one medium to another. Encyclopædia Britannica, Inc.

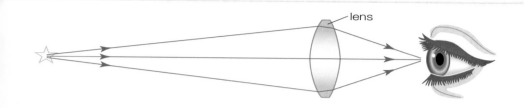

A double convex lens, or converging lens, focuses the diverging, or blurred, light rays from a distant object by refracting (bending) the rays twice. At the front side of the lens, the rays are bent toward the normal (the perpendicular to the surface) because the glass is a denser medium than the air, and, at the back side of the lens, the rays are bent away from the normal as the rays pass into the less-dense medium of the air. This double bending causes the rays to converge at a focal point behind the lens so that a sharper image can be seen or photographed. Encyclopædia Britannica, Inc.

light passes into a denser medium, the ray is bent toward the normal. Conversely, light emerging obliquely from a denser medium is bent away from the normal. In the special case where the incident beam is perpendicular to the boundary (that is, equal to the normal), there is no change in the direction of the light as it enters the second medium.

Snell's law governs the imaging properties of lenses. Light rays passing through a lens are bent at both surfaces of the lens. With proper design of the curvatures of the surfaces, various focusing effects can be realized. For example, rays initially diverging from a point source of light can be redirected by a lens to converge at a point in space, forming a focused image. The optics of the human eye is centred around the focusing properties of the cornea and the crystalline lens. Light rays from distant objects pass through these two components and are focused into a sharp image on the light-sensitive retina. Other optical imaging systems range from simple single-lens applications, such as the magnifying glass, the eyeglass, and the contact lens, to complex configurations of multiple lenses. It is not unusual for a modern camera to have a half dozen

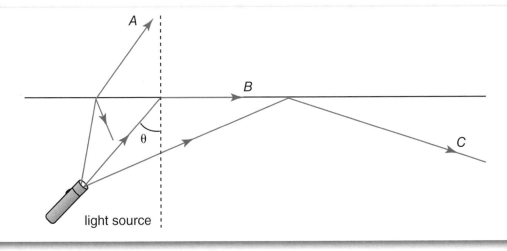

light source

Total internal reflection. When a light ray strikes the interface between two mediums, it is refracted through an angle that depends on the index of refraction of each material and the ray's angle of incidence, as measured relative to the normal (perpendicular) between the surfaces. At the critical angle of incidence (Θ), light is refracted such that it just remains within the original medium, as shown in ray B. For any light ray, such as C, that strikes the interface at a larger angle, all of the light is reflected internally. For angles less than the critical angle, such as A, some of the light passes through into the second medium. Encyclopædia Britannica, Inc.

or more separate lens elements, chosen to produce specific magnifications, minimize light losses via unwanted reflections, and minimize image distortion caused by lens aberrations.

TOTAL INTERNAL REFLECTION

One interesting consequence of the law of refraction is associated with light passing into a medium with a lower index of refraction. As previously mentioned, in this case light rays are bent away from the normal of the interface between the media. At what is called the critical angle of incidence (Θ), the refracted rays make an angle of 90° with the normal—in other words, they just skim the boundary of the two media. The sine of the critical angle is easily derived from the law of refraction: $\sin \Theta = {^{n_2}}\!/\!{_{n_1}}$.

For any incident angle greater than the critical angle, light rays are completely reflected inside the material. This phenomenon, called total internal reflection, is commonly taken advantage of to "pipe" light in a curved path. When light is directed down a narrow fibre of glass or plastic, the light repeatedly reflects off the fibre-air interface at a large incident angle—larger than the critical angle (for a glass-air interface the critical angle is about 42°). Optical fibres with diameters from 10 to 50 micrometres can transmit light over long distances with little loss of intensity. Optical communications uses sequences of light pulses to transmit information through an optical fibre network. Medical instruments such as endoscopes rely on the total internal reflection of light through an optical fibre bundle to image internal organs.

DISPERSION

Through his careful investigation of the refraction of white light as it passed through a glass prism, Isaac Newton was famously credited with the discovery that white light consists of a spectrum of colours. The dispersion of white light into its constituent colours is caused by a variation of the index of refraction of glass with colour. This effect, known as chromatic dispersion, results from the fact that the speed of light in glass depends on the wavelength of the light. The speed slightly decreases with decreasing wavelength; this means that the index of refraction, which is inversely proportional to the speed, slightly increases with decreasing wavelength. For glass, the index of refraction for red light (the longest visible wavelength) is about

A prism spreads white light into its various component wavelengths, or colours. © Getty Images

1 percent less than that for violet light (the shortest visible wavelength).

The focusing properties of glass lenses, being determined by their indices of refraction, are slightly dependent on colour. When a single lens images a distant white-light point source, such as a star, the image is slightly distorted because of dispersion in the lens; this effect is called chromatic aberration. In an effort to improve upon the chromatic aberration of the refracting telescope, Newton invented the reflecting telescope, in which the imaging and magnification are accomplished with mirrors.

Dispersion is not restricted to glass; all transparent media exhibit some dispersion. Many beautiful optical effects are explained by the phenomena of dispersion, refraction, and reflection. Principal among them is the

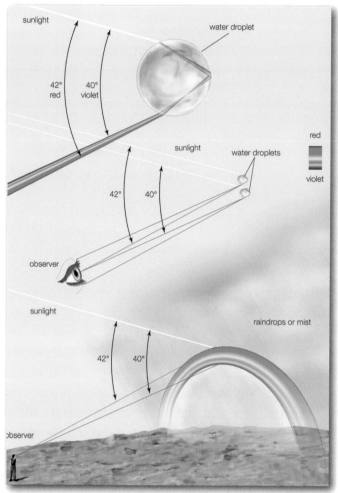

The rainbow effect. As sunlight enters water droplets in the atmosphere, its constituent colours (wavelengths) are bent (refracted) by slightly different amounts during its passage from the air into the water. A portion of the light striking the back of each water droplet is internally reflected and then refracted a second time as it reemerges into the air. Violet light is refracted most and reemerges at an angle of about 40° compared with the incident sunlight; red light is refracted least and reemerges at an angle of 42° compared with the incident sunlight. In order for observers to see a rainbow, they must have the Sun behind them such that the angle between the incident sunlight and their line of sight is about 42°. Thus, a rainbow forms a full circular arc with a central angle from the observer of 42°. However, the lower portion of the arc is obscured by the surface of the Earth; consequently, the maximum arc (a semicircle) can be seen near sunset. Encyclopædia Britannica, Inc.

rainbow, for which René Descartes and Newton are credited with the first solid quantitative analyses. A rainbow is formed when sunlight is refracted by spherical water droplets in the atmosphere; two refractions and one reflection, combined with the chromatic dispersion of water, produce the primary arcs of colour. The laws of geometrical optics also explain the formation of mirages and halos and the rarely observed "green flash" of a setting Sun.

The rules of geometrical optics, developed through centuries of observation, can be derived from the classical electromagnetic-wave model of light. However, as long as the physical dimensions of the objects that light encounters (and the apertures through which it passes) are significantly greater than the wavelength of the electromagnetic wave, there is no need for the mathematical formalism of the wave model. In those circumstances, light is adequately modeled as a collection of rays following the rules of geometrical optics. Most everyday optical phenomena can be handled within this approximation, since the wavelengths of visible light are relatively short (400 to 700 nm). However, as the dimensions of objects and apertures approach the wavelength of light, the wave character of light cannot be disregarded. Many optical effects, often subtle in nature, cannot be understood without a wave model. For example, on close inspection the shadows of objects in parallel light are seen not to be infinitely sharp. This is a consequence of the "bending" of waves around corners—a phenomenon best explained by the wave model. Another class of phenomena involves the polarization of light waves. These issues are addressed below.

LIGHT AS A WAVE

Newton's corpuscular model of light was championed by most of the European scientific community throughout the 1700s, but by the start of the 19th century it was facing challenges. About 1802, English physician and physicist Thomas Young showed that an interference pattern is produced when light from two sources overlaps. Though it took some time for Young's contemporaries to accept fully the implications of his landmark discovery, it conclusively demonstrated that light has wavelike characteristics. Young's work ushered in a period of intense experimental and theoretical activity that culminated 60 years later in a fully developed wave theory of light. By the latter years of the 19th century, corpuscular theories were abandoned. Before describing Young's work, an introduction to the relevant features of waves is in order.

CHARACTERISTICS OF WAVES

From ripples on a pond to deep ocean swells, sound waves, and light, all waves share some basic characteristics. Broadly speaking, a wave is a disturbance that propagates through space. Most waves move through a supporting medium, with the disturbance being a physical displacement of the medium. The time dependence of the displacement at any single point in space is often an oscillation about some equilibrium position. For example, a sound wave travels through the medium of air, and the disturbance is a small collective displacement of air molecules—individual molecules oscillate back and forth as the wave passes.

Unlike particles, which have well-defined positions and trajectories, waves are not localized in space. Rather, waves fill regions of space, and their evolutions in time are not described by simple trajectories. Nevertheless, some waves are more localized than others, and so it is useful to distinguish two broad classes. (1) A wave pulse is a relatively localized disturbance. For example, when a stone is dropped into a pond, the resulting ripples, which constitute a surface wave, extend over only a small portion of the surface at any instant of time. (2) At the opposite extreme, periodic waves can extend over great distances. In the example above, if the water surface is repeatedly disturbed at one point for a long period of time, the surface ripples eventually will blanket a large area.

A simple and useful example of a periodic wave is a harmonic wave. The wavelength λ of the wave is the physical separation between successive crests. The maximum

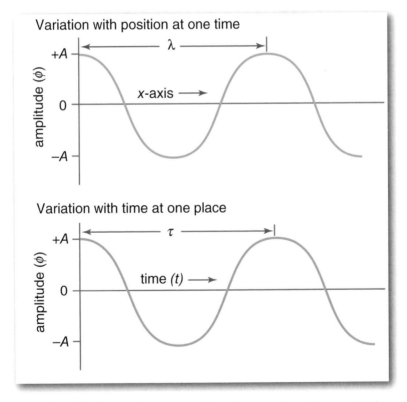

Snapshots of a harmonic wave can be taken at a fixed time to display the wave's variation with position (top) *or at a fixed location to display the wave's variation with time* (bottom). Encyclopædia Britannica, Inc.

displacement of the wave, or amplitude, is denoted by A. The time between successive oscillations is called the period τ of the wave. The number of oscillations per second is the wave frequency f, which is the reciprocal of the period, $1/\tau$.

Harmonic waves propagate with well-defined velocities that are related to their frequency and wavelength. Fixing attention on a single point in space, the number of wave crests that pass that point per second is the wave frequency f. The distance traveled past that point by any one crest in one second—the wave velocity v—is equal to the distance between crests λ multiplied by the frequency: $v = \lambda f$.

The properties of harmonic waves are illustrated in the mathematical expression for the displacement in both space and time. For a harmonic wave traveling in the x-direction, the spatial and time dependence of the displacement ϕ is

$$\phi(x,t) = A\cos\left(\frac{2\pi x}{\lambda} - 2\pi f t\right).$$

INTERFERENCE

A defining characteristic of all waves is superposition, which describes the behaviour of overlapping waves. The superposition principle states that when two or more waves overlap in space, the resultant disturbance is equal to the algebraic sum of the individual disturbances. (This is sometimes violated for large disturbances.) This simple underlying behaviour leads to a number of effects that are collectively called interference phenomena.

There are two extreme limits to interference effects. In constructive interference the crests of two waves coincide, and the waves are said to be in phase with each other.

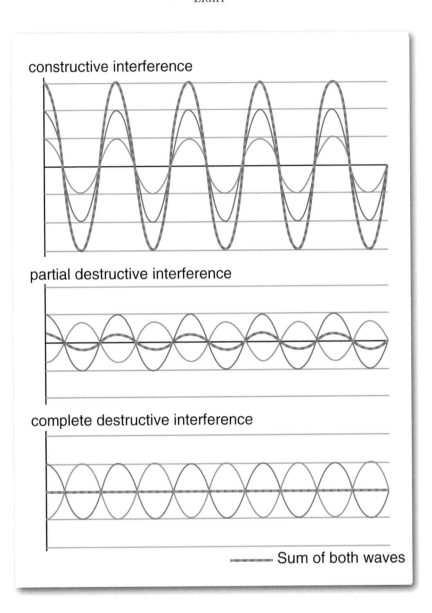

constructive interference

partial destructive interference

complete destructive interference

━━━━ Sum of both waves

When two waves of identical wavelength are in phase, they form a new wave with an amplitude equal to the sum of their individual amplitudes (constructive interference). When two waves are of completely opposite phase, they either form a new wave of reduced amplitude (partial destructive interference) or cancel each other out (complete destructive interference). Much more complicated constructive and destructive interference patterns emerge when waves with different wavelengths interact. Encyclopædia Britannica, Inc.

Their superposition results in a reinforcement of the disturbance; the amplitude of the resulting combined wave is the sum of the individual amplitudes. Conversely, in destructive interference the crest of one wave coincides with the valley of a second wave, and they are said to be out of phase. The amplitude of the combined wave equals the difference between the amplitudes of the individual waves. In the special case where those individual amplitudes are equal, the destructive interference is complete, and the net disturbance to the medium is zero.

Young's Double-Slit Experiment

The observation of interference effects definitively indicates the presence of overlapping waves. Thomas Young

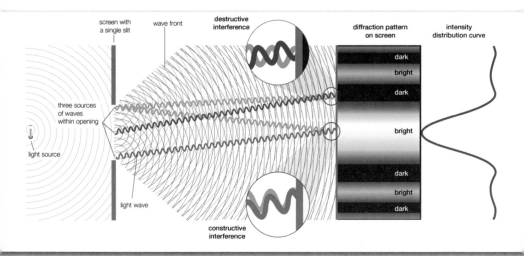

Young's double-slit experiment. When monochromatic light passing through two narrow slits illuminates a distant screen, a characteristic pattern of bright and dark fringes is observed. This interference pattern is caused by the superposition of overlapping light waves originating from the two slits. Regions of constructive interference, corresponding to bright fringes, are produced when the path difference from the two slits to the fringe is an integral number of wavelengths of the light. Destructive interference and dark fringes are produced when the path difference is a half-integral number of wavelengths. Encyclopædia Britannica, Inc.

postulated that light is a wave and is subject to the super-position principle; his great experimental achievement was to demonstrate the constructive and destructive interference of light (*c.* 1801). In a modern version of Young's experiment, differing in its essentials only in the source of light, a laser equally illuminates two parallel slits in an otherwise opaque surface. The light passing through the two slits is observed on a distant screen. When the widths of the slits are significantly greater than the wavelength of the light, the rules of geometrical optics hold—the light casts two shadows, and there are two illuminated regions on the screen. However, as the slits are narrowed in width, the light diffracts into the geometrical shadow, and the light waves overlap on the screen. (Diffraction is itself caused by the wave nature of light, being another example of an interference effect—it is discussed in more detail below.) The superposition principle determines the resulting intensity pattern on the illuminated screen. Constructive interference occurs whenever the difference in paths from the two slits to a point on the screen equals an integral number of wavelengths (0, λ, 2λ, . . .). This path difference guarantees that crests from the two waves arrive simultaneously. Destructive interference arises from path differences that equal a half-integral number of wavelengths ($\lambda/2$, $3\lambda/2$, . . .). Young used geometrical arguments to show that the superposition of the two waves results in a series of equally spaced bands, or fringes, of high intensity, corresponding to regions of constructive interference, separated by dark regions of complete destructive interference.

An important parameter in the double-slit geometry is the ratio of the wavelength of the light λ to the spacing of the slits d. If λ/d is much smaller than 1, the spacing between consecutive interference fringes will be small, and the interference effects may not be observable.

Using narrowly separated slits, Young was able to separate the interference fringes. In this way he determined the wavelengths of the colours of visible light. The very short wavelengths of visible light explain why interference effects are observed only in special circumstances—the spacing between the sources of the interfering light waves must be very small to separate regions of constructive and destructive interference.

Observing interference effects is challenging because of two other difficulties. Most light sources emit a continuous range of wavelengths, which result in many overlapping interference patterns, each with a different fringe spacing. The multiple interference patterns wash out the most pronounced interference effects, such as the regions of complete darkness. Second, for an interference pattern to be observable over any extended period of time, the two sources of light must be coherent with respect to each other. This means that the light sources must maintain a constant phase relationship. For example, two harmonic waves of the same frequency always have a fixed phase relationship at every point in space, being either in phase, out of phase, or in some intermediate relationship. However, most light sources do not emit true harmonic waves; instead, they emit waves that undergo random phase changes millions of times per second. Such light is called incoherent. Interference still occurs when light waves from two incoherent sources overlap in space, but the interference pattern fluctuates randomly as the phases of the waves shift randomly. Detectors of light, including the eye, cannot register the quickly shifting interference patterns, and only a time-averaged intensity is observed. Laser light is approximately monochromatic (consisting of a single wavelength) and is highly coherent; it is thus an ideal source for revealing interference effects.

After 1802, Young's measurements of the wavelengths of visible light could be combined with the relatively crude determinations of the speed of light available at the time in order to calculate the approximate frequencies of light. For example, the frequency of green light is about 6×10^{14} Hz (hertz, or cycles per second). This frequency is many orders of magnitude larger than the frequencies of common mechanical waves. For comparison, humans can hear sound waves with frequencies up to about 2×10^4 Hz. Exactly what was oscillating at such a high rate remained a mystery for another 60 years.

THIN-FILM INTERFERENCE

Observable interference effects are not limited to the double-slit geometry used by Thomas Young. The phenomenon of thin-film interference results whenever light reflects off two surfaces separated by a distance comparable to its wavelength. The "film" between the surfaces can be a vacuum, air, or any transparent liquid or solid. In visible light, noticeable interference effects are restricted to films with thicknesses on the order of a few micrometres. A familiar example is the film of a soap bubble. Light reflected from a bubble is a superposition of two waves — one reflecting off the front surface and a second reflecting off the back surface. The two reflected waves overlap in space and interfere. Depending on the thickness of the soap film, the two waves may interfere constructively or destructively. A full analysis shows that, for light of a single wavelength λ, there are constructive interference for film thicknesses equal to $\lambda/4$, $3\lambda/4$, $5\lambda/4$, . . . and destructive interference for thicknesses equal to $\lambda/2$, λ, $3\lambda/2$, ...

When white light illuminates a soap film, bright bands of colour are observed as different wavelengths suffer destructive interference and are removed from the reflection. The remaining reflected light appears as the complementary colour of the removed wavelength (e.g., if red light is removed by destructive interference, the reflected light will appear as cyan). Thin films of oil on water produce a similar effect. In nature, the feathers of certain birds, including peacocks and hummingbirds, and the shells of some beetles display iridescence, in which the colour on reflection changes with the viewing angle. This is caused by the interference of reflected light waves from thinly layered structures or regular arrays of reflecting rods. In a similar fashion, pearls and abalone shells are iridescent from the interference caused by reflections from multiple layers of nacre. Gemstones such as opal exhibit beautiful interference effects arising from the scattering of light from regular patterns of microscopic spherical particles.

There are many technological applications of interference effects in light. Common antireflection coatings on camera lenses are thin films with thicknesses and indices of refraction chosen to produce destructive interference on reflection for visible light. More-specialized coatings, consisting of multiple layers of thin films, are designed to transmit light only within a narrow range of wavelengths and thus act as wavelength filters. Multilayer coatings are also used to enhance the reflectivity of mirrors in astronomical telescopes and in the optical cavities of lasers. The precision techniques of interferometry measure small changes in relative distances by monitoring the fringe shifts in the interference patterns of reflected light. For example, the curvatures of surfaces in optical components are monitored to fractions of an optical wavelength with interferometric methods.

Diffraction

The subtle pattern of light and dark fringes seen in the geometrical shadow when light passes an obstacle, first observed by the Jesuit mathematician Francesco Grimaldi in the 17th century, is an example of the wave phenomenon of diffraction. Diffraction is a product of the superposition of waves—it is an interference effect. Whenever a wave is obstructed, those portions of the wave not affected by the obstruction interfere with one another in the region of space beyond the obstruction. The mathematics of diffraction is considerably complicated, and a detailed, systematic theory was not worked out until 1818 by the French physicist Augustin-Jean Fresnel.

The Dutch scientist Christiaan Huygens first stated the fundamental principle for understanding diffraction: every point on a wave front can be considered a secondary source of spherical wavelets. The shape of the advancing wave front is determined by the envelope of the overlapping spherical wavelets. If the wave is unobstructed, Huygens's principle will not be needed for determining its evolution—the rules of geometrical optics will suffice. (However, note that the light rays of geometrical optics are always perpendicular to the advancing wavefront; in this sense, the progress of a light ray is ultimately always determined by Huygens's principle.) Huygens's principle becomes necessary when a wave meets an obstacle or an aperture in an otherwise opaque surface. Thus, for a plane wave passing through a small aperture, only wavelets originating within the aperture contribute to the transmitted wave, which is seen to spread into the region of the aperture's geometric shadow.

Fresnel incorporated Young's principle of interference into Huygens's construction and calculated the detailed intensity patterns produced by interfering secondary wavelets. For a viewing screen a distance L from a slit of width a, light of wavelength λ produces a central intensity maximum that is approximately $\lambda L/a$ in width. This result highlights the most important qualitative feature of diffraction: the effect is normally apparent only when the sizes of obstacles or apertures are on the order of the wavelength of the wave. For example, audible sound waves have wavelengths of about one metre, which easily diffract around commonplace objects. This is why sound is heard around corners. On the other hand, visible light has wavelengths of a fraction of a micrometre, and it therefore does not noticeably bend around large objects. Only the most careful measurements by Young, Fresnel, and their early 19th-century contemporaries revealed the details of the diffraction of visible light.

DIFFRACTION EFFECTS

The diffraction of light produces some interesting phenomena. The counterintuitive Poisson's spot defies our intuition. The atmospheric glories delight us with their beauty.

POISSON'S SPOT

Fresnel presented much of his work on diffraction as an entry to a competition on the subject sponsored by the French Academy of Sciences. The committee of judges included a number of prominent advocates of Newton's corpuscular model of light, one of whom, Siméon-Denis Poisson, pointed out that Fresnel's model predicted a seemingly absurd result: If a parallel beam of light falls on a small spherical obstacle, there will be a bright spot at the centre of the circular shadow—a spot nearly as bright as if the obstacle were not there at all. An experiment was subsequently performed by the French physicist François Arago, and Poisson's spot was seen, vindicating Fresnel.

CIRCULAR APERTURES AND IMAGE RESOLUTION

Circular apertures also produce diffraction patterns. When a parallel beam of light passes through a converging lens, the rules of geometrical optics predict that the light comes to a tight focus behind the lens, forming a point image. In reality, the pattern in the lens's image plane is complicated by diffraction effects. The lens, considered as a circular aperture with diameter D, produces a two-dimensional diffraction pattern with a central intensity maximum of angular width about $\lambda/\underline{D}$. Angular width refers to the angle, measured in radians, that is defined by the two intensity minima on either side of the central maximum.

Diffraction effects from circular apertures have an important practical consequence: the intensity patterns in optical images produced by circular lenses and mirrors are limited in their ability to resolve closely spaced features. Each point in the object is imaged into a diffraction pattern of finite width, and the final image is a sum of individual diffraction patterns. Lord Rayleigh, a leading figure of late 19th-century physics, showed that the images of two point sources are resolvable only if their angular separation, relative to an imaging element of diameter D, is greater than about $1.2\lambda/D$ ("Rayleigh's criterion").

Circular aperture diffraction effects limit the resolving power of telescopes and microscopes. This is one of the reasons why the best astronomical telescopes have large-diameter mirrors; in addition to the obvious advantage of an increased light-gathering capability, larger mirrors decrease the resolvable angular separation of astronomical objects. To minimize diffraction effects, optical microscopes are sometimes designed to use ultraviolet light rather than longer-wavelength visible light. Nevertheless, diffraction is often the limiting factor in the ability of a microscope to resolve the fine details of objects.

The late 19th-century French painter Georges Seurat created a new technique, known as pointillism, based on diffraction effects. His paintings consist of thousands of closely spaced small dots of colour. When viewed up close, the individual points of colour are apparent to the eye. Viewed from afar, the individual points cannot be resolved because of the diffraction of the images produced by the lens of the eye. The overlapping images on the retina combine to produce colours other than those used in the individual dots of paint. The same physics underlies the use of closely spaced arrays of red, blue, and green phosphors on television screens and computer monitors; diffraction effects in the eye mix the three primary colours to produce a wide range of hues.

ATMOSPHERIC DIFFRACTION EFFECTS

Diffraction is also responsible for certain optical effects in the Earth's atmosphere. A set of concentric coloured rings, known as an atmospheric corona, often overlapping to produce a single diffuse whitish ring, is sometimes observed around the Moon. The corona is produced as light reflected from the Moon diffracts through water droplets or ice crystals in Earth's upper atmosphere. When the droplets are of uniform diameter, the different colours are clearly distinct in the diffraction pattern. A related and beautiful atmospheric phenomenon is the glory. Seen in backscattered light from water droplets, commonly forming a fog or mist, the glory is a set of rings of coloured light surrounding the shadow of the observer. The rings of light, with angular diameters of a few degrees, are created by the interplay of refraction, reflection, and diffraction in the water droplets. The glory, once a phenomenon rarely observed, is now frequently seen by airline travelers as coloured rings surrounding their airplane's shadow on a nearby cloud. Finally, the primary and secondary arcs of a rainbow are adequately explained by geometrical optics. However,

Diffraction rings, or the glory, occur most commonly when the Sun shines on a cloud or fog. The radius of the rings is dependent on the size of the cloud droplets — the smaller the droplets, the larger the radii. Moreover, the droplets must be nearly uniform in size for the phenomenon to appear. Harald Edens the more subtle supernumerary bows—weak arcs of light occasionally seen below the primary arc of colours—are caused by diffraction effects in the water droplets that form the rainbow.

THE DOPPLER EFFECT

In 1842 Austrian physicist Christian Doppler established that the apparent frequency of sound waves from an approaching source is greater than the frequency emitted by the source and that the apparent frequency of a receding source is lower. The Doppler effect, which is easily noticed with approaching or receding police sirens, also applies to light waves. The light from an approaching source is shifted up in frequency, or blueshifted, while light from a receding source is shifted down in frequency, or redshifted. The frequency shift depends on the velocity of the source relative to the observer; for velocities much less than the speed of light, the shift is proportional to the velocity.

The observation of Doppler shifts in atomic spectral lines is a powerful tool to measure relative motion in astronomy. Most notably, redshifted light from distant galaxies is the primary evidence for the general expansion of the universe. There are a host of other astronomical applications, including the determination of binary star orbits and the rotation rates of galaxies. The most common terrestrial application of the Doppler effect occurs in radar systems. Electromagnetic waves reflected from a moving object undergo Doppler shifts that can then be used to determine the object's speed. In these applications, ranging from monitoring automobile speeds to monitoring wind speeds in the atmosphere, radio waves or microwaves are used instead of visible light.

LIGHT AS ELECTROMAGNETIC RADIATION

In spite of theoretical and experimental advances in the first half of the 19th century that established the wave properties of light, the nature of light was not yet revealed—the identity of the wave oscillations remained a mystery. This situation dramatically changed in the 1860s when the Scottish physicist James Clerk Maxwell, in a watershed theoretical treatment, unified the fields of electricity, magnetism, and optics. In his formulation of electromagnetism, Maxwell described light as a propagating wave of electric and magnetic fields. More generally, he predicted the existence of electromagnetic radiation: coupled electric and magnetic fields traveling as waves at a speed equal to the known speed of light. In 1888 German physicist Heinrich Hertz succeeded in demonstrating the existence of long-wavelength electromagnetic waves and showed that their properties are consistent with those of the shorter-wavelength visible light.

ELECTRIC AND MAGNETIC FIELDS

The subjects of electricity and magnetism were well developed by the time Maxwell began his synthesizing work. English physician William Gilbert initiated the careful study of magnetic phenomena in the late 16th century. In the late 1700s an understanding of electric phenomena was pioneered by Benjamin Franklin, Charles-Augustin de Coulomb, and others. Siméon-Denis Poisson, Pierre-Simon Laplace, and Carl Friedrich Gauss developed powerful mathematical descriptions of electrostatics and magnetostatics that stand to the present time. The first connection between electric and magnetic effects was discovered by Danish physicist Hans Christian Ørsted in 1820 when he found that electric currents produce magnetic forces. Soon after, French physicist André-Marie Ampère developed a mathematical formulation (Ampère's law) relating currents to magnetic effects. In 1831 the great English experimentalist Michael Faraday discovered electromagnetic induction, in which a moving magnet (more generally, a changing magnetic flux) induces an electric current in a conducting circuit.

Faraday's conception of electric and magnetic effects laid the groundwork for Maxwell's equations. Faraday visualized electric charges as producing fields that extend through space and transmit electric and magnetic forces to other distant charges. The notion of electric and magnetic fields is central to the theory of electromagnetism, and so it requires some explanation. A field is used to represent any physical quantity whose value changes from one point in space to another. For example, the temperature of Earth's atmosphere has a definite value at every point above the surface of Earth; to specify the atmospheric temperature completely thus requires specifying a distribution of numbers—one for each spatial point. The temperature "field" is simply a mathematical accounting of those numbers; it may be expressed as a function of the spatial coordinates. The values of the temperature field can also vary with time; therefore, the field is more generally expressed as a function of spatial coordinates and time: $T(x, y, z, t)$, where T is the temperature field, x, y, and z are the spatial coordinates, and t is the time.

Temperature is an example of a scalar field; its complete specification requires only one number for each spatial point. Vector fields, on the other hand, describe physical quantities that have a direction and magnitude at each point in space. A familiar example is the velocity field of a fluid. Electric and magnetic fields are also vector fields; the electric field is written as $E(x, y, z, t)$ and the magnetic field as $B(x, y, z, t)$.

Maxwell's Equations

In the early 1860s, Maxwell completed a study of electric and magnetic phenomena. He presented a mathematical formulation in which the values of the electric and magnetic fields at all points in space can be calculated from a knowledge of the sources of the fields. By Faraday's time, it was known that electric charges are the source of electric fields and that electric currents (charges in motion) are the source of magnetic fields. Faraday's electromagnetic induction showed that there is a second source of electric fields—changing magnetic fields. In a significant step in the development of his theory, Maxwell postulated that changing electric fields are sources of magnetic fields. In its modern form, Maxwell's electromagnetic theory is expressed as four partial differential equations for the fields E and B. Known as Maxwell's equations, these four statements relating the fields to their sources, along with the expression for the forces exerted by the fields on electric charges, constitute the whole of classical electromagnetism.

Electromagnetic Waves and the Electromagnetic Spectrum

A manipulation of the four equations for the electric and magnetic fields led Maxwell to wave equations for the fields, the solutions of which are traveling harmonic waves. Though the mathematical treatment is detailed, the underlying origin of the waves can be understood qualitatively: changing magnetic fields produce electric fields, and changing electric fields produce magnetic fields. This implies the possibility of an electromagnetic field in which a changing electric field continually gives rise to a changing magnetic field, and vice versa.

ELECTROMAGNETIC WAVES

Electromagnetic waves do not represent physical displacements that propagate through a medium like mechanical sound and water waves; instead, they describe propagating oscillations in the strengths of electric and magnetic fields. Maxwell's wave equation showed that the speed of the waves, labeled c, is determined by a combination of constants in the laws of electrostatics and magnetostatics—in modern notation:

$$c = \frac{1}{\sqrt{\varepsilon_o \mu_o}}$$

where ε_o, the permittivity of free space, has an experimentally determined value of 8.85×10^{-12} square coulomb per newton square metre, and μ_o, the magnetic permeability of free space, has a value of 1.26×10^{-6} newton square seconds per square coulomb. The calculated speed, about 3×10^8 metres per second, agreed with the known speed of light. In an 1864 lecture before the Royal Society of London, "A Dynamical Theory of the Electro-Magnetic Field," Maxwell asserted:

> We have strong reason to conclude that light itself— including radiant heat and other radiation, if any—is an electromagnetic disturbance in the form of waves propagated through the electro-magnetic field according to electro-magnetic laws.

Maxwell's achievement ranks as one of the greatest advances of physics. For the physicist of the late 19th century, the study of light became a study of an electromagnetic phenomenon—the fields of electricity, magnetism, and optics were unified in one grand design. While an understanding of light has undergone some profound changes since the 1860s as a result of the discovery of light's quantum mechanical nature, Maxwell's electromagnetic wave model remains completely adequate for many purposes.

THE ELECTROMAGNETIC SPECTRUM

Heinrich Hertz's production in 1888 of what are now called radio waves, his verification that these waves travel at the same speed as visible light, and his measurements of their reflection, refraction, diffraction, and polarization properties were a convincing demonstration of the existence of Maxwell's waves. Visible light is but one example of a much broader set of phenomena—an electromagnetic spectrum with no theoretical upper or lower limit to frequencies and wavelengths. While there are no theoretical distinctions between electromagnetic waves of any wavelength, the spectrum is conventionally divided into different regions on the basis of historical developments, the methods of production and detection of the waves, and their technological uses.

SOURCES OF ELECTROMAGNETIC WAVES

The sources of classical electromagnetic waves are accelerating electric charges. (Note that acceleration refers to a change in velocity, which occurs whenever a particle's speed or its direction of motion changes.) A common example is the generation of radio waves by oscillating electric charges in an antenna. When a charge moves in a linear antenna

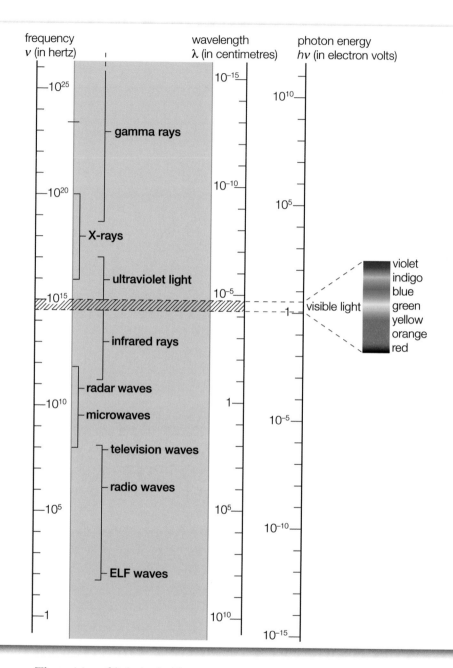

The position of light in the electromagnetic spectrum. The narrow range of visible light is shown enlarged at the right. Encyclopædia Britannica, Inc.

with an oscillation frequency f, the oscillatory motion constitutes an acceleration, and an electromagnetic wave with the same frequency propagates away from the antenna. At frequencies above the microwave region, with a few prominent exceptions, the classical picture of an accelerating electric charge producing an electromagnetic wave is less and less applicable. In the infrared, visible, and ultraviolet regions, the primary radiators are the charged particles in atoms and molecules. In this regime a quantum mechanical radiation model is far more relevant.

THE SPEED OF LIGHT

Measurements of the speed of light have challenged scientists for centuries. For millennia, it was believed that the speed of light was infinite. However, science has not yet advanced to the point of measuring something as fast as light.

EARLY MEASUREMENTS

The assumption that the speed is infinite was dispelled by the Danish astronomer Ole Rømer in 1676. French physicist Armand-Hippolyte-Louis Fizeau was the first to succeed in a terrestrial measurement in 1849, sending a light beam along a 17.3-km (10.75 miles) round-trip path across the outskirts of Paris. At the light source, the exiting beam was chopped by a rotating toothed wheel; the measured rotational rate of the wheel at which the beam, upon its return, was eclipsed by the toothed rim was used to determine the beam's travel time. Fizeau reported a light speed that differs by only about 5 percent from the currently accepted value. One year later, French physicist Jean-Bernard-Léon Foucault improved the accuracy of the technique to about 1 percent.

In the same year, Foucault showed that the speed of light in water is less than its speed in air by the ratio of the indices of refraction of air and water:

$$v_{water} = \frac{n_{air}}{n_{water}} v_{air} \approx 0.75 v_{air}.$$

This measurement established the index of refraction of a material as the ratio of the speed of light in vacuum to the speed within the material. The more general finding, that light is slowed in transparent media, directly

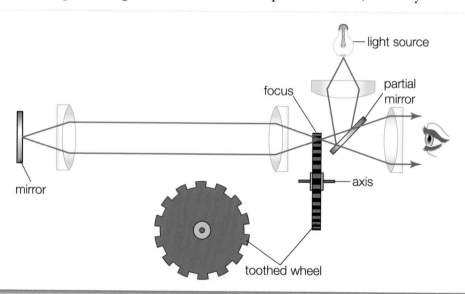

In 1849, Armand Fizeau sent light pulses through a rotating toothed wheel. A distant mirror on the other side reflected the pulses back through gaps in the wheel. By rotating the wheel at a certain speed, each light pulse that went through a gap on the way out was blocked by the next tooth as it came around. Knowing the distance to the mirror and the speed of rotation of the wheel enabled Fizeau to obtain one of the earliest measurements of the speed of light. Encyclopædia Britannica, Inc.

contradicted Isaac Newton's assertion that light corpuscles travel faster in media than in vacuum and settled any lingering 19th-century doubts about the corpuscle–wave debate.

THE MICHELSON-MORLEY EXPERIMENT

The German-born American physicist A.A. Michelson set the early standard for measurements of the speed of light in the late 1870s, determining a speed within 0.02 percent of the modern value. Michelson's most noteworthy measurements of the speed of light, however, were yet to come. From the first speculations on the wave nature of light by Huygens through the progressively more refined theories of Young, Fresnel, and Maxwell, it was assumed that an underlying physical medium supports the transmission of light, in much the same way that air supports the transmission of sound. Called the ether, or the luminiferous ether, this medium was thought to permeate all of space. The inferred physical properties of the ether were problematic—to support the high-frequency transverse oscillations of light, it would have to be very rigid, but its lack of effect on planetary motion and the fact that it was not observed in any terrestrial circumstances required it to be tenuous and chemically undetectable. While there is no reference to the properties of a supporting medium in the mathematics of Maxwell's electromagnetic theory, even he subscribed to the ether's existence, writing an article on the subject for the 9th edition of *Encyclopædia Britannica* in the 1870s. In 1887, Michelson, in collaboration with American chemist Edward Morley, completed a precise set of optical measurements designed to detect the motion of Earth through the ether as it orbited the Sun.

The measurements in the Michelson-Morley experiment were based on the assumption that an observer at rest in the ether would determine a different speed from an

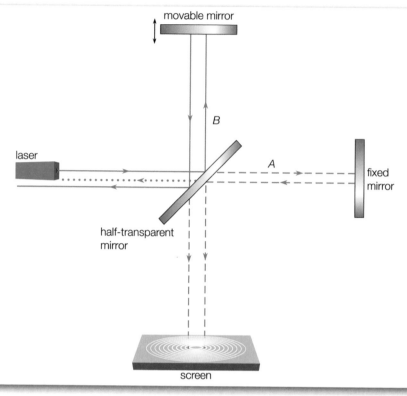

The Michelson interferometer consists of a half-transparent mirror oriented at a 45° angle to a light beam so that the light is divided into two equal parts (A and B), one of which is transmitted to a fixed mirror and the other of which is reflected to a movable mirror. The half-transparent mirror has the same effect on the returning beams, splitting each of them into two beams. Thus, two diminished light beams reach the screen, where interference patterns can be observed by varying the position of the movable mirror. Encyclopædia Britannica, Inc.

observer moving through the ether. Because Earth's speed relative to the Sun is about 29,000 metres (95,000 feet) per second, or about 0.01 percent of the speed of light, Earth provides a convenient vantage point for measuring any change in the relative speed of light due to motion. Using a Michelson optical interferometer, interference effects between two light beams traveling parallel to, and perpendicular to, Earth's orbital motion were monitored during the course of its orbit. The instrument was capable of detecting a difference in light speeds along the two paths of the interferometer as small as 5,000 metres (16,000 feet) per second (less than 2 parts in 100,000 of the speed of light). No difference was found. If Earth indeed moved through the ether, that motion seemed to have no effect on the measured speed of light.

What is now known as the most famous experimental null result in physics was reconciled in 1905 when Albert Einstein, in his formulation of special relativity, postulated that the speed of light is the same in all reference frames; i.e., the measured speed of light is independent of the relative motion of the observer and the light source. The hypothetical ether, with its preferred reference frame, was eventually abandoned as an unnecessary construct.

FUNDAMENTAL CONSTANT OF NATURE

Since Einstein's work, the speed of light is considered a fundamental constant of nature. Its significance is far broader than its role in describing a property of electromagnetic waves. It serves as the single limiting velocity in the universe, being an upper bound to the propagation speed of signals and to the speeds of all material particles. In the famous relativity equation, $E = mc^2$, the speed of light (c) serves as a constant of proportionality linking the formerly disparate concepts of mass (m) and energy (E).

Measurements of the speed of light were successively refined in the 20th century, eventually reaching a precision limited by the definitions of the units of length and time — the metre and the second. In 1983 the 17th General Conference on Weights and Measures fixed the speed of light as a defined constant at exactly 299,792,458 metres per second. The metre became a derived unit, equaling the distance traveled by light in 1/299,792,458 of a second.

POLARIZATION

A rope can be snapped so that a wave movement travels from one end to the other; the motion of the wave can be from side to side, up and down, or in any direction perpendicular to the rope. Similarly, an unpolarized light wave travels in a single direction but vibrates in random directions perpendicular to its travel. When a light wave vibrates in only one direction, it is called polarized.

TRANSVERSE WAVES

Waves come in two varieties. In a longitudinal wave the oscillating disturbance is parallel to the direction of propagation. A familiar example is a sound wave in air— the oscillating motions of the air molecules are induced in the direction of the advancing wave. Transverse waves

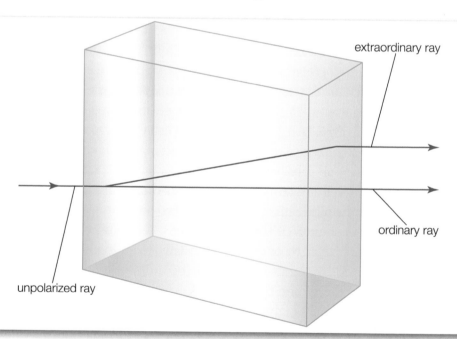

Double refraction showing two rays emerging when a single light ray strikes a calcite crystal at a right angle to one face. Encyclopædia Britannica, Inc.

consist of disturbances that are at right angles to the direction of propagation; for example, as a wave travels horizontally through a body of water, its surface bobs up and down.

A number of puzzling optical effects, first observed in the mid-17th century, were resolved when light was understood as a wave phenomenon and the directions of its oscillations were uncovered. The first so-called polarization effect was discovered by the Danish physician Erasmus Bartholin in 1669. Bartholin observed double refraction, or birefringence, in calcite (a common crystalline form of calcium carbonate). When light passes through calcite, the crystal splits the light, producing two images offset from each other. Newton was aware of this effect and speculated that perhaps his corpuscles of light had an asymmetry or "sidedness" that could explain the formation of the two images. Huygens, a contemporary of Newton, could account for double refraction with his elementary wave theory, but he did not recognize the true implications of the effect. Double refraction remained a mystery until Thomas Young, and independently the French physicist Augustin-Jean Fresnel, suggested that light waves are transverse. This simple notion provided a natural and uncomplicated framework for the analysis of polarization effects. (The polarization of the entering light wave can be described as a combination of two perpendicular polarizations, each with its own wave speed. Because of their different wave speeds, the two polarization components have different indices of refraction, and they therefore refract differently through the material, producing two images.) Fresnel quickly developed a comprehensive model of transverse light waves that accounted for double refraction and a host of other optical effects. Forty years later, Maxwell's electromagnetic theory elegantly provided the basis for the transverse nature of light.

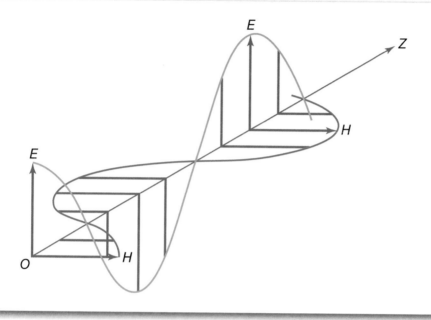

Electromagnetic wave, showing that electric field vector E *and magnetic field vector* H *are in phase.* Encyclopædia Britannica, Inc.

Maxwell's electromagnetic waves are transverse, with the electric and magnetic fields oscillating in directions perpendicular to the propagation direction. The fields are also perpendicular to one another, with the electric field direction, magnetic field direction, and propagation direction forming a right-handed coordinate system. For a wave with frequency f and wavelength λ (related by $\lambda f = c$) propagating in the positive x-direction, the fields are described mathematically by

$$\vec{E}(x,t) = E_0 \cos\left(\frac{2\pi x}{\lambda} - 2\pi f t\right)\hat{y}$$

$$\vec{B}(x,t) = B_0 \cos\left(\frac{2\pi x}{\lambda} - 2\pi f t\right)\hat{z}.$$

The equations show that the electric and magnetic fields are in phase with each other; at any given point in space, they reach their maximum values, E_o and B_o, at the same time. The amplitudes of the fields are not independent; Maxwell's equations show that $E_o = cB_o$ for all electromagnetic waves in a vacuum.

In describing the orientation of the electric and magnetic fields of a light wave, it is common practice to specify only the direction of the electric field; the magnetic field direction then follows from the requirement that the fields are perpendicular to one another, as well as the direction of wave propagation. A linearly polarized wave has the property that the fields oscillate in fixed directions as the wave propagates. Other polarization states are possible. In a circularly polarized light wave, the electric and magnetic field vectors rotate about the propagation direction while maintaining fixed amplitudes. Elliptically polarized light refers to a situation intermediate between the linear and circular polarization states.

Unpolarized Light

The atoms on the surface of a heated filament, which generate light, act independently of one another. Each of their emissions can be approximately modeled as a short "wave train" lasting from about 10^{-9} to 10^{-8} second. The electromagnetic wave emanating from the filament is a superposition of these wave trains, each having its own polarization direction. The sum of the randomly oriented wave trains results in a wave whose direction of polarization changes rapidly and randomly. Such a wave is said to be unpolarized. All common sources of light, including the Sun, incandescent and fluorescent lights, and flames, produce unpolarized light. However, natural light is often partially polarized because of multiple scatterings and reflections.

SOURCES OF POLARIZED LIGHT

Polarized light can be produced in circumstances where a spatial orientation is defined. One example is synchrotron radiation, where highly energetic charged particles move in a magnetic field and emit polarized electromagnetic waves. There are many known astronomical sources of synchrotron radiation, including emission nebulae, supernova remnants, and active galactic nuclei; the polarization of astronomical light is studied in order to infer the properties of these sources.

Natural light is polarized in passage through a number of materials, the most common being polaroid. Invented by the American physicist Edwin Land, a sheet of polaroid consists of long-chain hydrocarbon molecules aligned in

Polarized lenses selectively block light of horizontal orientation—resulting in a dramatic decrease in glare, which consists mostly of light reflected off horizontal surfaces. Polarized lenses are commonly used in sunglasses, binoculars, telescopes, and cameras. Encyclopædia Britannica, Inc.

one direction through a heat-treatment process. The molecules preferentially absorb any light with an electric field parallel to the alignment direction. The light emerging from a polaroid is linearly polarized with its electric field perpendicular to the alignment direction. Polaroid is used in many applications, including sunglasses and camera filters, to remove reflected and scattered light.

In 1808 the French physicist Étienne-Louis Malus discovered that, when natural light reflects off a nonmetallic surface, it is partially polarized. The degree of polarization depends on the angle of incidence and the index of refraction of the reflecting material. At one extreme, when the tangent of the incident angle of light in air equals the index of refraction of the reflecting material, the reflected light is 100 percent linearly polarized; this is

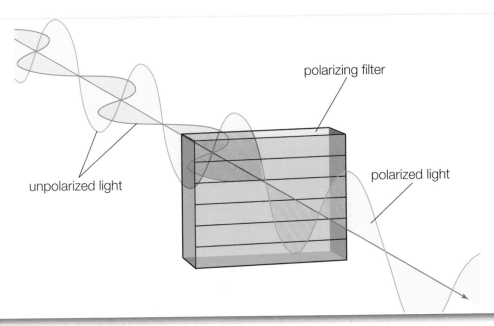

A polarizing filter has its molecules all aligned in the same direction. Light waves with the same orientation as the filter are absorbed by the molecules' vibrations, thereby reducing the intensity of the light passing through the filter. Encyclopædia Britannica, Inc.

known as Brewster's law after its discoverer, the Scottish physicist David Brewster. The direction of polarization is parallel to the reflecting surface. Because daytime glare typically originates from reflections off horizontal surfaces such as roads and water, polarizing filters are often used in sunglasses to remove horizontally polarized light, hence selectively removing glare.

The scattering of unpolarized light by very small objects, with sizes much less than the wavelength of the light (called Rayleigh scattering, after the English scientist Lord Rayleigh), also produces a partial polarization. When sunlight passes through the Earth's atmosphere, it is scattered by air molecules. The scattered light that reaches the ground is partially linearly polarized, the extent of its polarization depending on the scattering angle. Because human eyes are not sensitive to the polarization of light, this effect generally goes unnoticed. However, the eyes of many insects are responsive to polarization properties, and they use the relative polarization of ambient sky light as a navigational tool. A common camera filter employed to reduce background light in bright sunshine is a simple linear polarizer designed to reject Rayleigh scattered light from the sky.

Polarization effects are observable in optically anisotropic materials (in which the index of refraction varies with polarization direction) such as birefringent crystals and some biological structures and in optically active materials. Technological applications include polarizing microscopes, liquid crystal displays, and optical instrumentation for materials testing.

ENERGY TRANSPORT

The transport of energy by light plays a critical role in life. About 10^{22} joules of solar radiant energy reaches Earth each day. Perhaps half of that energy reaches Earth's surface, the rest being absorbed or scattered in the atmosphere. In turn, Earth continuously reradiates electromagnetic energy (predominantly in the infrared). Together, these energy-transport processes determine Earth's energy balance, setting its average temperature and driving its global weather patterns. The transformation of solar energy into chemical energy by photosynthesis in plants maintains life on Earth. The fossil fuels that power industrial society—natural gas, petroleum, and coal—are ultimately stored organic forms of solar energy deposited on Earth millions of years ago.

The electromagnetic-wave model of light accounts naturally for the origin of energy transport. In an electromagnetic wave, energy is stored in the electric and magnetic fields; as the fields propagate at the speed of light, the energy content is transported. The proper measure of energy transport in an electromagnetic wave is its irradiance, or intensity, which equals the rate at which energy passes a unit area oriented perpendicular to the direction of propagation. The time-averaged irradiance I for a harmonic electromagnetic wave is related to the amplitudes of the electric and magnetic fields: $I = \varepsilon_0 c^2 E_0 B_0 /2$ watts per square metre.

The irradiance of sunlight at the top of Earth's atmosphere is about 1,350 watts per square metre; this factor is referred to as the solar constant. Considerable efforts have gone into developing technologies to transform this solar energy into directly usable thermal or electric energy.

RADIATION PRESSURE

In addition to carrying energy, light transports momentum and is capable of exerting mechanical forces on objects. When an electromagnetic wave is absorbed by an object, the wave exerts a pressure (P) on the object that equals the wave's irradiance (I) divided by the speed of light (c): $P = I/c$ newtons per square metre.

Most natural light sources exert negligibly small forces on objects; this subtle effect was first demonstrated in 1903 by the American physicists Ernest Fox Nichols and Gordon Hull. However, radiation pressure is consequential in a number of astronomical settings. Perhaps most important, the equilibrium conditions of stellar structure are determined largely by the opposing forces of gravitational attraction on the one hand and radiation pressure and thermal pressure on the other. The outward force of the light escaping the core of a star acts to balance the inward gravitational forces on the outer layers of the star. Another, visually dramatic, example of radiation pressure is the formation of cometary tails, in which dust particles released by cometary nuclei are pushed by solar radiation into characteristic trailing patterns.

Terrestrial applications of radiation pressure became feasible with the advent of lasers in the 1960s. In part because of the small diameters of their output beams and the excellent focusing properties of the beams, laser intensities are generally orders of magnitude larger than the intensities of natural light sources. On the largest scale, the most powerful laser systems are designed to compress and heat target materials in nuclear fusion inertial confinement schemes. The radiation forces from table-top laser systems are used to manipulate atoms and microscopic objects. The techniques of laser cooling and trapping, pioneered by the Nobelists Steven Chu, William Phillips, and Claude Cohen-Tannoudji, slow a gas of atoms in an "optical molasses" of intersecting laser beams. Temperatures below 10^{-6} K (one-millionth of a degree above absolute zero) have been achieved. "Optical tweezers" is a related technique in which a tightly focused laser beam exerts a radiation force large enough to deflect, guide, and trap micron-sized objects ranging from dielectric spheres to biological samples such as viruses, single living cells, and organelles within cells.

INTERACTIONS OF LIGHT WITH MATTER

The transmission of light through a piece of glass, the reflections and refractions of light in a raindrop, and the scattering of sunlight in Earth's atmosphere are examples of interactions of light with matter. On an atomic scale, these interactions are governed by the quantum mechanical natures of matter and light, but many are adequately explained by the interactions of classical electromagnetic radiation with charged particles.

The electric and magnetic fields of the wave exert forces on the bound electrons of the atom, causing them to oscillate at the frequency of the wave. Oscillating charges are sources of electromagnetic radiation; the oscillating electrons radiate waves at the same frequency as the incoming fields. This constitutes the microscopic origin of the scattering of an electromagnetic wave. The electrons initially absorb energy from the incoming wave as they are set in motion, and they redirect that energy in the form of scattered light of the same frequency.

Through interference effects, the superposition of the reradiated waves from all of the participating atoms determines the net outcome of the scattering interactions. Two examples illustrate this point. As a light beam passes through transparent glass, the reradiated waves within the glass interfere destructively in all directions except the original propagation direction of the beam, resulting in little or no light's being scattered out of the original beam. Therefore, the light advances without loss through the glass. When sunlight passes through the Earth's upper atmosphere, on the other hand, the reradiated waves generated by the gaseous molecules do not suffer destructive interference, so that a significant amount of light is scattered in many directions. The outcomes of these two scattering interactions are quite different, primarily because of differences in the densities of the scatterers. Generally, when the mean spacing between scatterers is significantly less than the wavelength of the light (as in glass), destructive interference effects significantly limit the amount of lateral scattering; when the mean spacing is greater than, or on the order of, the wavelength and the scatterers are randomly distributed in space (as in the upper atmosphere), interference effects do not play a significant role in the lateral scattering.

Lord Rayleigh's analysis in 1871 of the scattering of light by atoms and molecules in the atmosphere showed that the intensity of the scattered light increases as the fourth power of its frequency; this strong dependence on frequency explains the colour of the sunlit sky. Being at the high-frequency end of the visible spectrum, blue light is scattered far more by air molecules than the lower-frequency colours; the sky appears blue. On the other hand, when sunlight passes through a long column of air, such as at sunrise or sunset, the high-frequency components are selectively scattered out of the beam and the remaining light appears reddish.

NONLINEAR INTERACTIONS

The interactions of light waves with matter become progressively richer as intensities are increased. The field of nonlinear optics describes interactions in which the response of the atomic oscillators is no longer simply proportional to the intensity of the incoming light wave. Nonlinear optics has many significant applications in communications and photonics, information processing, schemes for optical computing and storage, and spectroscopy.

Nonlinear effects generally become observable in a material when the strength of the electric field in the light wave is appreciable in comparison with the electric fields within the atoms of the material. Laser sources, particularly pulsed sources, easily achieve the required light intensities for this regime. Nonlinear effects are characterized by the generation of light with frequencies differing from the frequency of the incoming light beam. Classically, this is understood as resulting from the large driving forces of the electric fields of the incoming wave on the atomic oscillators. As an illustration, consider second harmonic generation, the first nonlinear effect observed in a crystal (1961). When high-intensity light of frequency f passes through an appropriate nonlinear crystal (quartz was used in the first observations), a fraction of that light is converted to light of frequency $2f$. Higher harmonics can also be generated with appropriate media, as well as combinations of frequencies when two or more light beams are used as input.

QUANTUM THEORY OF LIGHT

By the end of the 19th century, the battle over the nature of light as a wave or a collection of particles seemed over. James Clerk Maxwell's synthesis of electric, magnetic, and optical phenomena and the discovery by Heinrich Hertz of electromagnetic waves were theoretical and experimental triumphs of the first order. Along with Newtonian mechanics and thermodynamics, Maxwell's electromagnetism took its place as a foundational element of physics. However, just when everything seemed to be settled, a period of revolutionary change was ushered in at the beginning of the 20th century. A new interpretation of the emission of light by heated objects and new experimental methods that opened the atomic world for study led to a radical departure from the classical theories of Newton and Maxwell—quantum mechanics was born. Once again the question of the nature of light was reopened.

BLACKBODY RADIATION

Blackbody radiation refers to the spectrum of light emitted by any heated object; common examples include the heating element of a toaster and the filament of a light bulb. The spectral intensity of blackbody radiation peaks at a frequency that increases with the temperature of the emitting body: room temperature objects (about 300 K [27 °C, or 80 °F]) emit radiation with a peak intensity in the far infrared; radiation from toaster filaments and light bulb filaments (about 700 K [427 °C, or 800 °F] and 2,000 K [1,727 °C, or 3,140 °F], respectively) also peak in the infrared, though their spectra extend progressively into the visible; while the 6,000 K (5,727 °C, or 10,340 °F) surface of the Sun emits blackbody radiation that peaks in the centre of the visible range. In the late 1890s, calculations of the spectrum of blackbody radiation based on classical electromagnetic theory and thermodynamics could not duplicate the results of careful measurements. In fact, the calculations predicted the absurd result that, at any temperature, the spectral intensity increases without limit as a function of frequency.

In 1900 the German physicist Max Planck succeeded in calculating a blackbody spectrum that matched experimental results by proposing that the elementary oscillators at the surface of any object (the detailed structure of the oscillators was not relevant) could emit and absorb electromagnetic radiation only in discrete packets, with the energy of a packet being directly proportional to the frequency of the radiation, $E = hf$. The constant of proportionality, *h*, which Planck determined by comparing his theoretical results with the existing experimental data, is now called Planck's constant and has the approximate value 6.626×10^{-34} joule·second.

PHOTONS

Planck did not offer a physical basis for his proposal; it was largely a mathematical construct needed to match the calculated blackbody spectrum to the observed spectrum. In 1905 Albert Einstein gave a ground-breaking physical interpretation to Planck's mathematics when he proposed that electromagnetic radiation itself is granular, consisting of quanta, each with an energy *hf*. He based his conclusion on thermodynamic arguments applied to a radiation field that obeys Planck's radiation law. The term *photon*, which is now applied to the energy quantum of light, was later coined by the American chemist G.N. Lewis.

Einstein supported his photon hypothesis with an analysis of the photoelectric effect, a process, discovered by Hertz in 1887, in which electrons are ejected from a metallic surface illuminated by light. Detailed measurements showed that the onset of the effect is determined solely by the frequency of the light and the makeup of the surface and is independent of the light intensity. This behaviour was puzzling in the context of classical electromagnetic waves, whose energies are proportional to intensity and independent of frequency. Einstein supposed that a minimum amount of energy is required to liberate an electron from a surface—only photons with energies greater than this minimum can induce electron emission. This requires a minimum light frequency, in agreement with experiment. Einstein's prediction of the dependence of the kinetic energy of the ejected electrons on the light frequency, based on his photon model, was experimentally verified by the American physicist Robert Millikan in 1916.

In 1922 American Nobelist Arthur Compton treated the scattering of X-rays from electrons as a set of collisions between photons and electrons. Adapting the relation between momentum and energy for a classical electromagnetic wave to an individual photon, $p = E/c = hf/c = h/\lambda$, Compton used the conservation laws of momentum and energy to derive an expression for the wavelength shift of scattered X-rays as a function of their scattering angle. His formula matched his experimental findings, and the Compton effect, as it became known, was considered further convincing evidence for the existence of particles of electromagnetic radiation.

The energy of a photon of visible light is very small, being on the order of 4×10^{-19} joule. A more convenient energy unit in this regime is the electron volt (eV). One electron volt equals the energy gained by an electron when its electric potential is changed by one volt: $1\,eV = 1.6 \times 10^{-19}$ joule. The spectrum of visible light includes photons with energies ranging from about 1.8 eV (red light) to about 3.1 eV (violet light). Human vision cannot detect individual photons, although, at the peak of its spectral response (about 510 nm, in the green), the dark-adapted eye comes close. Under normal daylight conditions, the discrete nature of the light entering the human eye is completely obscured by the very large number of photons involved. For example, a standard 100-watt light bulb emits on the order of 10^{20} photons per second; at a distance of 10 metres from the bulb, perhaps 10^{11} photons per second will enter a normally adjusted pupil of a diameter of 2 mm.

Photons of visible light are energetic enough to initiate some critically important chemical reactions, most notably photosynthesis through absorption by chlorophyll molecules. Photovoltaic systems are engineered to convert light energy to electric energy through the absorption of visible photons by semiconductor materials. More-energetic ultraviolet photons (4 to 10 eV) can initiate photochemical reactions such as molecular dissociation and atomic and molecular ionization. Modern methods for detecting light are based on the response of materials to individual photons. Photoemissive detectors, such as photomultiplier tubes, collect electrons emitted by the photoelectric effect; in photoconductive detectors the absorption of a photon causes a change in the conductivity of a semiconductor material.

A number of subtle influences of gravity on light, predicted by Einstein's general theory of relativity, are most easily understood in the context of a photon model of light and are presented here. (However, note that general relativity is not itself a theory of quantum physics.)

Through the famous relativity equation $E = mc^2$, a photon of frequency f and energy $E = hf$ can be considered to have an effective mass of $m = hf/c^2$. Note that this effective mass is distinct from the "rest mass" of a photon, which is zero. General relativity predicts that the path of light is deflected in the gravitational field of a massive object; this can be somewhat simplistically understood as resulting from a gravitational attraction proportional to the effective mass of the photons. In addition, when light travels toward a massive object, its energy increases, and its frequency thus increases (gravitational blueshift). Gravitational redshift describes the converse situation where light traveling away from a massive object loses energy and its frequency decreases.

QUANTUM MECHANICS

The first two decades of the 20th century left the status of the nature of light confused. That light is a wave phenomenon was indisputable; there were countless examples of interference effects — the signature of waves — and a well-developed electromagnetic wave theory. However, there was also undeniable evidence that light consists of a collection of particles with well-defined energies and momenta. This paradoxical wave-particle duality was soon seen to be shared by all elements of the material world.

In 1923 the French physicist Louis de Broglie suggested that wave-particle duality is a feature common to light and all matter. In direct analogy to photons, de Broglie proposed that electrons with momentum p should exhibit wave properties with an associated wavelength $\lambda = h/p$. Four years later, de Broglie's hypothesis of matter waves, or de Broglie waves, was experimentally confirmed by Clinton Davisson and Lester Germer at Bell Laboratories with their observation of electron diffraction effects.

A radically new mathematical framework for describing the microscopic world, incorporating de Broglie's hypothesis, was formulated in 1926–27 by the German physicist Werner Heisenberg and the Austrian physicist Erwin Schrödinger, among others. In quantum mechanics, the dominant theory of 20th-century physics, the Newtonian notion of a classical particle with a well-defined trajectory is replaced by the wave function, a nonlocalized function of space and time. The interpretation of the wave function, originally suggested by the German physicist Max Born, is statistical — the wave function provides the means for calculating the probability of finding a particle at any point in space. When a measurement is made to detect a particle, it always appears as pointlike, and its position immediately after the measurement is well defined. But before a measurement is made, or between successive measurements, the particle's position is not well defined; instead, the state of the particle is specified by its evolving wave function.

The quantum mechanics embodied in the 1926–27 formulation is nonrelativistic—that is, it applies only to particles whose speeds are significantly less than the speed of light. The quantum mechanical description of light was not fully realized until the late 1940s. However, light and matter share a common central feature—a complementary relation between wave and particle aspects—that can be illustrated without resorting to the formalisms of relativistic quantum mechanics.

WAVE-PARTICLE DUALITY

The same interference pattern demonstrated in Young's double-slit experiment is produced when a beam of matter, such as electrons, impinges on a double-slit apparatus. Concentrating on light, the interference pattern clearly demonstrates its wave properties. But what of its particle properties? Can an individual photon be followed through the two-slit apparatus, and if so, what is the origin of the resulting interference pattern? The superposition of two waves, one passing through each slit, produces the pattern in Young's apparatus. Yet, if light is considered a collection of particle-like photons, each can pass only through one slit or the other. Soon after Einstein's photon hypothesis in 1905, it was suggested that the two-slit interference pattern might be caused by the interaction of photons that passed through different slits. This interpretation was ruled out in 1909 when the English physicist Geoffrey Taylor reported a diffraction pattern in the shadow of a needle recorded on a photographic plate exposed to a very weak light source, weak enough that only one photon could be present in the apparatus at any one time. Photons were not interfering with one another; each photon was contributing to the diffraction pattern on its own.

In modern versions of this two-slit interference experiment, the photographic plate is replaced with a detector that is capable of recording the arrival of individual photons. Each photon arrives whole and intact at one point on the detector. It is impossible to predict the arrival position of any one photon, but the cumulative effect of many independent photon impacts on the detector results in the gradual buildup of an interference pattern. The magnitude of the classical interference pattern at any one point is therefore a measure of the probability of any one photon's arriving at that point. The interpretation of this seemingly paradoxical behaviour (shared by light and matter), which is in fact predicted by the laws of quantum mechanics, has been debated by the scientific community since its discovery. The American physicist Richard Feynman summarized the situation in 1965:

> We choose to examine a phenomenon which is impossible, absolutely impossible, to explain in any classical way, and which has in it the heart of quantum mechanics. In reality, it contains the only mystery.

In a wholly unexpected fashion, quantum mechanics resolved the long wave-particle debate over the nature of light by rejecting both models. The behaviour of light cannot be fully accounted for by a classical wave model or by a classical particle model. These pictures are useful in their respective regimes, but ultimately they are approximate, complementary descriptions of an underlying reality that is described quantum mechanically.

QUANTUM OPTICS

Quantum optics, the study and application of the quantum interactions of light with matter, is an active and expanding field of experiment and theory. Progress in the development of light sources and detection techniques since the early 1980s has allowed increasingly sophisticated optical tests of the foundations of quantum mechanics. Basic quantum effects such as single photon interference, along with more esoteric issues such as the meaning of the measurement process, have been more clearly elucidated. Entangled states of two or more photons with highly correlated properties (such as polarization direction) have been generated and used to test the fundamental issue of nonlocality in quantum mechanics. Novel technological applications of quantum optics are also under study, including quantum cryptography and quantum computing.

EMISSION AND ABSORPTION PROCESSES

That materials, when heated in flames or put in electrical discharges, emit light at well-defined and characteristic frequencies was known by the mid-19th century. The study of the emission and absorption spectra of atoms was crucial to the development of a successful theory of atomic structure. Attempts to describe the origin of the emission and absorption lines (i.e., the frequencies of emission and absorption) of even the simplest atom, hydrogen, in the framework of classical mechanics and electromagnetism failed miserably.

BOHR MODEL

In 1913, Danish physicist Niels Bohr proposed a model for the hydrogen atom that succeeded in explaining the regularities of its spectrum. In what is known as the Bohr atomic model, the orbiting electrons in an atom are found in only certain allowed "stationary states" with well-defined energies. An atom can absorb or emit one photon when an electron makes a transition from one stationary state, or energy level, to another. Conservation of energy determines the energy of the photon and thus the frequency of the emitted or absorbed light. Though Bohr's model was superseded by quantum mechanics, it still offers a useful, though simplistic, picture of atomic transitions.

SPONTANEOUS EMISSION

When an isolated atom is excited into a high-energy state, it generally remains in the excited state for a short time before emitting a photon and making a transition to a lower energy state. This fundamental process is called spontaneous emission. The emission of a photon is a probabilistic event; that is, the likelihood of its occurrence is described by a probability per unit time. For many excited states of atoms, the average time before the spontaneous emission of a photon is on the order of 10^{-9} to 10^{-8} second.

STIMULATED EMISSION

The absorption of a photon by an atom is also a probabilistic event, with the probability per unit time being proportional to the intensity of the light falling on the atom. In 1917 Einstein, though not knowing the exact mechanisms for the emission and absorption of photons, showed through thermodynamic arguments that there must be a third type of radiative transition in an atom— stimulated emission. In stimulated emission the presence of photons with an appropriate energy triggers an atom in an excited state to emit a photon of identical energy and to make a transition to a lower state. As with absorption, the probability of stimulated emission is proportional to the intensity of the light bathing the atom. Einstein mathematically expressed the statistical nature of the three possible radiative transition routes (spontaneous emission, stimulated emission, and absorption) with the so-called Einstein coefficients and quantified the relations between the three processes. One of the early successes of quantum mechanics was the correct prediction of the numerical values of the Einstein coefficients for the hydrogen atom.

Einstein's description of the stimulated emission process showed that the emitted photon is identical in every respect to the stimulating photons, having the same energy and polarization, traveling in the same direction, and being in phase with those photons. Some 40 years after Einstein's work, the laser was invented, a device that is directly based on the stimulated emission process. (The acronym laser stands for "light amplification by stimulated emission of radiation.") Laser light, because of the underlying properties of stimulated emission, is highly monochromatic, directional, and coherent. Many modern spectroscopic techniques for probing atomic and molecular structure and dynamics, as well as innumerable technological applications, take advantage of these properties of laser light.

QUANTUM ELECTRODYNAMICS

The foundations of a quantum mechanical theory of light and its interactions with matter were developed in the late 1920s and '30s by Paul Dirac, Werner Heisenberg, Pascual Jordan, Wolfgang Pauli, and others. The fully developed theory, called quantum electrodynamics (QED), is credited to the independent work of Richard Feynman, Julian S. Schwinger, and Tomonaga Shin'ichirō. QED describes the interactions of electromagnetic radiation with charged particles and the interactions of charged particles with one another. The electric and magnetic fields described in Maxwell's equations are quantized, and photons appear as excitations of those quantized fields. In QED, photons serve as carriers of electric and magnetic forces. For example, two identical charged particles electrically repel one another because they are exchanging what are called virtual photons. (Virtual photons cannot be directly detected; their existence violates the conservation laws of energy and momentum.) Photons can also be freely emitted by charged particles, in which case they are detectable as light. Though the mathematical complexities of QED are formidable, it is a highly successful theory that has now withstood decades of precise experimental tests. It is considered the prototype field theory in physics; great efforts have gone into adapting its core concepts and calculational approaches to the description of other fundamental forces in nature.

QED provides a theoretical framework for processes involving the transformations of matter into photons and photons into matter. In pair creation, a photon interacting with an atomic nucleus (to conserve momentum) disappears, and its energy is converted into an electron and a positron (a particle-antiparticle pair). In pair annihilation, an electron-positron pair disappears, and two high-energy photons are created. These processes are of central importance in cosmology—once again demonstrating that light is a primary component of the physical universe.

CHAPTER 5
ELECTROMAGNETIC RADIATION

In terms of classical theory, electromagnetic radiation is the flow of energy at the universal speed of light through free space or through a material medium in the form of the electric and magnetic fields that make up electromagnetic waves such as radio waves, visible light, and gamma rays. In such a wave, time-varying electric and magnetic fields are mutually linked with each other at right angles and perpendicular to the direction of motion. An electromagnetic wave is characterized by its intensity and the frequency v of the time variation of the electric and magnetic fields.

GENERAL CONSIDERATIONS

In terms of the modern quantum theory, electromagnetic radiation is the flow of photons (also called light quanta) through space. Photons are packets of energy hv that always move with the universal speed of light. The symbol h is Planck's constant, while the value of v is the same as that of the frequency of the electromagnetic wave of classical theory. Photons having the same energy hv are all alike, and their number density corresponds to the intensity of the radiation. Electromagnetic radiation exhibits a multitude of phenomena as it interacts with charged particles in atoms, molecules, and larger objects of matter. These phenomena as well as the ways in which electromagnetic radiation is created and observed, the manner in which such radiation occurs in nature, and its technological uses depend on its frequency v. The spectrum of frequencies of electromagnetic radiation extends from very low values over the range of radio waves, television waves, and microwaves to visible light and beyond to the substantially higher values of ultraviolet light, X-rays, and gamma rays.

OCCURRENCE AND IMPORTANCE

Close to 0.01 percent of the mass/energy of the entire universe occurs in the form of electromagnetic radiation. All human life is immersed in it and modern communications technology and medical services are particularly dependent on one or another of its forms. In fact, all living things on Earth depend on the electromagnetic radiation received from the Sun and on the transformation of solar energy by photosynthesis into plant life or by biosynthesis into zooplankton, the basic step in the food chain in oceans. The eyes of many animals, including those of humans, are adapted to be sensitive to and hence to see the most abundant part of the Sun's electromagnetic radiation—namely, light, which comprises the visible portion of its wide range of frequencies. Green plants also have high sensitivity to the maximum intensity of solar electromagnetic radiation, which is absorbed by a substance called chlorophyll that is essential for plant growth via photosynthesis.

Practically all the fuels that modern society uses—gas, oil, and coal—are stored forms of energy received from the Sun as electromagnetic radiation millions of years ago. Only the energy from nuclear reactors does not originate from the Sun.

Everyday life is pervaded by man-made electromagnetic radiation: food is heated in microwave ovens, airplanes are guided by radar waves, television sets receive electromagnetic waves transmitted by broadcasting stations, and infrared waves from heaters provide warmth. Infrared waves also are given off and received by automatic self-focusing cameras that electronically measure and set the correct distance to the object to be photographed. As soon as the Sun sets, incandescent or fluorescent lights are turned on to provide artificial illumination, and cities glow brightly with the colourful fluorescent and neon lamps of advertisement signs. Familiar too is ultraviolet radiation, which the eyes cannot see but whose effect is felt as pain from sunburn. Ultraviolet light represents a kind of electromagnetic radiation that can be harmful to life. Such is also true of X-rays, which are important in medicine as they allow physicians to observe the inner parts of the body but exposure to which should be kept to a minimum. Less familiar are gamma rays, which come from nuclear reactions and radioactive decay and are part of the harmful high-energy radiation of radioactive materials and nuclear weapons.

THE ELECTROMAGNETIC SPECTRUM

The brief account of familiar phenomena given above surveyed electromagnetic radiation from small frequencies ν (long wave radios) to exceedingly high values of ν (gamma rays). Going from the ν values of radio waves to those of visible light is like comparing the thickness of this page with the distance of Earth from the Sun, which represents an increase by a factor of a million billion. Similarly, going from the ν values of visible light to the very much larger ones of gamma rays represents another increase in frequency by a factor of a million billion. This extremely large range of ν values is called the electromagnetic spectrum. The number ν is shared by both the classical and the modern interpretation of electromagnetic radiation. In classical language, ν is the frequency of the temporal changes in an electromagnetic wave. The frequency of a wave is related to its speed c and wavelength λ in the following way. If 10 complete waves pass by in one second, one observes 10 wriggles, and one says that the frequency of such a wave is v = 10 cycles per second (10 hertz [Hz]). If the wavelength of the wave is, say, λ = 3 cm (1.18 inches), then it is clear that a wave train 30 cm (11.81 inches) long has passed in that one second to produce the 10 wriggles that were observed. Thus, the speed of the wave is 30 cm per second, and one notes that in general the speed is $c = \lambda v$. The speed of electromagnetic radiation of all kinds is the same universal constant that is defined to be exactly c = 299,792,458 metres per second (186,282 miles per second). The energy of modern-day photons is $h v$. One commonly uses as the unit of energy electron volt (eV), which is the energy that can be given to an electron by a one-volt battery. It is clear that the range of wavelengths λ and of photon energies $h v$ are equally as large as the spectrum of v values.

Because the wavelengths and energy quanta $h v$ of electromagnetic radiation of the various parts of the spectrum are so different in magnitude, the sources of the radiations, the interactions with matter, and the detectors employed are correspondingly different. This is why the same electromagnetic radiation is called by different names in various regions of the spectrum.

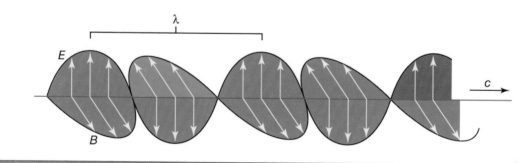

Radiation fields in which vectors {E vector} and {B vector} are perpendicular to each other and to the direction of propagation. Encyclopædia Britannica, Inc.

In spite of these obvious differences of scale, all forms of electromagnetic radiation obey certain general rules that are well understood and that allow one to calculate with very high precision their properties and interactions with charged particles in atoms, molecules, and large objects. Electromagnetic radiation is, classically speaking, a wave of electric and magnetic fields propagating at the speed of light c through empty space. In this wave the electric and magnetic fields change their magnitude and direction each second. This rate of change is the frequency v measured in cycles per second—namely, in hertz. The electric and magnetic fields are always perpendicular to one another and at right angles to the direction of propagation. There is as much energy carried by the electric component of the wave as by the magnetic component, and the energy is proportional to the square of the field strength.

GENERATION OF ELECTROMAGNETIC RADIATION

Electromagnetic radiation is produced whenever a charged particle, such as an electron, changes its velocity— i.e., whenever it is accelerated or decelerated. The energy of the electromagnetic radiation thus produced comes from the charged particle and is therefore lost by it. A common example of this phenomenon is the oscillating charge or current in a radio antenna. The antenna of a radio transmitter is part of an electric resonance circuit in which the charge is made to oscillate at a desired frequency. An electromagnetic wave so generated can be received by a similar antenna connected to an oscillating electric circuit in the tuner that is tuned to that same frequency. The electromagnetic wave in turn produces an oscillating motion of charge in the receiving antenna. In general, one can say that any system which emits electromagnetic radiation of a given frequency can absorb radiation of the same frequency.

Such man-made transmitters and receivers become smaller with decreasing wavelength of the electromagnetic wave and prove impractical in the millimetre range. At even shorter wavelengths down to the wavelengths of X-rays, which are one million times smaller, the oscillating charges arise from moving charges in molecules and atoms.

One may classify the generation of electromagnetic radiation into two categories: (1) systems or processes that produce radiation covering a broad continuous spectrum of frequencies and (2) those that emit (and absorb) radiation of discrete frequencies that are characteristic of particular systems. The Sun with its continuous spectrum is an example of the first, while a radio transmitter tuned to one frequency exemplifies the second category.

CONTINUOUS SPECTRA OF ELECTROMAGNETIC RADIATION

Such spectra are emitted by any warm substance. Heat is the irregular motion of electrons, atoms, and molecules; the higher the temperature, the more rapid is the motion. Since electrons are much lighter than atoms, irregular thermal motion produces irregular oscillatory charge motion, which reflects a continuous spectrum of frequencies. Each oscillation at a particular frequency can be considered a tiny "antenna" that emits and receives electromagnetic radiation. As a piece of iron is heated to increasingly high temperatures, it first glows red, then yellow, and finally white. In short, all the colours of the visible spectrum are represented. Even before the iron begins to glow red, one can feel the emission of infrared waves by the heat sensation on the skin. A white-hot piece of iron also emits ultraviolet radiation, which can be detected by a photographic film.

Not all materials heated to the same temperature emit the same amount and spectral distribution of electromagnetic waves. For example, a piece of glass heated next to iron looks nearly colourless, but it feels hotter to the skin (it emits more infrared rays) than does the iron. This observation illustrates the rule of reciprocity: a body radiates strongly at those frequencies that it is able to absorb, because for both processes it needs the tiny antennas of that range of frequencies. Glass is transparent in the visible range of light because it lacks possible electronic absorption at these particular frequencies. As a consequence, glass cannot glow red because it cannot absorb red. On the other hand, glass is a better emitter/absorber in the infrared than iron or any other metal that strongly reflects such lower frequency electromagnetic waves. This selective emissivity and absorptivity is important for understanding the greenhouse effect and many other phenomena in nature. The tungsten filament of a light bulb has a temperature of 2,500 K (2,227 °C, or 4,040 °F) and emits large amounts of visible light but relatively little infrared because metals, as mentioned above, have small emissivities in the infrared range. This is of course fortunate, since one wants light from a light bulb but not much heat. The light emitted by a candle originates from very hot carbon soot particles in the flame, which strongly absorb and thus emit visible light. By contrast, the gas flame of a kitchen range is pale, even though it is hotter than a candle flame, because of the absence of soot. Light from the stars originates from the high temperature of the gases at their surface. A wide spectrum of radiation is emitted from the Sun's surface, the temperature of which is about 6,000 K (5,727 °C, or 10,340 °F). The radiation output is 60 million watts for every square metre of solar surface, which is equivalent to the amount produced by an average-size commercial power-generating station that can supply electric power for about 30,000 households.

The spectral composition of a heated body depends on the materials of which the body consists. That is not the case for an ideal radiator or absorber. Such an ideal object absorbs and thus emits radiation of all frequencies equally and fully. A radiator/absorber of this kind is called a blackbody, and its radiation spectrum is referred to as blackbody radiation, which depends on only one parameter, its temperature. Scientists devise and study such ideal objects because their properties can be known exactly. This information can then be used to determine and understand why real objects, such as a piece of iron or glass, a cloud, or a star, behave differently.

A good approximation of a blackbody is a piece of coal or, better yet, a cavity in a piece of coal that is visible through a small opening. There is one property of blackbody radiation which is familiar to everyone but which is actually quite mysterious. As the piece of coal is heated to higher and higher temperatures, one first observes a dull red glow, followed by a change in colour to bright red; as the temperature is increased further, the colour changes to yellow and finally to white. White is not itself a colour but rather the visual effect of the combination of all primary colours. The fact that white glow is observed at high temperatures means that the colour blue has been added to the ones observed at lower temperatures. This colour change with temperature is mysterious because one would expect, as the energy (or temperature) is increased, just more of the same and not something entirely different. For example, as one increases the power of a radio amplifier, one hears the music louder but not at a higher pitch.

The change in colour or frequency distribution of the electromagnetic radiation coming from heated bodies at different temperatures remained an enigma for centuries.

The solution of this mystery by the German physicist Max Planck initiated the era of modern physics at the beginning of the 20th century. He explained the phenomenon by proposing that the tiny antennas in the heated body are quantized, meaning that they can emit electromagnetic radiation only in finite energy quanta of size hv. The universal constant h is called Planck's constant in his honour. For blue light $hv = 3$ eV, whereas $hv = 1.8$ eV for red light. Since high-frequency antennas of vibrating charges in solids have to emit larger energy quanta hv than lower-frequency antennas, they can only do so when the temperature, or the thermal atomic motion, becomes high enough. Hence, the average pitch, or peak frequency, of blackbody electromagnetic radiation increases with temperature.

The many tiny antennas in a heated chunk of material are, as noted above, to be identified with the accelerating and decelerating charges in the heat motion of the atoms of the material. There are other sources of continuous spectra of electromagnetic radiation that are not associated with heat but still come from accelerated or decelerated charges. X-rays are, for example, produced by abruptly stopping rapidly moving electrons. This deceleration of the charges produces *bremsstrahlung* ("braking radiation"). In an X-ray tube, electrons moving with an energy of $E_{max} = 10,000$ to $50,000$ eV (10–50 keV) are made to strike a piece of metal. The electromagnetic radiation produced by this sudden deceleration of electrons is a continuous spectrum extending up to the maximum photon energy $hv = E_{max}$.

By far the brightest continuum spectra of electromagnetic radiation come from synchrotron radiation sources. These are not well known because they are predominantly used for research and only recently have they been considered for commercial and medical applications. Because any change in motion is an acceleration, circulating currents of electrons produce electromagnetic radiation. When these circulating electrons move at relativistic speeds (i.e., those approaching the speed of light), the brightness of the radiation increases enormously. This radiation was first observed at the General Electric Company in 1947 in an electron synchrotron (hence the name of this radiation), which is a type of particle accelerator that forces relativistic electrons into circular orbits using powerful magnetic fields. The intensity of synchrotron radiation is further increased more than a thousandfold by wigglers and undulators that move the beam of relativistic electrons to and fro by means of other magnetic fields.

The conditions for generating *bremsstrahlung* as well as synchrotron radiation exist in nature in various forms. Acceleration and capture of charged particles by the gravitational field of a star, black hole, or galaxy is a source of energetic cosmic X-rays. Gamma rays are produced in other kinds of cosmic objects—namely, supernovae, neutron stars, and quasars.

DISCRETE-FREQUENCY SOURCES AND ABSORBERS OF ELECTROMAGNETIC RADIATION

These are commonly encountered in everyday life. Familiar examples of discrete-frequency electromagnetic radiation include the distinct colours of lamps filled with different fluorescent gases characteristic of advertisement signs, the colours of dyes and pigments, the bright yellow of sodium lamps, the blue-green hue of mercury lamps, and the specific colours of lasers.

Sources of electromagnetic radiation of specific frequency are typically atoms or molecules. Every atom or molecule can have certain discrete internal energies, which are called quantum states. An atom or molecule can therefore change its internal energy only by discrete amounts.

By going from a higher to a lower energy state, a quantum hv of electromagnetic radiation is emitted of a magnitude that is precisely the energy difference between the higher and lower state. Absorption of a quantum hv brings the atom from a lower to a higher state if hv matches the energy difference. All like atoms are identical, but all different chemical elements of the periodic table have their own specific set of possible internal energies. Therefore, by measuring the characteristic and discrete electromagnetic radiation that is either emitted or absorbed by atoms or molecules, one can identify which kind of atom or molecule is giving off or absorbing the radiation. This provides a means of determining the chemical composition of substances. Since one cannot subject a piece of a distant star to conventional chemical analysis, studying the emission or absorption of starlight is the only way to determine the composition of stars or of interstellar gases and dust.

The Sun, for example, not only emits the continuous spectrum of radiation that originates from its hot surface but also emits discrete radiation quanta hv that are characteristic of its atomic composition. Many of the elements can be detected at the solar surface, but the most abundant is helium. This is so because helium is the end product of the nuclear fusion reaction that is the fundamental energy source of the Sun. This particular element was named helium (from the Greek word *helios*, meaning "Sun") because its existence was first discovered by its characteristic absorption energies in the Sun's spectrum. The helium of the cooler outer parts of the solar atmosphere absorbs the characteristic light frequencies from the lower and hotter regions of the Sun.

The characteristic and discrete energies hv found as emission and absorption of electromagnetic radiation by atoms and molecules extend to X-ray energies. As high-energy electrons strike the piece of metal in an X-ray tube, electrons are knocked out of the inner energy shell of the atoms. These vacancies are then filled by electrons from the second or third shell; emitted in the process are X-rays having hv values that correspond to the energy differences of the shells. One therefore observes not only the continuous spectrum of the *bremsstrahlung* discussed above but also X-ray emissions of discrete energies hv that are characteristic of the specific elemental composition of the metal struck by the energetic electrons in the X-ray tube.

The discrete electromagnetic radiation energies hv emitted or absorbed by all substances reflect the discreteness of the internal energies of all material things. This means that window glass and water are transparent to visible light; they cannot absorb these visible light quanta because their internal energies are such that no energy difference between a higher and a lower internal state matches the energy hv of visible light. The coefficient of absorption of water is a function of frequency v of electromagnetic radiation. An absorption coefficient $\alpha = 10^{-4}$ cm^{-1} means that the intensity of electromagnetic radiation is only one-third its original value after passing through 100 metres (330 feet) of water. When $\alpha = 1$ cm^{-1}, only a layer 1 cm thick is needed to decrease the intensity to one-third its original value, and, for $\alpha = 10^3$ cm, a layer of water having a thickness of this page is sufficient to attenuate electromagnetic radiation by that much. The transparency of water to visible light, marked by the vertical dashed lines, is a remarkable feature that is significant for life on Earth.

All things look so different and have different colours because of their different sets of internal discrete energies, which determine their interaction with electromagnetic radiation. The words *looking* and *colours* are associated with the human detectors of electromagnetic radiation, the eyes. Since there are instruments available for detecting electromagnetic radiation of any frequency, one can imagine that things "look" different at all energies of the spectrum because different materials have their own characteristic sets of discrete internal energies. Even the nuclei of atoms are composites of other elementary particles and thus can be excited to many discrete internal energy states. Since nuclear energies are much larger than atomic energies, the energy differences between internal energy states are substantially larger, and the corresponding electromagnetic radiation quanta $h\nu$ emitted or absorbed when nuclei change their energies are even bigger than those of X-rays. Such quanta given off or absorbed by atomic nuclei are called gamma rays.

PROPERTIES AND BEHAVIOUR

Electromagnetic radiation displays some of the same wave phenomena that sound does. Light waves can interfere with one another, and they are subject to the Doppler effect. However, some effects (such as the scattering of light), depending on the frequency, are quite different.

SCATTERING, REFLECTION, AND REFRACTION

If a charged particle interacts with an electromagnetic wave, it experiences a force proportional to the strength of the electric field and thus is forced to change its motion in accordance with the frequency of the electric field wave. In doing so, it becomes a source of electromagnetic radiation of the same frequency, as described in the previous section. The energy for the work done in accelerating the charged particle and emitting this secondary radiation comes from and is lost by the primary wave. This process is called scattering.

Since the energy density of the electromagnetic radiation is proportional to the square of the electric field strength, and the field strength is caused by acceleration of a charge, the energy radiated by such a charge oscillator increases with the square of the acceleration. On the other hand, the acceleration of an oscillator depends on the frequency of the back-and-forth oscillation. The acceleration increases with the square of the frequency. This leads to the important result that the electromagnetic energy radiated by an oscillator increases very rapidly—namely, with the square of the square or, as one says, with the fourth power of the frequency. Doubling the frequency thus produces an increase in radiated energy by a factor of 16.

This rapid increase in scattering with the frequency of electromagnetic radiation can be seen on any sunny day: it is the reason the sky is blue and the setting Sun is red. The higher-frequency blue light from the Sun is scattered much more by the atoms and molecules of Earth's atmosphere than is the lower-frequency red light. Hence the light of the setting Sun, which passes through a thick layer of atmosphere, has much more red than yellow or blue light, while light scattered from the sky contains much more blue than yellow or red light.

The process of scattering, or reradiating part of the electromagnetic wave by a charge oscillator, is fundamental to understanding the interaction of electromagnetic radiation with solids, liquids, or any matter that contains a very large number of charges and thus an enormous number of charge oscillators. This also explains why a substance that has charge oscillators of certain frequencies absorbs and emits radiation of those frequencies.

When electromagnetic radiation falls on a large collection of individual small charge oscillators, as in a piece of glass or metal or a brick wall, all of these oscillators perform oscillations in unison, following the beat of the electric wave. As a result, all the oscillators emit secondary

radiation in unison (or coherently), and the total secondary radiation coming from the solid consists of the sum
of all these secondary coherent electromagnetic waves.
This sum total yields radiation that is reflected from the
surface of the solid and radiation that goes into the solid
at a certain angle with respect to the normal of (i.e., a line
perpendicular to) the surface. The latter is the refracted
radiation that may be attenuated (absorbed) on its way
through the solid.

SUPERPOSITION AND INTERFERENCE

When two electromagnetic waves of the same frequency
superpose in space, the resultant electric and magnetic
field strength of any point of space and time is the sum
of the respective fields of the two waves. When one forms
the sum, both the magnitude and the direction of the
fields need be considered, which means that they sum like
vectors. In the special case when two equally strong waves
have their fields in the same direction in space and time
(i.e., when they are in phase), the resultant field is twice
that of each individual wave. The resultant intensity, being
proportional to the square of the field strength, is therefore not two but four times the intensity of each of the
two superposing waves.

By contrast, the superposition of a wave that has an
electric field in one direction (positive) in space and time
with a wave of the same frequency having an electric field
in the opposite direction (negative) in space and time
leads to cancellation and no resultant wave at all (zero
intensity). Two waves of this sort are termed out of phase.
The first example, that of in-phase superposition yielding four times the individual intensity, constitutes what is
called constructive interference. The second example, that
of out-of-phase superposition yielding zero intensity,

is destructive interference. Since the resultant field at any point and time is the sum of all individual fields at that point and time, these arguments are easily extended to any number of superposing waves. One finds constructive, destructive, or partial interference for waves having the same frequency and given phase relationships.

Propagation and Coherence

Once generated, an electromagnetic wave is self-propagating because a time-varying electric field produces a time-varying magnetic field and vice versa. When an oscillating current in an antenna is switched on for, say, eight minutes, then the beginning of the electromagnetic train reaches the Sun just when the antenna is switched off because it takes a few seconds more than eight minutes for electromagnetic radiation to reach the Sun. This eight-minute wave train, which is as long as the Sun–Earth distance, then continues to travel with the speed of light past the Sun into the space beyond.

Except for radio waves transmitted by antennas that are switched on for many hours, most electromagnetic waves come in many small pieces. The length and duration of a wave train are called coherence length and coherence time, respectively. Light from the Sun or from a light bulb comes in many tiny bursts lasting about a millionth of a millionth of a second and having a coherence length of about one centimetre (.39 inch). The discrete radiant energy emitted by an atom as it changes its internal energy can have a coherence length several hundred times longer (one to 10 metres [3. 28 feet to 32.8 feet) unless the radiating atom is disturbed by a collision.

The time and space at which the electric and magnetic fields have a maximum value or are zero between the reversal of their directions are different for different wave trains. It is therefore clear that the phenomenon of interference can arise only from the superposition of part of a wave train with itself. This can be accomplished, for instance, with a half-transparent mirror that reflects half the intensity and transmits the other half of each of the billion billion wave trains of a given light source, say, a yellow sodium discharge lamp. One can allow one of these half beams to travel in direction A and the other in direction B. By reflecting each half beam back, one can then superpose the two half beams and observe the resultant total. If one half beam has to travel a path ½ wavelength or ³⁄₂ or ⁵⁄₂ wavelength longer than the other, then the superposition yields no light at all because the electric and magnetic fields of every half wave train in the two half beams point in opposite directions and their sum is therefore zero. The important point is that cancellation occurs between each half wave train and its mate. This is an example of destructive interference. By adjusting the path lengths A and B such that they are equal or differ by λ, 2λ, 3λ . . ., the electric and magnetic fields of each half wave train and its mate add when they are superposed. This is constructive interference, and, as a result, one sees strong light.

The interferometer discussed above was designed by the American physicist Albert A. Michelson in 1880 (while he was studying with Hermann von Helmholtz in Berlin) for the purpose of measuring the effect on the speed of light of the motion of the ether through which light was believed to travel.

SPEED OF ELECTROMAGNETIC RADIATION AND THE DOPPLER EFFECT

Electromagnetic radiation, or in modern terminology the photons $h\nu$, always travel in free space with the universal speed c—i.e., the speed of light. This is actually a very puzzling situation which was first experimentally verified by Michelson and Edward Williams Morley, another

American scientist, in 1887 and which is the basic axiom of Albert Einstein's theory of relativity. Although there is no doubt that it is true, the situation is puzzling because it is so different from the behaviour of normal particles; that is to say, for little or not so little pieces of matter. When one chases behind a normal particle (e.g., an airplane) or moves in the opposite direction toward it, one certainly will measure very different speeds of the airplane relative to oneself. One would detect a very small relative speed in the first case and a very large one in the second. Moreover, a bullet shot forward from the airplane and another toward the back would appear to be moving with different speeds relative to oneself. This would not at all be the case when one measures the speed of electromagnetic radiation: irrespective of one's motion or that of the source of the electromagnetic radiation, any measurement by a moving observer will result in the universal speed of light. This must be accepted as a fact of nature.

What happens to pitch or frequency when the source is moving toward the observer or away from him? It has been established from sound waves that the frequency is higher when a sound source is moving toward the observer and lower when it is moving away from him. This is the Doppler effect, named after the Austrian physicist Christian Doppler, who first described the phenomenon in 1842. Doppler predicted that the effect also occurs with electromagnetic radiation and suggested that it be used for measuring the relative speeds of stars. This means that a characteristic blue light emitted, for example, by an excited helium atom as it changes from a higher to a lower internal energy state would no longer appear blue when one looks at this light coming from helium atoms that move very rapidly away from the Earth with, say, a galaxy. When the speed of such a galaxy away from the Earth is large, the light may appear yellow; if the speed is still larger, it may appear red or even infrared. This is actually what happens, and the speed of galaxies as well as of stars relative to the Earth is measured from the Doppler shift of characteristic atomic radiation energies $h\nu$.

COSMIC BACKGROUND ELECTROMAGNETIC RADIATION

As one measures the relative speeds of galaxies using the Doppler shift of characteristic radiation emissions, one finds that all galaxies are moving away from one another. Those that are moving the fastest are systems that are the farthest away (Hubble's law). The speeds and distances give the appearance of an explosion. Extrapolating backward in time, one obtains an estimate as to when this explosion, dubbed the big bang, might have occurred. This time is calculated to be somewhere between 15 billion and 20 billion years ago, which is considered to be the age of the universe. From this early stage onward, the universe expanded and cooled. The American scientists Robert W. Wilson and Arno Penzias determined in 1965 that the whole universe can be conceived of as an expanding blackbody filled with electromagnetic radiation which now corresponds to a temperature of 2.74 K (-270.41 °C or -454.74 °F), only a few degrees above absolute zero. Because of this low temperature, most of the radiation energy is in the microwave region of the electromagnetic spectrum. The intensity of this radiation corresponds, on average, to about 400 photons in every cubic centimetre of the universe. It has been estimated that there are about one billion times more photons in the universe than electrons, nuclei, and all other things taken together. The presence of this microwave cosmic background radiation supports the predictions of big-bang cosmology.

EFFECT OF GRAVITATION

The energy of the quanta of electromagnetic radiation is subject to gravitational forces just like a mass of magnitude $m = h\nu/c^2$. This is so because the relationship of energy E and mass m is $E = mc^2$. As a consequence, light traveling toward Earth gains energy and its frequency is shifted toward the blue (shorter wavelengths), whereas light traveling "up" loses energy and its frequency is shifted toward the red (longer wavelengths). These shifts are very small but have been detected by the American physicists Robert V. Pound and Glen A. Rebka.

The effect of gravitation on light increases with the strength of the gravitational attraction. Thus, a light beam from a distant star does not travel along a straight line when passing a star like the Sun but is deflected toward it. This deflection can be strong around very heavy cosmic objects, which then distort the light path acting as a gravitational lens.

Under extreme conditions the gravitational force of a cosmic object can be so strong that no electromagnetic radiation can escape the gravitational pull. Such an object, called a black hole, is therefore not visible and its presence can only be detected by its gravitational effect on other visible objects in its vicinity.

THE GREENHOUSE EFFECT OF THE ATMOSPHERE

The temperature of the terrestrial surface environment is controlled not only by the Sun's electromagnetic radiation but also in a sensitive way by Earth's atmosphere. As noted earlier, each substance absorbs and emits electromagnetic radiation of some energies $h\nu$ and does not do so in other ranges of energy. These regions of transparency and opaqueness are governed by the particular distribution of internal energies of the substance.

Earth's atmosphere acts much like the glass panes of a greenhouse: it allows sunlight, particularly its visible range, to reach and warm Earth, but it largely inhibits the infrared radiation emitted by the heated terrestrial surface from escaping into space. Since the atmosphere becomes thinner and thinner with increasing altitude above Earth, there is less atmospheric absorption in the higher regions of the atmosphere. At an altitude of 100 km (60 miles), the fraction of atmosphere is one 10-millionth of that on the ground. Below 10 million hertz (10^7 Hz), the absorption is caused by the ionosphere, a layer in which atoms and molecules in the atmosphere are ionized by the Sun's ultraviolet radiation. In the infrared region, the absorption is caused by molecular vibrations and rotations. In the ultraviolet and X-ray regions, the absorption is due to electronic excitations in atoms and molecules.

Without water vapour and carbon dioxide (CO_2), which are, together with certain industrial pollutants, the main infrared-absorbing species in the atmosphere, Earth would experience the extreme temperature variations between night and day that occur on the Moon. Earth would then be a frozen planet, like Mars, with an average temperature of 200 K (-73 °C, or -100 °F), and not be able to support life. Scientists believe that Earth's temperature and climate in general will be affected as the composition of the atmosphere is altered by an increased release and accumulation of carbon dioxide and other gaseous pollutants.

FORMS OF ELECTROMAGNETIC RADIATION

Electromagnetic radiation appears in a wide variety of forms and manifestations. Yet, these diverse phenomena are understood to comprise a single aspect of nature, following simple physical principles. Common to all forms is the fact that electromagnetic radiation interacts with and is generated by electric charges. The apparent differences in the phenomena arise from the question in which environment and under what circumstances can charges respond on the time scale of the frequency v of the radiation.

At smaller frequencies v (smaller than 10^{12} hertz), electric charges typically are the freely moving electrons in the metal components of antennas or the free electrons and ions in space that give rise to phenomena related to radio waves, radar waves, and microwaves. At higher frequencies (10^{12} to 5×10^{14} hertz), in the infrared region of the spectrum, the moving charges are primarily associated with the rotations and vibrations of molecules and the motions of atoms bonded together in materials. Electromagnetic radiation in the visible range to X-rays have frequencies that correspond to charges within atoms, whereas gamma rays are associated with frequencies of charges within atomic nuclei. The characteristics of electromagnetic radiation occurring in the different regions of the spectrum are described in this section.

Radio Waves

Radio waves are used for wireless transmission of sound messages, or information, for communication, as well as for maritime and aircraft navigation. The information is imposed on the electromagnetic carrier wave as amplitude modulation (AM) or as frequency modulation (FM) or in digital form (pulse modulation). Transmission therefore involves not a single-frequency electromagnetic wave but rather a frequency band whose width is proportional to the information density. The width is about 10,000 Hz for telephone, 20,000 Hz for high-fidelity sound, and five megahertz (MHz = one million hertz) for high-definition television. This width and the decrease in efficiency of generating electromagnetic waves with decreasing frequency sets a lower frequency limit for radio waves near 10,000 Hz.

Because electromagnetic radiation travels in free space in straight lines, scientists questioned the efforts of the Italian physicist and inventor Guglielmo Marconi to develop long-range radio. The curvature of Earth limits the line-of-sight distance from the top of a 100-metre (330-foot) tower to about 30 km (19 miles). Marconi's unexpected success in transmitting messages over more than 2,000 km (1,200 miles) led to the discovery of the Kennelly–Heaviside layer, more commonly known as the ionosphere. This region is an approximately 300-km-thick (200 mile) layer starting about 100 km (60 miles) above Earth's surface in which the atmosphere is partially ionized by ultraviolet light from the Sun, giving rise to enough electrons and ions to affect radio waves. Because of the Sun's involvement, the height, width, and degree of ionization of the stratified ionosphere vary from day to night and from summer to winter.

Radio waves transmitted by antennas in certain directions are bent or even reflected back to Earth by the ionosphere. They may bounce off Earth and be reflected by the ionosphere repeatedly, making radio transmission around the globe possible. Long-distance communication is further facilitated by the so-called ground wave. This form of electromagnetic wave closely follows the surface of Earth, particularly over water, as a result of the wave's interaction with the terrestrial surface. The range of the ground wave (up to 1,600 km [1,000 miles]) and the bending and reflection of the sky wave by the ionosphere depend on the frequency of the waves. Under normal ionospheric conditions 40 MHz is the highest-frequency radio wave that can be reflected from the ionosphere. In order to accommodate the large band width of transmitted signals, television frequencies are necessarily higher

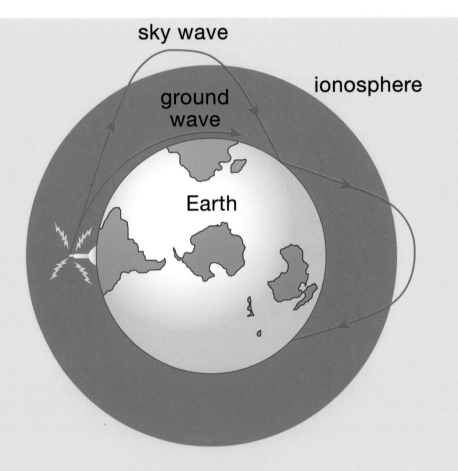

© 1994 Encyclopaedia Britannica, Inc.

Radio-wave transmission reaching beyond line of sight by means of the sky wave reflected by the ionosphere and by means of the ground wave.

than 40 MHz. Television transmitters must therefore be placed on high towers or on hilltops.

As a radio wave travels from the transmitting to the receiving antenna, it may be disturbed by reflections from buildings and other large obstacles. Disturbances arise when several such reflected parts of the wave reach the receiving antenna and interfere with the reception of the wave. Radio waves can penetrate nonconducting materials such as wood, bricks, and concrete fairly well. They cannot pass through electrical conductors such as water or metals. Above $v = 40$ MHz, radio waves from deep space can penetrate the Earth's atmosphere. This makes radio astronomy observations with ground-based telescopes possible.

Whenever transmission of electromagnetic energy from one location to another is required with minimal energy loss and disturbance, the waves are confined to a limited region by means of wires, coaxial cables, and, in the microwave region, waveguides. Unguided or wireless transmission is naturally preferred when the locations of receivers are unspecified or too numerous, as in the case of radio and television communications. Cable television, as the name implies, is an exception. In this case electromagnetic radiation is transmitted by a coaxial cable system to users either from a community antenna or directly from broadcasting stations. The shielding of this guided transmission from disturbances provides high-quality signals.

In a coaxial cable there is a potential difference between the inner and outer conductors and so electric field lines E extend from one conductor to the other. The conductors carry opposite currents that produce the magnetic field lines B. The electric and magnetic fields are perpendicular to each other and perpendicular to the direction of propagation. At any cross section of the cable, the directions of the E and B field lines change to their opposite with the frequency ν of the radiation. This direction reversal of the fields does not change the direction of propagation along the conductors. The speed of propagation is again the universal speed of light if the region between the conductors consists of air or free space.

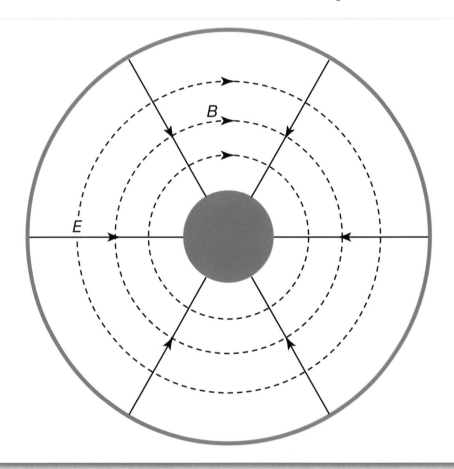

Cross section of a coaxial cable carrying high-frequency current. Electric field lines E *(solid)* and magnetic field lines B (dashed) *are mutually perpendicular and perpendicular to the electromagnetic wave propagation, which is toward the viewer.* Encyclopædia Britannica, Inc.

A combination of radio waves and strong magnetic fields is used by magnetic resonance imaging (MRI) to produce diagnostic pictures of parts of the human body and brain without apparent harmful effects. This imaging technique has thus found increasingly wider application in medicine.

Extremely low-frequency (ELF) waves are of interest for communications systems for submarines. The relatively weak absorption by seawater of electromagnetic radiation at low frequencies and the existence of prominent resonances of the natural cavity formed by the Earth and the ionosphere make the range between 5 and 100 Hz attractive for this application.

There is evidence that ELF waves and the oscillating magnetic fields that occur near electric power transmission lines or electric heating blankets have adverse effects on human health and the electrochemical balance of the brain. Prolonged exposure to low-level and low-frequency magnetic fields have been reported to increase the risk of developing leukemia, lymphoma, and brain cancer in children.

MICROWAVES

The microwave region extends from 1,000 to 300,000 MHz (or 1-mm to 30-cm wavelengths). Although microwaves were first produced and studied in 1886 by Hertz, their practical application had to await the invention of suitable generators, such as the klystron and magnetron.

Microwaves are the principal carriers of high-speed telegraphic data transmissions between stations on the Earth and also between ground-based stations and satellites and space probes. A system of synchronous satellites about 36,000 km (22,000 miles) above Earth is used for international broadband telegraphy of all kinds of communications—e.g., television, telephone, and fax.

Microwave transmitters and receivers are parabolic dish antennas. They produce microwave beams whose spreading angle is proportional to the ratio of the wavelength of the constituent waves to the diameter of the dish. The beams can thus be directed like a searchlight. Radar beams consist of short pulses of microwaves. One can determine the distance of an airplane or ship by measuring the time it takes such a pulse to travel to the object and, after reflection, back to the radar dish antenna. Moreover, by making use of the change in frequency of the reflected wave pulse caused by the Doppler effect, one can measure the speed of objects. Microwave radar is therefore widely used for guiding airplanes and vessels and for detecting speeding motorists. Microwaves can penetrate clouds of smoke, but are scattered by water droplets, and so are used for mapping meteorologic disturbances and in weather forecasting.

Microwaves play an increasingly wide role in heating and cooking food. They are absorbed by water and fat in foodstuffs (e.g., in the tissue of meats) and produce heat from the inside. In most cases, this reduces the cooking time a hundredfold. Such dry objects as glass and ceramics, on the other hand, are not heated in the process, and metal foils are not penetrated at all.

The heating effect of microwaves destroys living tissue when the temperature of the tissue exceeds 43 °C (109 °F). Accordingly, exposure to intense microwaves in excess of 20 milliwatts of power per square centimetre of body surface is harmful. The lens of the human eye is particularly affected by waves with a frequency of 3,000 MHz, and repeated and extended exposure can result in cataracts. Radio waves and microwaves of far less power (microwatts per square centimetre) than the 10 to 20 milliwatts per square centimetre needed to produce heating in living tissue can have adverse effects on the electrochemical balance of the brain and the development of a fetus if these waves are modulated or pulsed at low frequencies between 5 and 100 hertz, which are of the same magnitude as brain wave frequencies.

Various types of microwave generators and amplifiers have been developed. Vacuum-tube devices, the klystron and the magnetron, continue to be used on a wide scale, especially for higher-power applications. Klystrons are primarily employed as amplifiers in radio relay systems and for dielectric heating, while magnetrons have been adopted for radar systems and microwave ovens. Solid-state technology has yielded several devices capable of producing, amplifying, detecting, and controlling microwaves. Notable among these are the Gunn diode and the tunnel (or Esaki) diode. Another type of device, the maser (acronym for "microwave amplification by stimulated emission of radiation") has proved useful in such areas as radio astronomy, microwave radiometry, and long-distance communications.

Astronomers have discovered what appears to be natural masers in some interstellar clouds. Observations of radio radiation from interstellar hydrogen (H_2) and certain other molecules indicate amplification by the maser process. Also, as was mentioned above, microwave cosmic background radiation has been detected and is considered by many to be the remnant of the primeval fireball postulated by the big-bang cosmological model.

Infrared Radiation

Beyond the red end of the visible range but at frequencies higher than those of radar waves and microwaves is the infrared region of the electromagnetic spectrum, between frequencies of 10^{12} and 5×10^{14} Hz (or wavelengths from 0.1 to 7.5×10^{-5} centimetre). William Herschel, a German-born British musician and self-taught astronomer, discovered this form of radiation in 1800 by exploring, with the aid of a thermometer, sunlight dispersed into its colours by a glass prism. Infrared radiation is absorbed and emitted by the rotations and vibrations of chemically bonded atoms or groups of atoms and thus by many kinds of materials. For instance, window glass that is transparent to visible light absorbs infrared radiation by the vibration of its constituent atoms. Infrared radiation is strongly absorbed by water and by the atmosphere. Although invisible to the eye, infrared radiation can be detected as warmth by the skin. Nearly 50 percent of the Sun's radiant energy is emitted in the infrared region of the electromagnetic spectrum, with the rest primarily in the visible region.

Atmospheric haze and certain pollutants that scatter visible light are nearly transparent to parts of the infrared spectrum because the scattering efficiency increases with the fourth power of the frequency. Infrared photography of distant objects from the air takes advantage of this phenomenon. For the same reason, infrared astronomy enables researchers to observe cosmic objects through large clouds of interstellar dust that scatter infrared radiation substantially less than visible light. However, since water vapour, ozone, and carbon dioxide in the atmosphere absorb large parts of the infrared spectrum most infrared astronomical observations are carried out at high altitude by balloons, rockets, or spacecraft.

An infrared photograph of a landscape enhances objects according to their heat emission: blue sky and water appear nearly black, whereas green foliage and unexposed skin show up brightly. Infrared photography can reveal pathological tissue growths (thermography) and defects in electronic systems and circuits due to their increased emission of heat.

The infrared absorption and emission characteristics of molecules and materials yield important information about the size, shape, and chemical bonding of molecules and of atoms and ions in solids. The energies of rotation and vibration are quantized in all systems. The infrared radiation energy $h\nu$ emitted or absorbed by a given molecule or substance is therefore a measure of the difference of some of the internal energy states. These in turn are determined by the atomic weight and molecular bonding forces. For this reason, infrared spectroscopy is a powerful tool for determining the internal structure of molecules and substances or, when such information is already known and tabulated, for identifying the amounts of those species in a given sample. Infrared spectroscopic techniques are often used to determine the composition and hence the origin and age of archaeological specimens and for detecting forgeries of art and other objects, which, when inspected under visible light, resemble the originals.

Infrared radiation plays an important role in heat transfer and is integral to the so-called greenhouse effect, influencing the thermal radiation budget of Earth on a global scale and affecting nearly all biospheric activity. Virtually every object at Earth's surface emits electromagnetic radiation primarily in the infrared region of the spectrum.

Man-made sources of infrared radiation include, besides hot objects, infrared light-emitting diodes (LEDs) and lasers. LEDs are small, inexpensive optoelectronic devices made of such semiconducting materials as gallium arsenide. Infrared LEDs are employed as optoisolators and as light sources in some fibre-optics-based communications systems. Powerful optically pumped infrared lasers have been developed using carbon dioxide and carbon monoxide. Carbon dioxide infrared lasers are used to induce and alter chemical reactions and in isotope separation. They also are employed in LIDAR (light radar) systems. Other applications of infrared light include its use in the rangefinders of automatic self-focusing cameras, security alarm systems, and night-vision optical instruments.

Instruments for detecting infrared radiation include heat-sensitive devices such as thermocouple detectors, bolometers (some of these are cooled to temperatures close to absolute zero so that the thermal radiation of the detector system itself is greatly reduced), photovoltaic cells, and photoconductors. The latter are made of semiconductor materials (e.g., silicon and lead sulfide) whose electrical conductance increases when exposed to infrared radiation.

VISIBLE RADIATION

Visible light is the most familiar form of electromagnetic radiation and makes up that portion of the spectrum to which the eye is sensitive. This span is very narrow; the frequencies of violet light are only about twice those of red. The corresponding wavelengths extend from 7×10^{-5} cm (red) to 4×10^{-5} cm (violet). The energy of a photon from the centre of the visible spectrum (yellow) is $h\nu = 2.2$ eV. This is one million times larger than the energy of a photon of a television wave and one billion times larger than that of radio waves in general.

Life on Earth could not exist without visible light, which represents the peak of the Sun's spectrum and close to one-half of all of its radiant energy. Visible light is essential for photosynthesis, which enables plants to produce the carbohydrates and proteins that are the food sources for animals. Coal and oil are sources of energy accumulated from sunlight in plants and microorganisms millions of years ago, and hydroelectric power is extracted from one step of the hydrologic cycle kept in motion by sunlight at the present time.

Considering the importance of visible sunlight for all aspects of terrestrial life, one cannot help being awed by the absorption spectrum of water. The remarkable transparency of water centred in the narrow regime of visible light is the result of the characteristic distribution of internal energy states of water. Absorption is strong toward the infrared on account of molecular vibrations and intermolecular oscillations. In the ultraviolet region, absorption of radiation is caused by electronic excitations. Light of frequencies having absorption coefficients larger than $\alpha = 10 \text{ cm}^{-1}$ cannot even reach the retina of the human eye because its constituent liquid consists mainly of water that absorbs such frequencies of light.

Since the 1970s an increasing number of devices have been developed for converting sunlight into electricity. Unlike various conventional energy sources, solar energy does not become depleted by use and does not pollute the environment. Two branches of development may be noted—namely, photothermal and photovoltaic technologies. In photothermal devices, sunlight is used to heat a substance, as, for example, water, to produce steam with which to drive a generator. Photovoltaic devices, on the other hand, convert the energy in sunlight directly to electricity by use of the photovoltaic effect in a semiconductor junction. Solar panels consisting of photovoltaic devices made of gallium arsenide have conversion efficiencies of more than 20 percent and are used to provide electric power in many satellites and space probes. Large-area solar panels can be made with amorphous semiconductors that have conversion efficiencies of about 10 percent.

Solar cells have replaced dry cell batteries in some portable electronic instruments, and solar energy power stations of 60-megawatts capacity have been built.

The intensity and spectral composition of visible light can be measured and recorded by essentially any process or property that is affected by light. Detectors make use of a photographic process based on silver halide, the photo-emission of electrons from metal surfaces, the generation of electric current in a photovoltaic cell, and the increase in electrical conduction in semiconductors.

Glass fibres constitute an effective means of guiding and transmitting light. A beam of light is confined by total internal reflection to travel inside such an optical fibre, whose thickness may be anywhere between one hundredth of a millimetre and a few millimetres. Many thin optical fibres can be combined into bundles to achieve image reproduction. The flexibility of these fibres or fibre bundles permits their use in medicine for optical exploration of internal organs. Optical fibres connecting the continents provide the capability to transmit substantially larger amounts of information than other systems of international telecommunications. Another advantage of optical fibre communication systems is that transmissions cannot easily be intercepted and are not disturbed by lower atmospheric and stratospheric disturbances.

Optical fibres integrated with miniature semiconductor lasers and light-emitting diodes, as well as with light detector arrays and photoelectronic imaging and recording materials, form the building blocks of a new optoelectronics industry. Some familiar commercial products are optoelectronic copying machines, laser printers, compact disc players, fax machines, optical recording media, and optical disc mass-storage systems of exceedingly high bit density.

ULTRAVIOLET RADIATION

The German physicist Johann Wilhelm Ritter, having learned of Herschel's discovery of infrared waves, looked beyond the violet end of the visible spectrum of the Sun and found (in 1801) that there exist invisible rays that darken silver chloride even more efficiently than visible light. This spectral region extending between visible light and X-rays is designated ultraviolet. Sources of this form of electromagnetic radiation are hot objects like the Sun, synchrotron radiation sources, mercury or xenon arc lamps, and gaseous discharge tubes filled with gas atoms (e.g., mercury, deuterium, or hydrogen) that have internal electron energy levels which correspond to the photons of ultraviolet light.

When ultraviolet light strikes certain materials, it causes them to fluoresce—i.e., they emit electromagnetic radiation of lower energy, such as visible light. The spectrum of fluorescent light is characteristic of a material's composition and thus can be used for screening minerals, detecting bacteria in spoiled food, identifying pigments, or detecting forgeries of artworks and other objects (the aged surfaces of ancient marble sculptures, for instance, fluoresce yellow-green, whereas a freshly cut marble surface fluoresces bright violet).

Optical instruments for the ultraviolet region are made of special materials, such as quartz, certain silicates, and metal fluorides, which are transparent at least in the near ultraviolet. Far-ultraviolet radiation is absorbed by nearly all gases and materials and thus requires reflection optics in vacuum chambers.

Ultraviolet radiation is detected by photographic plates and by means of the photoelectric effect in photomultiplier tubes. Also, ultraviolet radiation can be converted to visible light by fluorescence before detection.

The relatively high energy of ultraviolet light gives rise to certain photochemical reactions. This characteristic is exploited to produce cyanotype impressions on fabrics and for blueprinting design drawings. Here, the fabric or paper is treated with a mixture of chemicals that react upon exposure to ultraviolet light to form an insoluble blue compound. Electronic excitations caused by ultraviolet radiation also produce changes in the colour and transparency of photosensitive and photochromic glasses. Photochemical and photostructural changes in certain polymers constitute the basis for photolithography and the processing of the microelectronic circuits.

Although invisible to the eyes of humans and most vertebrates, near-ultraviolet light can be seen by many insects. Butterflies and many flowers that appear to have identical colour patterns under visible light are distinctly different when viewed under the ultraviolet rays perceptible to insects.

An important difference between ultraviolet light and electromagnetic radiation of lower frequencies is the ability of the former to ionize, meaning that it can knock an electron out from atoms and molecules. All high-frequency electromagnetic radiation beyond the visible—i.e., ultraviolet light, X-rays, and gamma rays—is ionizing and therefore harmful to body tissues, living cells, and DNA (deoxyribonucleic acid). The harmful effects of ultraviolet light to humans and larger animals are mitigated by the fact that this form of radiation does not penetrate much further than the skin.

The body of a sunbather is struck by 10^{21} photons every second, and 1 percent of these, or more than a billion billion per second, are photons of ultraviolet radiation. Tanning and natural body pigments help to protect the skin to some degree, preventing the destruction of skin cells by ultraviolet light. Nevertheless, overexposure to the ultraviolet component of sunlight can cause skin cancer, cataracts of the eyes, and damage to the body's immune system. Fortunately a layer of ozone (O_3) in the stratosphere absorbs the most damaging ultraviolet rays, which have wavelengths of 2,000 and 2,900 angstroms (one angstrom [Å] = 10^{-10} metre), and attenuates those with wavelengths between 2,900 and 3,150 Å. Without this protective layer of ozone, life on Earth would not be possible. The ozone layer is produced at an altitude of about 10 to 50 km (6 to 30 miles) above Earth's surface by a reaction between upward-diffusing molecular oxygen (O_2) and downward-diffusing ionized atomic oxygen (O^+). Many scientists believe that this life-protecting stratospheric ozone layer is being reduced by chlorine atoms in chlorofluorocarbon (or Freon) gases released into the atmosphere by aerosol propellants, air-conditioner coolants, solvents used in the manufacture of electronic components, and other sources.

Ionized atomic oxygen, nitrogen, and nitric oxide are produced in the upper atmosphere by absorption of solar ultraviolet radiation. This ionized region is the ionosphere, which affects radio communications and reflects and absorbs radio waves of frequencies below 40 MHz.

X-RAYS

X-rays are electromagnetic radiation of extremely short wavelength and high frequency, with wavelengths ranging from about 10^{-8} to 10^{-12} metre and corresponding frequencies from about 10^{16} to 10^{20} hertz (Hz).

X-rays are commonly produced by accelerating (or decelerating) charged particles; examples include a beam of electrons striking a metal plate in an X-ray tube and a circulating beam of electrons in a synchrotron particle accelerator or storage ring. In addition, highly excited

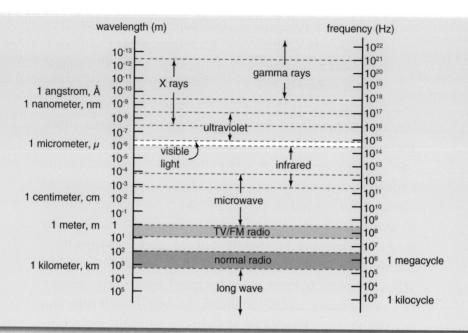

The relationship of X-rays to other electromagnetic radiation within the electromagnetic spectrum. Encyclopædia Britannica, Inc.

atoms can emit X-rays with discrete wavelengths characteristic of the energy level spacings in the atoms. The X-ray region of the electromagnetic spectrum falls far outside the range of visible wavelengths. However, the passage of X-rays through materials, including biological tissue, can be recorded with photographic films and other detectors. The analysis of X-ray images of the body is an extremely valuable medical diagnostic tool.

X-rays are a form of ionizing radiation—when interacting with matter, they are energetic enough to cause neutral atoms to eject electrons. Through this ionization process the energy of the X-rays is deposited in the matter. When passing through living tissue, X-rays can cause harmful biochemical changes in genes, chromosomes, and other cell components. The biological effects of ionizing radiation, which are complex and highly dependent on the length and intensity of exposure, are still under active study. X-ray radiation therapies take advantage of these effects to combat the growth of malignant tumours.

X-rays were discovered in 1895 by German physicist Wilhelm Konrad Röntgen while investigating the effects of electron beams (then called cathode rays) in electrical discharges through low-pressure gases. Röntgen uncovered a startling effect—namely, that a screen coated with a fluorescent material placed outside a discharge tube would glow even when it was shielded from the direct visible and ultraviolet light of the gaseous discharge. He deduced that an invisible radiation from the tube passed through the air and caused the screen to fluoresce. Röntgen was able to show that the radiation responsible for the fluorescence originated from the point where the electron beam struck the glass wall of the discharge tube. Opaque objects placed between the tube and the screen proved to be transparent to the new form of radiation; Röntgen dramatically demonstrated this by producing a photographic image of the bones of the human hand. His discovery of so-called Röntgen rays was met with worldwide scientific and popular excitement, and, along with the discoveries of radioactivity (1896) and the electron (1897), it ushered in the study of the atomic world and the era of modern physics.

FUNDAMENTAL CHARACTERISTICS

X-rays are a form of electromagnetic radiation. Their basic physical properties are identical to those of the more familiar components of the electromagnetic spectrum—visible light, infrared radiation, and ultraviolet radiation.

Wave Nature

As with other forms of electromagnetic radiation, X-rays can be described as coupled waves of electric and magnetic fields traveling at the speed of light (about 300,000 km, or 186,000 miles, per second). Their characteristic wavelengths and frequencies can be demonstrated and measured through the interference effects that result from the overlap of two or more waves in space. X-rays also exhibit particle-like properties; they can be described as a flow of photons carrying discrete amounts of energy and momentum. This dual nature is a property of all forms of radiation and matter and is comprehensively described by the theory of quantum mechanics.

Though it was immediately suspected, following Röntgen's discovery, that X-rays were a form of electromagnetic radiation, this proved very difficult to establish. X-rays are distinguished by their very short wavelengths, typically 1,000 times shorter than the wavelengths of visible light. Because of this, and because of the practical difficulties of producing and detecting the new form of radiation, the nature of X-rays was only gradually unraveled in the early decades of the 20th century.

In 1906 the British physicist Charles Glover Barkla first demonstrated the wave nature of X-rays by showing that they can be "polarized" by scattering from a solid. Polarization refers to the orientation of the oscillations in a transverse wave; all electromagnetic waves are transverse oscillations of electric and magnetic fields. The very short wavelengths of X-rays, hinted at in early diffraction studies in which the rays were passed through narrow slits, was firmly established in 1912 by the pioneering work of the German physicist Max von Laue and his students Walter Friedrich and Paul Knipping. Laue suggested that the ordered arrangements of atoms in crystals could serve as natural three-dimensional diffraction gratings. Typical atomic spacings in crystals are approximately 1 angstrom (1×10^{-10} metre), ideal for producing diffraction effects in electromagnetic radiation of comparable wavelength.

Friedrich and Knipping verified Laue's predictions by photographing diffraction patterns produced by the passage of X-rays through a crystal of zinc sulfide. These experiments demonstrated that X-rays have wavelengths of about 1 angstrom and confirmed that the atoms in crystals are arranged in regular structures.

In the following year, the British physicist William Lawrence Bragg devised a particularly simple model of the scattering of X-rays from the parallel layers of atoms in a crystal. The Bragg law shows how the angles at which X-rays are most efficiently diffracted from a crystal are related to the X-ray wavelength and the distance between the layers of atoms. Bragg's physicist father, William Henry Bragg, based his design of the first X-ray spectrometer on his son's analysis. The pair used their X-ray spectrometer in making seminal studies of both the distribution of wavelengths in X-ray beams and the crystal structures of many common solids—an achievement for which they shared the Nobel Prize for Physics in 1915.

Particle Nature

In the early 1920s, experimental studies of the scattering of X-rays from solids played a key role in establishing the particle nature of electromagnetic radiation. In 1905 German physicist Albert Einstein had proposed that electromagnetic radiation is granular, consisting of quanta (later called photons) each with an energy hf, where h is Planck's constant (about 6.6×10^{-34} joule·second) and f is the frequency of the radiation. Einstein's hypothesis was strongly supported in subsequent studies of the photoelectric effect and by the successes of Danish physicist Niels Bohr's model of the hydrogen atom and its characteristic emission and absorption spectra. Further verification came in 1922 when American physicist Arthur Compton successfully treated the scattering of X-rays from the atoms in a solid as a set of collisions between X-ray photons and the loosely bound outer electrons of the atoms.

Adapting the relation between momentum and energy for a classical electromagnetic wave to an individual photon, Compton used conservation of energy and conservation of momentum arguments to derive an expression for the wavelength shift of scattered X-rays as a function of their scattering angle. In the so-called Compton effect, a colliding photon transfers some of its energy and momentum to an electron, which recoils. The scattered photon must thus have less energy and momentum than the incoming photon, resulting in scattered X-rays of slightly lower frequency and longer wavelength. Compton's careful measurements of this small effect, coupled with his successful theoretical treatment (independently derived by the Dutch scientist Peter Debye), provided convincing evidence for the existence of photons. The approximate wavelength range of the X-ray portion of the electromagnetic spectrum, 10^{-8} to 10^{-12} metre, corresponds to a range of photon energies from about 100 eV (electron volts) to 1 MeV (million electron volts).

APPLICATIONS

The defining characteristics of X-rays—their ability to penetrate optically opaque materials, their wavelengths of atomic dimension, the high energy of individual X-ray photons—led to a wide range of industrial, medical, and scientific applications. Specialized X-ray sources, detectors, and analysis techniques have been developed to address a range of questions from the study of the interactions of the simplest molecules to the structure of the human brain.

X-ray images of the body are an indispensable diagnostic tool in modern medicine. Medical imaging allows for the nonintrusive detection of dental cavities, bone

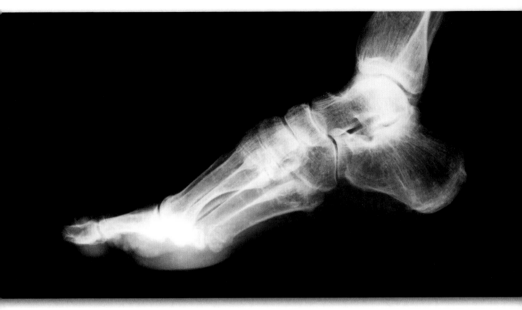

X-ray of a human foot. © Vadim Kozlovsky/Shutterstock.com

fractures, foreign objects, and diseased conditions such as cancer. Standard X-ray images easily differentiate between bone and soft tissue; additional contrast between different areas of soft tissue is afforded by the injection of a contrast medium—a liquid or gas that is comparatively opaque to X-rays. In the 1970s a powerful new X-ray imaging technique, computed tomography (CT), was developed. Now in widespread use, CT scans produce detailed high-resolution cross-sectional images of internal organs and structures; they are far more sensitive to small density variations than conventional X-ray images.

As with other forms of ionizing radiation, X-rays cause biochemical changes in living cells. A high-energy X-ray photon deposits its energy by liberating electrons from atoms and molecules. These free electrons may themselves ionize additional neutral species. Through this process, reactive ions and free radicals are formed, leading to further chemical reactions. The resulting radiation-induced chemistry can break the molecular bonds needed for cell growth and can induce genetic damage. While there are significant health risks associated with exposure to X-rays, radiation therapies exploit the above effects to treat cancerous tumours and blood disorders such as leukemia. X-rays (and higher-energy gamma rays) are directed at target tissues; the consequent molecular damage blocks the growth of the diseased cells. Nearby normal cells, also exposed to the ionizing X-rays, are typically more capable of repair. In a related application, in agricultural industries the irradiation of some foods with X-rays and gamma rays is used to inhibit selectively the growth of bacteria.

X-rays are a powerful diagnostic tool for revealing the structure and composition of materials. The great utility of X-ray images derives from the differential absorption of X-rays by materials of different density, composition, and homogeneity. In a common application, X-rays are used for quick examination of the contents of airline baggage. In industry, X-ray images are used to detect flaws nondestructively in castings that are inaccessible to direct observation. X-ray microscopes are capable of magnifying X-ray absorption images so as to resolve features on scales as small as about 40 nanometres (nm; billionths of a metre), or roughly 400 atomic diameters. This resolution, about five times greater than that achieved by the best visible light microscopes, is possible because of the small diffraction effects associated with the very short wavelengths of X-rays. X-ray microscopes usually operate with "soft" X-rays (wavelengths in the 1- to 10-nm range) and rely on reflective optics or "zone plates" to achieve focusing. Because water is relatively transparent in the soft X-ray region, these microscopes are ideal for studying biological materials in an aqueous environment. Another sophisticated absorption technique, called EXAFS ("extended X-ray absorption fine structure"), is capable of identifying the short-range ordering of atoms and molecules in unstable samples of crystals and amorphous solids.

X-ray diffraction techniques (or "X-ray crystallography") allow for the determination of crystal structures in inorganic, organic, and biological materials. The detailed atomic structure of the double-helix polymer deoxyribonucleic acid (DNA) was famously revealed by James Watson and Francis Crick via the X-ray crystallography studies of Maurice Wilkins. X-ray fluorescence is a complementary method for the quantitative analysis of the composition of materials. In this technique, a sample is exposed to either an electron beam or a beam of primary X-rays; the resulting atomic excitations lead to X-ray emissions with wavelengths characteristic of the elements in the sample. The electron microprobe uses this process to identify the constituents of sample regions as small as a few micrometres (millionths of a metre). X-ray fluorescence and diffraction techniques are valuable methods for the nondestructive analysis of art objects. Brushstroke techniques and the arrangements of painted-over pigments in oil paintings, the presence of coatings and varnishes, and the compositions of glasses, porcelain, and enamels are revealed through X-ray analysis.

Many of the above techniques are enhanced by the exceptionally high X-ray intensities produced in modern synchrotron light facilities. Extremely bright, short X-ray pulses, tuned to selected wavelength regions, are used to probe chemical reactions on surfaces, the electronic structures of semiconductors and magnetic materials, and the structure and function of proteins and biological macromolecules. Another promising source of high-intensity X-rays is the X-ray laser. While coherent X-rays (a signature of lasing) at the longer-wavelength end of the spectral region have been produced in the laboratory, the development of a practical device at shorter wavelengths remained a difficult technological challenge until 2009, when lasing was achieved with X-rays with a wavelength of 0.15 nm.

PRODUCTION OF X-RAYS

There are three common mechanisms for the production of X-rays: the acceleration of a charged particle, atomic transitions between discrete energy levels, and the radioactive decay of some atomic nuclei. Each mechanism leads to a characteristic spectrum of X-ray radiation.

In the theory of classical electromagnetism, accelerating electric charges emit electromagnetic waves. In the most common terrestrial source of X-rays, the X-ray tube, a beam of high-energy electrons impinges on a solid target. As the fast-moving electrons in the beam interact with the electrons and nuclei of the target atoms, they are repeatedly deflected and slowed. During this abrupt deceleration, the beam electrons emit bremsstrahlung (German: "braking radiation")—a continuous spectrum of electromagnetic radiation with a peak intensity in the X-ray region. Most of the energy radiated in an X-ray tube is contained in this continuous spectrum. Far more powerful (and far larger) sources of a continuum of X-rays are synchrotron particle accelerators and storage rings. In a synchrotron, charged particles (usually electrons or positrons) are accelerated to very high energies (typically billions of electron volts) and then confined to a closed orbit by strong magnets. When the charged particles are deflected by the magnetic fields (and hence accelerated via the change in their direction of motion), they emit so-called synchrotron radiation— a continuum whose intensity and frequency distribution are determined by the strength of the magnetic fields and the energy of the circulating particles. Specially designed synchrotron light sources are used worldwide for X-ray studies of materials.

In an X-ray tube, in addition to the continuous spectrum of radiation emitted by the decelerating electrons, there is also a spectrum of discrete X-ray emission lines that is characteristic of the target material. This "characteristic radiation" results from the excitation of the target atoms by collisions with the fast-moving electrons. Most commonly, a collision first causes a tightly bound inner-shell electron to be ejected from the atom; a loosely bound outer-shell electron then falls into the inner shell to fill the vacancy. In the process, a single photon is emitted by the atom with an energy equal to the difference between the inner-shell and outer-shell vacancy states. This energy difference usually corresponds to photon wavelengths in the X-ray region of the spectrum. Characteristic X-ray radiation can also be produced from a target material when it is exposed to a primary X-ray beam. In this case, the primary X-ray photons initiate the sequence of electron transitions that result in the emission of secondary X-ray photons.

In 1913 the English physicist Henry Moseley discovered a simple relationship between the wavelengths of the X-ray emission lines from a target and the atomic number of the target element—the wavelengths are inversely proportional to the square of the atomic number. Known as Moseley's law, this relationship proved to be a definitive tool in the determination of atomic numbers in the early days of atomic physics. X-ray fluoresence techniques, in which the wavelengths of characteristic X-rays are recorded following the excitation of a target, are now commonly used to identify the elemental constituents of materials.

X-ray emission is sometimes a by-product of a nuclear transformation. In the process of electron capture, an inner-shell atomic electron is captured by the atomic nucleus, initiating the transformation of a nuclear proton into a neutron and lowering the atomic number by one unit. The vacant inner-shell orbit is then quickly filled by an outer-shell electron, producing a characteristic X-ray photon. The relaxation of an excited nucleus to a lower-energy state also sometimes results in the emission of an X-ray photon. However, the photons emitted in most nuclear transitions of this type are of even higher energy than X-rays—they fall into the gamma-ray region of the electromagnetic spectrum.

Many astronomical sources of X-rays have been discovered over the past 50 years; collectively they are a rich resource of information about the universe. X-rays are emitted by the Sun's hot corona (outer atmosphere) and by the coronas of other ordinary stars in the Milky Way Galaxy. Many binary star systems emit copious X-rays; the strongest such sources produce, in the X-ray region alone, more than 1,000 times the entire energy output of the Sun. Supernova remnants are also strong sources of X-rays, which are sometimes associated with synchrotron radiation produced by high-energy charged particles circulating in intense magnetic fields and sometimes with atomic emissions from extremely hot gases (in the range of 10 million kelvins [18,000,000 °F or 10,000,000 °C]). Powerful extragalactic sources of X-rays, including active galaxies, quasars, and galactic clusters, are currently under intense scientific scrutiny; in some cases the exact mechanisms of X-ray production are still uncertain or unknown. As the Earth's atmosphere strongly absorbs X-rays, astronomical observations in the X-ray region must be made from orbiting satellites. The launch of the Chandra X-Ray Observatory in 1999 greatly advanced the observational capabilities of X-ray astronomy.

DETECTION OF X-RAYS

Photographic film was used by Röntgen as one of the first X-ray detectors, and this simple technique remains in wide use in medical applications. The process of exposure is initiated by X-ray photons ionizing radiation-sensitive silver halide crystals in an emulsion on the film surface; the resulting photochemical change of the affected crystals darkens the exposed area.

Photographic techniques, while much improved upon since the time of Röntgen and still extremely useful for qualitative applications, are not well-suited for more quantitative measurements of X-ray intensities and spectral content. A number of more effective detection methods have been developed. In a Geiger-Müller tube, or Geiger counter, incoming X-ray photons ionize atoms in a gas-filled volume. An applied high voltage induces further ionizations from collisions between liberated electrons and neutral atoms, creating an avalanche of charged particles and a large electrical pulse that is easily detected. More sophisticated detection schemes based on the ionization of gas atoms can discriminate between X-rays of different energies. Other common detection schemes rely on the ability of X-rays to produce visible fluorescence in crystals and charge separation in semiconductors.

GAMMA RAYS

The electromagnetic radiation with the shortest wavelength and highest energy is called a gamma ray. Gamma rays are produced in the disintegration of radioactive atomic nuclei and in the decay of certain subatomic particles. The commonly accepted definitions of the gamma-ray and X-ray regions of the electromagnetic spectrum include some wavelength overlap, with gamma-ray radiation having wavelengths that are generally shorter than a few tenths of an angstrom (10^{-10} metre) and gamma-ray photons having energies that are greater than tens of thousands of electron volts (eV). There is no theoretical upper limit to the energies of gamma-ray photons and no lower limit to gamma-ray wavelengths; observed energies presently extend up to a few trillion electron volts — these extremely high-energy photons are produced in astronomical sources through currently unidentified mechanisms.

The term *gamma ray* was coined by British physicist Ernest Rutherford in 1903 following early studies of the emissions of radioactive nuclei. Just as atoms have discrete energy levels associated with different configurations of the orbiting electrons, atomic nuclei have energy level structures determined by the configurations of the protons and neutrons that constitute the nuclei. While energy differences between atomic energy levels are typically in the 1- to 10-eV range, energy differences in nuclei usually fall in the 1-keV (thousand electron volts) to 10-MeV (million electron volts) range. When a nucleus makes a transition from a high-energy level to a lower-energy level, a photon is emitted to carry off the excess energy; nuclear energy-level differences correspond to photon wavelengths in the gamma-ray region.

When an unstable atomic nucleus decays into a more stable nucleus, the "daughter" nucleus is sometimes produced in an excited state. The subsequent relaxation of the daughter nucleus to a lower-energy state results in the emission of a gamma-ray photon. Gamma-ray spectroscopy, involving the precise measurement of gamma-ray photon energies emitted by different nuclei, can establish nuclear energy-level structures and allows for the identification of trace radioactive elements through their gamma-ray emissions. Gamma rays are also produced in the important process of pair annihilation, in which an electron and its antiparticle, a positron, vanish and two photons are created. The photons are emitted in opposite directions and must each carry 511 keV of energy—the rest mass energy of the electron and positron. Gamma rays can also be generated in the decay of some unstable subatomic particles, such as the neutral pion.

Gamma-ray photons, like their X-ray counterparts, are a form of ionizing radiation; when they pass through matter, they usually deposit their energy by liberating electrons from atoms and molecules. At the lower energy ranges, a gamma-ray photon is often completely absorbed by an atom and the gamma ray's energy transferred to a single ejected electron. Higher-energy gamma rays are more likely to scatter from the atomic electrons, depositing a fraction of their energy in each scattering event. Standard methods for the detection of gamma rays are based on the effects of the liberated atomic electrons in gases, crystals, and semiconductors.

Gamma rays can also interact with atomic nuclei. In the process of pair production, a gamma-ray photon with an energy exceeding twice the rest mass energy of the electron (greater than 1.02 MeV), when passing close to a nucleus, is directly converted into an electron-positron pair. At even higher energies (greater than 10 MeV), a gamma ray can be directly absorbed by a nucleus, causing the ejection of nuclear particles or the splitting of the nucleus in a process known as photofission.

Medical applications of gamma rays include the valuable imaging technique of positron emission tomography (PET) and effective radiation therapies to treat cancerous tumours. In a PET scan, a short-lived positron-emitting radioactive pharmaceutical, chosen because of its participation in a particular physiological process (e.g., brain function), is injected into the body. Emitted positrons quickly combine with nearby electrons and, through pair annihilation, give rise to two 511-keV gamma rays traveling in opposite directions. After detection of the gamma rays, a computer-generated reconstruction of the locations of the gamma-ray emissions produces an image that highlights the location of the biological process being examined.

As a deeply penetrating ionizing radiation, gamma rays cause significant biochemical changes in living cells. Radiation therapies make use of this property to selectively destroy cancerous cells in small localized tumours. Radioactive isotopes are injected or implanted near the tumour; gamma rays that are continuously emitted by the radioactive nuclei bombard the affected area and arrest the development of the malignant cells.

Airborne surveys of gamma-ray emissions from the Earth's surface search for minerals containing trace radioactive elements such as uranium and thorium. Aerial and ground-based gamma-ray spectroscopy is employed to support geologic mapping, mineral exploration, and identification of environmental contamination. Gamma rays were first detected from astronomical sources in the 1960s, and gamma-ray astronomy is now a well-established field of research. As with the study of astronomical X-rays, gamma-ray observations must be made above the strongly absorbing atmosphere of Earth—typically with orbiting satellites or high-altitude balloons. There are many intriguing and poorly understood astronomical gamma-ray sources, including powerful point sources tentatively identified as pulsars, quasars, and supernova remnants. Among the most fascinating unexplained astronomical phenomena are so-called gamma-ray bursts—brief, extremely intense emissions from sources that are apparently isotropically distributed in the sky.

CHAPTER 6
LASERS

A laser is a device that stimulates atoms or molecules to emit light at particular wavelengths and amplifies that light, typically producing a very narrow beam of radiation. The emission generally covers an extremely limited range of visible, infrared, ultraviolet, or X-ray wavelengths. Many different types of lasers have been developed, with highly varied characteristics. Laser is an acronym for "light amplification by the stimulated emission of radiation."

HISTORY

The laser is an outgrowth of a suggestion made by Albert Einstein in 1916 that under the proper circumstances atoms could release excess energy as light—either spontaneously or when stimulated by light. German physicist Rudolf Walther Ladenburg first observed stimulated emission in 1928, although at the time it seemed to have no practical use.

In 1951 Charles H. Townes, then at Columbia University in New York City, thought of a way to generate stimulated emission at microwave frequencies. At the end of 1953, he demonstrated a working device that focused "excited" ammonia molecules in a resonant microwave cavity, where they emitted a pure microwave frequency. Townes named the device a maser, for "microwave amplification by the stimulated emission of radiation." Aleksandr Mikhaylovich Prokhorov and Nikolay Gennadiyevich Basov of the P.N. Lebedev Physical Institute in Moscow independently described the theory of maser operation.

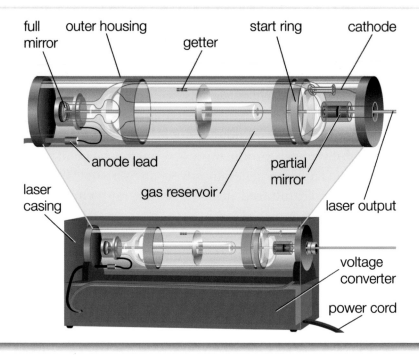

Basic laser components. Encyclopædia Britannica, Inc.

For their work all three shared the 1964 Nobel Prize for Physics.

An intense burst of maser research followed in the mid-1950s, but masers found only a limited range of applications as low-noise microwave amplifiers and atomic clocks. In 1957 Townes proposed to his brother-in-law and former postdoctoral student at Columbia University, Arthur L. Schawlow (then at Bell Laboratories), that they try to extend maser action to the much shorter wavelengths of infrared or visible light. Townes also had discussions with a graduate student at Columbia University, Gordon Gould, who quickly developed his own laser ideas. Townes and Schawlow published their ideas for an "optical maser" in a seminal paper in the Dec. 15, 1958, issue of *Physical Review*. Meanwhile, Gould coined the word *laser* and wrote a patent application. Whether Townes or Gould should be credited as the "inventor" of the laser thus became a matter of intense debate and led to years of litigation. Eventually, Gould received a series of four patents starting in 1977 that earned him millions of dollars in royalties.

The Townes-Schawlow proposal led several groups to try building a laser. The Gould proposal became the basis of a classified military contract. Success came first to Theodore H. Maiman, who took a different approach at Hughes Research Laboratories in Malibu, Calif. He fired bright pulses from a photographer's flash lamp to excite chromium atoms in a crystal of synthetic ruby, a material he chose because he had studied carefully how it absorbed and emitted light and calculated that it should work as a laser. On May 16, 1960, he produced red pulses from a ruby rod about the size of a fingertip. In December 1960, Ali Javan, William Bennett, Jr., and Donald Herriott at Bell Labs built the first gas laser, which generated a continuous infrared beam from a mixture of helium and neon. In 1962, Robert N. Hall and coworkers at the General Electric Research and Development Center in Schenectady, N.Y., made the first semiconductor laser.

While lasers quickly caught the public imagination, perhaps for their similarity to the "heat rays" of science fiction, practical applications took years to develop. A young physicist named Irnee D'Haenens, while working with Maiman on the ruby laser, joked that the device was "a solution looking for a problem," and the line lingered in the laser community for many years. Townes and Schawlow had expected laser beams to be used in basic research and to send signals through air or space. Gould envisioned more powerful beams capable of cutting and drilling many materials. A key early success came in late

1963 when two researchers at the University of Michigan, Emmett Leith and Juris Upatnieks, used lasers to make the first three-dimensional holograms.

Helium-neon lasers were the first lasers with broad commercial applications. Because they could be adjusted to generate a visible red beam instead of an infrared beam, they found immediate use projecting straight lines for alignment, surveying, construction, and irrigation. Soon eye surgeons were using pulses from ruby lasers to weld detached retinas back in place without cutting into the eye. The first large-scale application for lasers was the laser scanner for automated checkout in supermarkets, which was developed in the mid-1970s and became common a few years later. Compact disc audio players and laser printers for personal computers soon followed.

Lasers have become standard tools in diverse applications. Laser pointers highlight presentation points in lecture halls, and laser target designators guide smart bombs to their targets. Lasers weld razor blades, write patterns on objects on production lines without touching them, remove unwanted hair, and bleach tattoos. Laser rangefinders in space probes profiled the surfaces of Mars and the asteroid Eros in unprecedented detail. In the laboratory, lasers have helped physicists to cool atoms to within a tiny fraction of a degree of absolute zero.

FUNDAMENTAL PRINCIPLES

Laser emission is shaped by the rules of quantum mechanics, which limit atoms and molecules to having discrete amounts of stored energy that depend on the nature of the atom or molecule. These discrete amounts are called energy levels.

ENERGY LEVELS AND STIMULATED EMISSIONS

The lowest energy level for an individual atom occurs when its electrons are all in the nearest possible orbits to its nucleus. This condition is called the ground state. When one or more of an atom's electrons have absorbed energy, they can move to outer orbits, and the atom is then referred to as being "excited." Excited states are generally not stable; as electrons drop from higher-energy to lower-energy levels, they emit the extra energy as light.

Einstein recognized that this emission could be produced in two ways. Usually, discrete packets of light known as photons are emitted spontaneously, without outside intervention. Alternatively, a passing photon could stimulate an atom or molecule to emit light—if the passing photon's energy exactly matched the energy that an electron would release spontaneously when dropping to a lower-energy configuration. Which process dominates depends on the ratio of lower-energy to higher-energy configurations. Ordinarily, lower-energy configurations predominate. This means that a spontaneously emitted photon is more likely to be absorbed and raise an electron from a lower-energy configuration to a higher-energy configuration than to stimulate a higher-energy configuration to drop to a lower-energy configuration by emitting a second photon. As long as lower-energy states are more common, stimulated emission will die out.

However, if higher-energy configurations predominate (a condition known as population inversion), spontaneously emitted photons are more likely to stimulate further emissions, generating a cascade of photons. Heat alone does not produce a population inversion; some process must selectively excite the atoms or molecules. Typically,

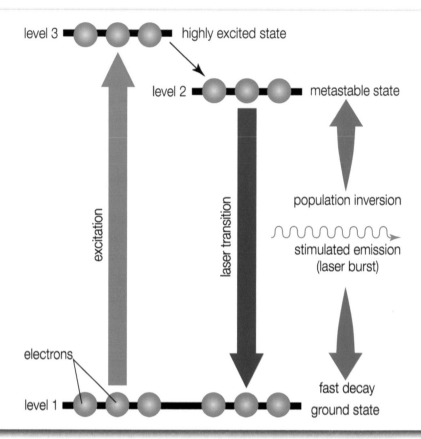

Three-level laser. A burst of energy excites electrons in more than half of the atoms from their ground state to a higher state, creating a population inversion. The electrons then drop into a long-lived state with slightly less energy, where they can be stimulated to quickly shed excess energy as a laser burst, returning the electrons to a stable ground state. Encyclopædia Britannica, Inc.

this is done by illuminating the laser material with bright light or by passing an electric current through it.

The simplest conceivable system, such as the ammonia maser built by Townes, has only two energy levels. More useful laser systems involve three or four energy levels. In a three-level laser, the material is first excited to a short-lived high-energy state that spontaneously drops to a somewhat lower-energy state with an unusually long

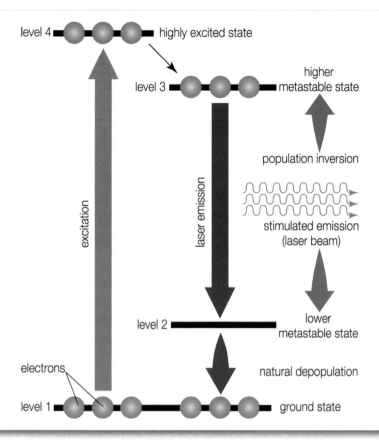

Four-level laser. A sustained laser beam can be achieved by using atoms that have two relatively stable levels between their ground state and a higher-energy excited state. As in a three-level laser, the atoms first drop to a long-lived metastable state where they can be stimulated to emit excess energy. However, instead of dropping to the ground state, they stop at another state above the ground state from which they can more easily be excited back up to the higher metastable state, thereby maintaining the population inversion needed for continuous laser operation. Encyclopædia Britannica, Inc.

lifetime, called a metastable state. The metastable state is important because it traps and holds the excitation energy, building up a population inversion that can be further stimulated to emit radiation, dropping the species back to the ground state. The ruby laser developed by Theodore Maiman is an example of a three-level laser.

Unfortunately, the three-level laser works only if the ground state is depopulated. As atoms or molecules emit light, they accumulate in the ground state, where they can absorb the stimulated emission and shut down laser action, so most three-level lasers can only generate pulses. This difficulty is overcome in the four-level laser, where an extra transition state is located between metastable and ground states. This allows many four-level lasers to emit a steady beam for days on end.

Laser Elements

Population inversions can be produced in a gas, liquid, or solid, but most laser media are gases or solids. Typically, laser gases are contained in cylindrical tubes and excited by an electric current or external light source, which is said to "pump" the laser. Similarly, solid-state lasers may use semiconductors or transparent crystals with small concentrations of light-emitting atoms.

An optical resonator is needed to build up the light energy in the beam. The resonator is formed by placing a pair of mirrors facing each other so that light emitted along the line between the mirrors is reflected back and forth. When a population inversion is created in the medium, light reflected back and forth increases in intensity with each pass through the laser medium. Other light leaks around the mirrors without being amplified. In an actual laser cavity, one or both mirrors transmit a fraction of the incident light. The fraction of light transmitted—that is, the laser beam—depends on the type of laser. If the laser generates a continuous beam, the amount of light added by stimulated emission on each round trip between the mirrors equals the light emerging in the beam plus losses within the optical resonator.

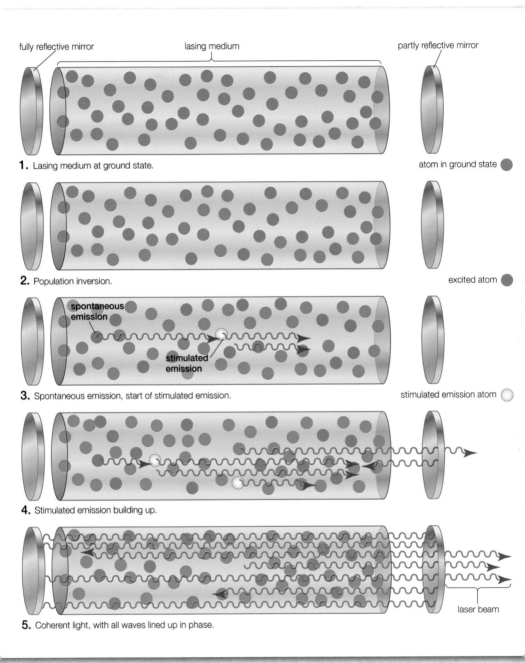

1. Lasing medium at ground state.

atom in ground state

2. Population inversion.

excited atom

3. Spontaneous emission, start of stimulated emission.

stimulated emission atom

4. Stimulated emission building up.

5. Coherent light, with all waves lined up in phase.

Stimulated emission in a laser cavity. Encyclopædia Britannica, Inc.

The combination of laser medium and resonant cavity forms what often is called simply a laser but technically is a laser oscillator. Oscillation determines many laser properties, and it means that the device generates light internally. Without mirrors and a resonant cavity, a laser would just be an optical amplifier, which can amplify light from an external source but not generate a beam internally. Elias Snitzer, a researcher at American Optical, demonstrated the first optical amplifier in 1961, but such devices were little used until the spread of communications based on fibre optics.

Laser Beam Characteristics

Laser light generally differs from other light in being focused in a narrow beam, limited to a narrow range of wavelengths (often called "monochromatic"), and consisting of waves that are in phase with each other. These properties arise from interactions between the process of stimulated emission, the resonant cavity, and the laser medium.

Stimulated emission produces a second photon identical to the one that stimulated the emission, so the new photon has the same phase, wavelength, and direction— that is, the two are coherent with respect to each other, with peaks and valleys in phase. Both the original and the new photon can then stimulate the emission of other identical photons. Passing the light back and forth through a resonant cavity enhances this uniformity, with the degree of coherence and the narrowness of the beam depending on the laser design.

Although a visible laser produces what looks like a point of light on the opposite wall of a room, the alignment, or collimation, of the beam is not perfect. The extent of beam spreading depends on both the distance between the laser mirrors and diffraction, which scatters light at the edge of an aperture. Diffraction is proportional to the laser wavelength divided by the size of the emitting aperture; the larger the aperture is, the more slowly the beam spreads. A red helium-neon laser emits from a one-millimetre (.0039 inch) aperture at a wavelength of 0.633 micrometre, generating a beam that diverges at an angle of about 0.057 degree, or one milliradian. Such a small angle of divergence will produce a one-metre spot at a distance of one kilometre (.62 mile). In contrast, a typical flashlight beam produces a similar one-metre spot within a few metres. Not all lasers produce tight beams, however. Semiconductor lasers emit light near one micrometre wavelength from an aperture of comparable size, so their divergence is 20 degrees or more, and external optics are needed to focus their beams.

The output wavelength depends on the laser material, the process of stimulated emission, and the optics of the laser resonator. For each transition between energy levels, a material can support stimulated emission over a limited range of wavelengths; the extent of that range varies with the nature of the material and the transition. The probability of stimulated emission varies with wavelength, and the process concentrates emission at wavelengths where that probability is the highest.

Resonant cavities support laser oscillation at wavelengths that meet a resonant condition—an integral number N of wavelengths λ must equal the distance light travels during a round trip between the mirrors. If the cavity length is L and the refractive index of the material in the laser cavity is n, the round-trip distance $2L$ must equal $N\lambda/n$, or $2L = N\lambda/n$. Each resonance is called a longitudinal mode. Except in semiconductor lasers, cavities are thousands of wavelengths long, so the wavelengths of adjacent modes are closely spaced—and usually the laser simultaneously emits light on two or more wavelengths within

0.1 percent of each other. These beams are monochromatic for most practical applications; other optics can be added to limit laser oscillation to a single longitudinal mode and an even narrower range of wavelengths. The best laboratory lasers emit a range of wavelengths that differ by less than 0.0000001 percent.

The narrower the range of wavelengths, the more coherent the beam—meaning the more precisely every light wave in the beam is in exact synchronization with every other one. This is measured by a quantity called coherence length. If the centre of the range of wavelengths emitted is λ and the range of wavelengths emitted is $\Delta\lambda$, this coherence length equals $\lambda^2/2\Delta\lambda$. Typical coherence lengths range from millimetres to metres. Such long coherence lengths are essential, for instance, to record holograms of three-dimensional objects.

Lasers can generate pulsed or continuous beams, with average powers ranging from microwatts to over a million watts in the most powerful experimental lasers. A laser is called continuous-wave if its output is nominally constant over an interval of seconds or longer; one example is the steady red beam from a laser pointer. Pulsed lasers concentrate their output energy into brief high-power bursts. These lasers can fire single pulses or a series of pulses at regular intervals. Instantaneous power can be extremely high at the peak of a very short pulse. Laboratory lasers have generated peak power exceeding 10^{15} watts for intervals of about 10^{-12} second.

Pulses can be compressed to extremely short duration, about 5 femtoseconds (5×10^{-15} second) in laboratory experiments, in order to "freeze" the action during events that occur very rapidly, such as stages in chemical reactions. Laser pulses also can be focused to concentrate high powers on small spots, much as a magnifier focuses sunlight onto a small spot to ignite a piece of paper.

TYPES OF LASERS

Crystals, glasses, semiconductors, gases, liquids, beams of high-energy electrons, and even gelatin doped with suitable materials can generate laser beams. In nature, hot gases near bright stars can generate strong stimulated emission at microwave frequencies, although these gas clouds lack resonant cavities, so they do not produce beams.

In crystal and glass lasers, such as Maiman's first ruby laser, light from an external source excites atoms, known as dopants, that have been added to a host material at low concentrations. Important examples include glasses and crystals doped with the rare-earth element neodymium and glasses doped with erbium or ytterbium, which can be drawn into fibres for use as fibre-optic lasers or amplifiers. Titanium atoms doped into synthetic sapphire can generate stimulated emission across an exceptionally broad range and are used in wavelength-tunable lasers.

Many different gases can function as laser media. The common helium-neon laser contains a small amount of neon and a much larger amount of helium. The helium atoms capture energy from electrons passing through the gas and transfer it to the neon atoms, which emit light. The best-known helium-neon lasers emit red light, but they also can be made to emit yellow, orange, green, or infrared light; typical powers are in the milliwatt range. Argon and krypton atoms that have been stripped of one or two electrons can generate milliwatts to watts of laser light at visible and ultraviolet wavelengths. The most powerful commercial gas laser is the carbon-dioxide laser, which can generate kilowatts of continuous power.

The most widely used lasers today are semiconductor diode lasers, which emit visible or infrared light when an electric current passes through them. The emission occurs at the interface between two regions doped with different materials. The *p-n* junction can act as a laser medium, generating stimulated emission and providing lasing action if it is inside a suitable cavity. Conventional edge-emitting semiconductor lasers have mirrors on opposite edges of the *p-n* junction, so light oscillates in the junction plane. Vertical-cavity surface-emitting lasers (VCSELs) have mirrors above and below the *p-n* junction, so light resonates perpendicular to the junction. The wavelength depends on the semiconductor compound.

A few other types of lasers are used in research. In dye lasers the laser medium is a liquid containing organic dye molecules that can emit light over a range of wavelengths; adjusting the laser cavity changes, or tunes, the output wavelength. Chemical lasers are gas lasers in which a chemical reaction generates the excited molecules that produce stimulated emission. In free-electron lasers stimulated emission comes from electrons passing through a magnetic field that periodically varies in direction and intensity, causing the electrons to accelerate and release light energy. Because the electrons do not transition between well-defined energy levels, some specialists question whether a free-electron laser should be called a laser, but the label has stuck. Depending on the energy of the electron beam and variations in the magnetic field, free-electron lasers can be tuned across a wide range of wavelengths. Both free-electron and chemical lasers can emit high powers.

LASER APPLICATIONS

Lasers deliver coherent, monochromatic, well-controlled, and precisely directed light beams. Although lasers are poor choices for general-purpose illumination, they are ideal for concentrating light in space, time, or particular wavelengths. For example, many people were first introduced to lasers by concerts in the early 1970s that incorporated laser light shows, in which moving laser beams of different colours projected changing patterns on planetarium domes, concert-hall ceilings, or outdoor clouds.

Most laser applications fall into one of a few broad categories: (1) transmission and processing of information, (2) precise delivery of energy, and (3) alignment, measurement, and imaging. These categories cover diverse applications, from pinpoint energy delivery for delicate surgery to heavy-duty welding and from the mundane alignment of suspended ceilings to laboratory measurements of atomic properties.

TRANSMISSION AND PROCESSING OF INFORMATION

Laser beams can be focused onto very small spots and switched on and off billions of times per second. These characteristics make lasers important tools in telecommunications and information processing.

LASER SCANNERS

In laser supermarket scanners, a rotating mirror scans a red beam while clerks move packages across the beam. Optical sensors detect light reflected from striped bar codes on packages, decode the symbol, and relay the information to a computer so that it can add the price to the bill.

OPTICAL DISCS

Tiny, inexpensive semiconductor lasers read data from a growing variety of optical compact disc formats to play music, display video recordings, and read computer software. Audio compact discs, using infrared lasers, were introduced around 1980; CD-ROMs (compact disc read-only memory) for computer data soon followed. Newer optical drives use more powerful lasers to record data on light-sensitive discs called CD-R (recordable) or CD-RW (read/write), which can be played in ordinary CD-ROM drives. DVDs (digital video, or versatile, discs) work similarly, but they use a shorter-wavelength red laser to read smaller spots, so the discs can hold enough information to play a digitized motion picture. A new generation of discs called Blu-ray uses blue-light lasers to read and store data at an even higher density.

Fibre-Optic Communication Systems

Fibre-optic communication systems that transmit signals more than a few kilometres also use semiconductor laser beams. The optical signals are sent at infrared wavelengths of 1.3 to 1.6 micrometres, where glass fibres are most transparent. This technology has become the backbone of the global telecommunications network, and most telephone calls traveling beyond the confines of a single town go part of the way through optical fibres.

Precise Delivery of Energy

Laser energy can be focused in space and concentrated in time so that it heats, burns away, or vaporizes many materials. Although the total energy in a laser beam may be small, the concentrated power on small spots or during short intervals can be enormous.

Industrial Uses

Although lasers cost much more than mechanical drills or blades, their different properties allow them to perform otherwise difficult tasks. A laser beam does not deform flexible materials as a mechanical drill would, so it can drill holes in materials such as soft rubber nipples for baby bottles. Likewise, laser beams can drill or cut into extremely hard materials without dulling bits or blades. For example, lasers have drilled holes in diamond dies used for drawing wire.

MEDICAL APPLICATIONS

Surgical removal of tissue with a laser is a physical process similar to industrial laser drilling. Carbon-dioxide lasers burn away tissue because their infrared beams are strongly absorbed by the water that makes up the bulk of living cells. A laser beam cauterizes the cuts, stopping bleeding in blood-rich tissues such as the female reproductive tract or the gums. Laser wavelengths near one micrometre can penetrate the eye, welding a detached retina back into place, or cutting internal membranes that often grow cloudy after cataract surgery. Less-intense laser pulses can destroy abnormal blood vessels that spread across the retina in patients suffering from diabetes, delaying the blindness often associated with the disease. Ophthalmologists surgically correct visual defects by removing tissue from the cornea, reshaping the transparent outer layer of the eye with intense ultraviolet pulses.

Through the use of optical fibres similar to the tiny strands of glass that carry information in telephone systems, laser light can be delivered to places within the body that the beams could not otherwise reach. One important example involves threading a fibre through the urethra and into the kidney so that the end of the fibre can deliver intense laser pulses to kidney stones. The laser energy splits the stones into fragments small enough to pass through the urethra without requiring surgical incisions. Fibres also can be inserted through small incisions to deliver laser energy to precise spots in the knee joint during arthroscopic surgery.

Another medical application for lasers is in the treatment of skin conditions. Pulsed lasers can bleach certain types of tattoos as well as dark-red birthmarks called portwine stains. Cosmetic laser treatments include removing unwanted body hair and wrinkles.

High-Energy Lasers

Scientists have shown that lasers can concentrate extremely high powers in either pulses or continuous beams. Major applications for these high-power levels are fusion research, nuclear weapons testing, and missile defense.

Laser-activated fusion. Interior of the U.S. Department of Energy's National Ignition Facility (NIF), located at Lawrence Livermore National Laboratory, Livermore, Calif. The NIF target chamber uses a high-energy laser to heat fusion fuel to temperatures sufficient for thermonuclear ignition. The facility is used for basic science, fusion energy research, and nuclear weapons testing. U.S. Department of Energy

Extremely high temperatures and pressures are needed to force atomic nuclei to fuse together, releasing energy. In the 1960s physicists at the Lawrence Livermore National Laboratory in California calculated that intense laser pulses could produce those conditions by heating and compressing tiny pellets containing mixtures of hydrogen isotopes. They suggested using these "microimplosions" both to generate energy for civilian use and to simulate the implosion of a hydrogen bomb, which involves similar processes. Since then, Livermore has built a series of lasers to test and refine these theories, primarily for the U.S. government's nuclear weapons program.

Military laser weapon research also dates back to the 1960s, but it attracted little attention until President Ronald Reagan launched the Strategic Defense Initiative in 1983. High-energy lasers offer a way to deliver destructive energy to targets at the speed of light, which is very attractive for fast-moving targets such as nuclear missiles. Military researchers have tested high-energy lasers for use as weapons on land, at sea, in the air, and in space, although no high-energy lasers have been placed in orbit. Experiments have shown that massive lasers can generate high powers; however, tests have also shown that the atmosphere distorts such powerful beams, causing them to spread out and miss their targets. These problems and the end of the Cold War slowed research on laser weapons, though interest continues in laser weapons to defend against smaller-scale missile attacks.

ALIGNMENT, MEASUREMENT, AND IMAGING

Laser beams are used often when precise measurements are needed. For example, laser ranging has been used to detect the minute movements of the continents. Many

Nobel Prizes for Physics have been awarded for work that could only be done with lasers.

SURVEYING

Surveyors and construction workers use laser beams to draw straight lines through the air. The beam itself is not visible in the air except where scattered by dust or haze, but it projects a bright point on a distant object. Surveyors bounce the beam off a mirror to measure direction and angle. The beam can set an angle for grading irrigated land, and a rotating beam can define a smooth plane for construction workers installing walls or ceilings.

Pulsed laser radar can measure distance in the same manner as microwave radar by timing how long it takes a laser pulse to bounce back from a distant object. For instance, in 1969 laser radar precisely measured the

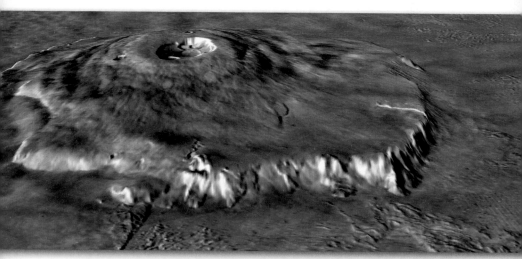

Olympus Mons, the highest point on Mars, in a computer-generated oblique view made by combining photos obtained by the Viking *mission in the 1970s with topographic data gathered by Mars Global Surveyor a quarter century later. The image clearly shows the shield volcano's relative flatness and gently sloping profile, the steep outward-facing cliff at its base (buried in places under lava that has flowed into the surrounding plains), and the complex caldera of intersecting craters at the summit.* NASA/JPL/MOLA Science Team distance from the Earth to the Moon, and in the 1970s military laser rangefinders were developed to measure the distance to battlefield targets accurately. Laser range finding is now widely used for remote sensing. Instruments flown on aircraft can profile the layers of foliage in a forest, and the Mars Global Surveyor used a laser altimeter to map elevations on the Martian surface.

INTERFEROMETRY AND HOLOGRAPHY

The coherence of laser light is crucial for interferometry and holography, which depend on interactions between

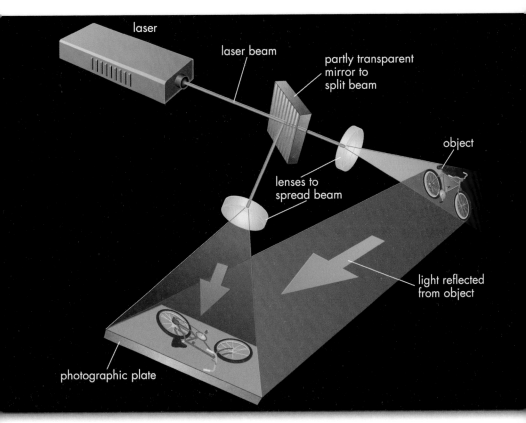

Holography uses no camera. Instead, two beams of light from a single laser shine on a piece of film. One of the beams reflects from the object. Encyclopædia Britannica, Inc.

light waves to make extremely precise measurements and to record three-dimensional images. The result of adding light waves together depends on their relative phases. If the peaks of one align with the valleys of the other, they will interfere destructively to cancel each other out; if their peaks align, they will interfere constructively to produce a bright spot. This effect can be used for measurement by splitting a beam into two identical halves that follow different paths. Changing one path just half a wavelength from the other will shift the two out of phase, producing a dark spot. This technique has proved invaluable for precise measurements of very small distances.

Holograms are made by splitting a laser beam into two identical halves, using one beam to illuminate an object. This object beam is then combined with the other half—the reference beam—in the plane of a photographic plate, producing a random-looking pattern of light and dark zones that record the wave front of light from the object. Later, when laser light illuminates that pattern from the same angle as the reference beam, it is scattered to reconstruct an identical wave front of light, which appears to the viewer as a three-dimensional image of the object. Holograms now can be mass-produced by an embossing process, as used on credit cards, and do not have to be viewed in laser light.

RESEARCH TOOL

The ability to control laser wavelength and pulse duration precisely has proved invaluable for fundamental research in physics and other sciences. Lasers have been particularly important in spectroscopy, the study of the light absorbed and emitted when atoms and molecules make transitions between energy levels, which can reveal the inner workings of atoms. Lasers can concentrate much more power into a narrow range of wavelengths than other light sources, which makes them invaluable in analyzing fine spectroscopic details.

For example, simultaneously illuminating samples with laser beams coming from opposite directions can cancel the effects of the random motions of atoms or molecules in a gas. This technique has greatly improved the precision of the measurement of the Rydberg constant, which is critical in calculations of atomic properties, and it earned Arthur Schawlow a share of the 1981 Nobel Prize for Physics. Nicolaas Bloembergen shared the prize for developing other types of high-precision laser spectroscopy.

Since that early work, laser spectroscopy has expanded considerably. Laser pulses have been used to take snapshots of chemical reactions as they occur, on time scales faster than atomic vibrations in a molecule. These techniques have given chemists new ways to understand chemical physics, and they earned Ahmed Zewail the 1999 Nobel Prize for Chemistry. Thanks to his work, the Nobel Committee wrote, "we have reached the end of the road: no chemical reactions take place faster than this."

Physicists also have used the subtle forces exerted by laser beams to slow and trap atoms, molecules, and small particles. Arthur Ashkin, a researcher at Bell Labs, showed that a tightly focused horizontal laser beam could trap atoms in the zone with highest light intensity, a technique called "optical tweezers" now used in a variety of research. Other research has shown that laser illumination can slow the motion of atoms if its wavelength is tuned to a point slightly off the wavelength of peak absorption. The atoms repeatedly absorb photons from the beam and then emit photons in random directions. The photon momentum slows the motion toward the laser beam. Placing the atoms at the junction of six laser beams aimed at right angles to each other slows their momentum in all directions, producing a clump of atoms less than 0.001 degree above absolute zero. Adding a magnetic field improves confinement and can reduce their temperature to less than one-millionth degree above absolute zero. These techniques have led to the creation of a new state of matter, called a Bose-Einstein condensate, and they earned Steven Chu, Claude Cohen-Tannoudji, and William D. Phillips the 1997 Nobel Prize for Physics.

CHAPTER 7
OPTICS

Optics is the branch of science concerned with the genesis and propagation of light, the changes that it undergoes and produces, and other phenomena closely associated with it.

Originally, the term *optics* was used only in relation to the eye and vision. Later, as lenses and other devices for aiding vision began to be developed, these were naturally called optical instruments, and the meaning of the term *optics* eventually became broadened to cover any application of light, even though the ultimate receiver is not the eye but a physical detector, such as a photographic plate or a television camera. In the 20th century, optical methods came to be applied extensively to regions of the electromagnetic radiation spectrum not visible to the eye, such as X-rays, ultraviolet, infrared, and microwave radio waves, and to this extent these regions are now often included in the general field of optics.

GEOMETRICAL OPTICS

There are two major branches of optics: physical and geometrical. Physical optics deals primarily with the nature and properties of light itself. Geometrical optics has to do with the principles that govern the image-forming properties of lenses, mirrors, and other devices that make use of light. It also includes optical data processing, which involves the manipulation of the information content of an image formed by coherent optical systems.

THE OPTICAL IMAGE

An optical image may be regarded as the apparent reproduction of an object by a lens or mirror system, employing light as a carrier. An entire image is generally produced simultaneously, as by the lens in a camera, but images may also be generated sequentially by point-by-point scanning, as in a television system or in the radio transmission of pictures across long distances in space. Nevertheless, the final detector of all images is invariably the human eye, and, whatever means is used to transmit and control the light, the final image must either be produced simultaneously or scanned so rapidly that the observer's persistence of vision will give him the mental impression of a complete image covering a finite field of view. For this to be effective the image must be repeated (as in motion pictures) or scanned (as in television) at least 40 times a second to eliminate flicker or any appearance of intermittency.

HISTORICAL BACKGROUND

To the ancients, the processes of image formation were full of mystery. Indeed, for a long time there was a great discussion as to whether, in vision, something moved from the object to the eye or whether something reached out from the eye to the object. By the beginning of the 17th century, however, it was known that rays of light travel in straight lines, and in 1604 Johannes Kepler, a German astronomer, published a book on optics in which he postulated that an extended object could be regarded as a multitude of separate points, each point emitting rays of light in all directions. Some of these rays would enter a lens, by which they would be bent around and made to converge to a point, the "image" of the object point whence the rays originated. The lens of the eye was not different from other lenses, and it formed an image of external objects on the retina, producing the sensation of vision.

There are two main types of image to be considered: real and virtual. A real image is formed outside the system, where the emerging rays actually cross; such an image can be caught on a screen or piece of film and is the kind of image formed by a slide projector or in a camera. A virtual image, on the other hand, is formed inside an instrument at the point where diverging rays would cross if they were extended backward into the instrument. Such an image is formed in a microscope or telescope and can be seen by looking into the eyepiece.

Kepler's concept of an image as being formed by the crossing of rays was limited in that it took no account of possible unsharpness caused by aberrations, diffraction, or even defocussing. In 1957 the Italian physicist Vasco Ronchi went the other way and defined an image as any recognizable nonuniformity in the light distribution over a surface such as a screen or film; the sharper the image, the greater the degree of nonuniformity. Today, the concept of an image often departs from Kepler's idea that an extended object can be regarded as innumerable separate points of light, and it is sometimes more convenient to regard an image as being composed of overlapping patterns of varying frequencies and contrasts; hence, the quality of a lens can be expressed by a graph connecting the spatial frequency of a parallel line object with the contrast in the image. This concept is investigated fully under "Optics and Information Theory."

Optics had progressed rapidly by the early years of the 19th century. Lenses of moderately good quality were being made for telescopes and microscopes, and in 1841 the great mathematician Carl Friedrich Gauss published his classical book on geometrical optics. In it he expounded the concept of the focal length and cardinal points of a lens system and developed formulas for calculating the position and size of the image formed by a lens of given focal length. Between 1852 and 1856 Gauss's theory was extended to the calculation of the five principal aberrations of a lens, thus laying the foundation for the formal procedures of lens design that were used for the next 100 years. Since about 1960, however, lens design has been almost entirely computerized, and the old methods of designing lenses by hand on a desk calculator are rapidly disappearing.

By the end of the 19th century numerous other workers had entered the field of geometrical optics, notably an English physicist, Lord Rayleigh (John William Strutt), and a German physicist, Ernst Karl Abbe. It is impossible to list all their accomplishments here. Since 1940 there has been a great resurgence in optics on the basis of information and communication theory.

Light Rays, Waves, and Wavelets

A single point of light, which may be a point in an extended object, emits light in the form of a continually expanding train of waves, spherical in shape and centred about the point of light. It is, however, often much more convenient to regard an object point as emitting fans of rays, the rays being straight lines everywhere perpendicular to the waves. When the light beam is refracted by a lens or reflected by a mirror, the curvature of the waves is changed, and the angular divergence of the ray bundle is similarly changed in such a way that the rays remain everywhere perpendicular to the waves. When aberrations are present, a convergent ray bundle does not shrink to a perfect point, and the emerging waves are then not truly spherical.

In 1690 Christiaan Huygens, a Dutch scientist, postulated that a light wave progresses because each point in it becomes the centre of a little wavelet travelling outward in all directions at the speed of light, each new wave being merely the envelope of all these expanding wavelets. When the wavelets reach the region outside the outermost rays of the light beam, they destroy each other by mutual interference wherever a crest of one wavelet falls upon a trough of another wavelet. Hence, in effect, no waves or wavelets are allowed to exist outside the geometrical light beam defined by the rays. The normal destruction of one wavelet by another, which serves to restrict the light energy to the region of the rectilinear ray paths, however, breaks down when the light beam strikes an opaque edge, for the edge then cuts off some of the interfering wavelets, allowing others to exist, which diverge slightly into the shadow area. This phenomenon is called diffraction, and it gives rise to a complicated fine structure at the edges of shadows and in optical images.

The Pinhole Camera

An excellent example of the working of the wavelet theory is found in the well-known pinhole camera. If the pinhole is large, the diverging geometrical pencil of rays leads to a blurred image, because each point in the object will be projected as a finite circular patch of light on the film. The spreading of the light at the boundary of a large pinhole by diffraction is slight. If the pinhole is made extremely small, however, the geometrical patch then becomes small, but the diffraction spreading is now great, leading once more to a blurred picture. There are thus two opposing effects present, and at the optimum hole size the two effects are just equal. This occurs when the hole diameter is equal to the square root of twice the wavelength (λ) times the distance (f) between the pinhole and film—i.e., $\sqrt{2\lambda f}$. For $f = 100$ mm and $\lambda = 0.0005$ mm, the optimum hole size becomes 0.32 mm. This is not very exact, and a 0.4-mm hole would probably be just as good in practice. A pinhole, like a camera lens, can be regarded as having an f-number, which is the ratio of focal length to aperture. In this example, the f-number is 100/0.32 = 310, designated f/310. Modern camera lenses have much greater apertures, in order to achieve light-gathering power, of around f/1.2–f/5.6.

Resolution and the Airy Disk

When a well-corrected lens is used in place of a pinhole, the geometrical ray divergence is eliminated by the focussing action of the lens, and a much larger aperture may be employed; in that case the diffraction spreading becomes small indeed. The image of a point formed by a perfect lens is a minute pattern of concentric and progressively fainter rings of light surrounding a central dot, the whole structure being called the Airy disk after George Biddell Airy, an English astronomer, who first explained the phenomenon in 1834. The Airy disk of a practical lens is small, its diameter being approximately equal to the f-number of the lens expressed in microns (0.001 mm). The Airy disk of an f/4.5 lens is therefore about 0.0045 mm in diameter (ten times the wavelength of blue light). Nevertheless, the Airy disk formed by a telescope or microscope objective can be readily seen with a bright point source of light if a sufficiently high eyepiece magnification is used.

The finite size of the Airy disk sets an inevitable limit to the possible resolving power of a visual instrument. Rayleigh found that two adjacent and equally bright stars can just be resolved if the image of one star falls somewhere near the innermost dark ring in the Airy disk of the other star; the resolving power of a lens can therefore be regarded as about half the f-number of the lens expressed in microns. The angular resolution of a telescope is equal to the angle subtended by the least resolvable image separation at the focal length of the objective, the light-gathering lens. This works out at about 4.5 seconds of arc divided by the diameter of the objective in inches.

THE RAYLEIGH LIMIT

As noted above, when a perfect lens forms an image of a point source of light, the emerging wave is a sphere centred about the image point. The optical paths from all points on the wave to the image are therefore equal, so that the expanding wavelets are all in phase (vibrating in unison) when they reach the image. In an imperfect lens, however, because of the presence of aberrations, the emerging wave is not a perfect sphere, and the optical paths from the wave to the image point are then not all equal. In such a case some wavelets will reach the image as a peak, some as a trough, and there will be much destructive interference leading to the formation of a sizable patch of light, much different from the minute Airy disk characteristic of a perfectly corrected lens. In 1879 Rayleigh studied the effects of phase inequalities in a star image and came to the conclusion that an image will not be seriously degraded unless the path differences between one part of the wave and another exceed one-quarter of the wavelength of light. As this difference represents only 0.125 micron (5×10^{-6} inch), it is evident that an optical system must be designed and constructed with almost superhuman care if it is to give the best possible definition.

RAY-TRACING METHODS

There are two kinds of ray-tracing methods. The first is called graphical and consists of tracing the optical path of a light ray. The second is called trigonometrical and uses mathematics for greater precision.

GRAPHICAL RAY TRACING

In 1621 Willebrord Snell, a professor of mathematics at Leiden, discovered a simple graphical procedure for determining the direction of the refracted ray at a surface when the incident ray is given. The mathematical form of the law of refraction was announced by the French mathematician René Descartes some 16 years later.

Snell's construction is as follows: The line *AP* represents a ray incident upon a refracting surface at *P*, the normal at *P* being *PN*. If the incident and refracted rays are extended to intersect any line *SS* parallel to the normal, the lengths *PQ* and *PR* along the rays will be proportional to the refractive indices *n* and *n'*. Hence, if *PQ* and the indices are known, *PR* can be found and the refracted ray drawn in.

A convenient modification of Snell's construction can readily be used to trace the path of a ray through a

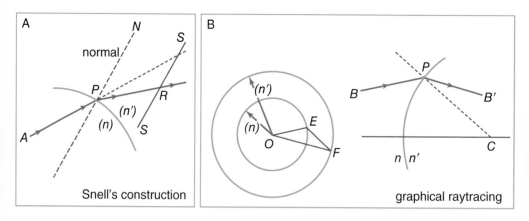

Graphic refraction procedures. Encyclopædia Britannica, Inc.

complete lens. In this modification, the incident ray *BP* strikes a refracting surface at *P*. The normal to the surface is *PC*. At any convenient place on the page two concentric circles are drawn about a point *O* with radii proportional to the refractive indices *n* and *n'*, respectively. A line *OE* is now drawn parallel to the incident ray *BP* extending as far as the circle representing the refractive index *n* of the medium containing the incident ray. From *E* a line is drawn parallel to the normal *PC* extending to *F* on the circle representing the refractive index *n'*. The line *OF* then represents the direction of the desired refracted ray, which may be drawn in at *PB'*. This process is repeated successively for all the surfaces in a lens. If a mirror is involved, the reflected ray may be found by drawing the normal line *EF* across the circle diagram to the incident-index circle on the other side.

TRIGONOMETRICAL RAY TRACING

No graphical construction can possibly be adequate to determine the aberration residual of a corrected lens, and for this an accurate trigonometrical computation must be

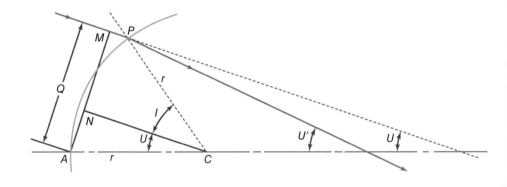

Trigonometrical ray tracing. Encyclopædia Britannica, Inc.

made and carried out to six or seven decimal places, the angles being determined to single seconds of arc or less. There are many procedures for calculating the path of a ray through a system of spherical refracting or reflecting surfaces; the typical procedure starts with a ray lying in the meridian plane, defined as the plane containing the lens axis and the object point. A ray in this plane is defined by its slope angle, U, and by the length of the perpendicular, Q, drawn from the vertex (A) of the surface on to the ray. By drawing a line parallel to the incident ray through the centre of curvature C, to divide Q into two parts at N, the relation is stated as $AN = r \sin U$, and $NM = r \sin I$. Hence

$$Q = r(\sin U + \sin I).$$ (2)

From this the first ray-tracing equation can be derived,

$$\sin I = \frac{Q}{r} - \sin U.$$ (3a)

Applying the law of refraction, equation (2), gives the second equation

$$\sin I' = \frac{n}{n'} - \sin I.$$ (3b)

Because the angle $PCA = U + I = U' + I'$, the slope of the refracted ray can be written as

$$U' = U + l - l';$$ (3c)

and, lastly, by adding primes to equation (2),

$$Q' = r(\sin U' + \sin l').$$

Having found the Q' of the refracted ray, transfer to the next surface can be performed by

$$Q_2 = Q'_1 - d \sin U'_1 ,$$

in which d is the axial distance from the first to the second refracting surface. After performing this calculation for all the surfaces in succession, the longitudinal distance from the last surface to the intersection point of the emergent ray with the lens axis is found by

$$L' = \frac{Q'}{\sin U'}.$$

Corresponding but much more complicated formulas are available for tracing a skew ray, that is, a ray that does not lie in the meridian plane but travels at an angle to it. After refraction at a surface, a skew ray intersects the meridian plane again at what is called the diapoint. By tracing the paths of a great many (100 or more) meridional and skew rays through a lens, with the help of an electronic computer, and plotting the assemblage of points at which all these rays pierce the focal plane after emerging from the lens, a close approximation to the appearance of a star image can be constructed, and a good idea of the expected performance of a lens can be obtained.

PARAXIAL, OR FIRST-ORDER, IMAGERY

In a lens that has spherical aberration, the various rays from an axial object point will in general intersect the lens axis at different points after emerging into the image space. By tracing several rays entering the lens at different heights (i.e., distances from the axis) and extrapolating from a graph connecting ray height with image position, it would be possible to infer where a ray running very close to the axis (a paraxial ray) would intersect the axis, although such a ray could not be traced directly by the ordinary trigonometrical formulas because the angles would be too small for the sine table to be of any use. Because the sine of a small angle is equal to the radian measure of the angle itself, however, a paraxial ray can be traced by reducing the ray-tracing formulas to their limiting case for small angles and thus determining the paraxial intersection point directly. When this is done, writing paraxial-ray data with lowercase letters, it is found that the Q and Q' above both become equal to the height of incidence y, and the formulas (3a), (3b), and (3c) become, in the paraxial limit:

$$i = \frac{y}{r'} - u \tag{4a}$$

$$i' = \frac{n}{n'}\, i \tag{4b}$$

$$u' = u + i - i'. \tag{4c}$$

The longitudinal distance from the last surface to the intersection point of the emerging paraxial ray with the lens axis becomes $l' = y/u'$.

Because all paraxial rays from a given object point unite at the same image point, the resulting longitudinal distance (l') is independent of the particular paraxial ray that is traced. Any nominal value for the height of incidence, y, may therefore be adopted, remembering that it is really an infinitesimal and y is only its relative magnitude. Thus, it is clear that the paraxial angles in equation (4) are really only auxiliaries, and they can be readily eliminated, giving the object–image distances for paraxial rays:

$$n'(l' - r)u' = n(l - r)u \tag{5}$$

and

$$\frac{n'}{l'} = \frac{n}{l} + \frac{n' - n}{r}. \tag{6}$$

MAGNIFICATION: THE OPTICAL INVARIANT

It is frequently as important to determine the size of an image as it is to determine its location. To obtain an expression for the magnification—that is, the ratio of the size of an image to the size of the object—the following process may be used: If an object point B lies to one side of the lens axis at a transverse distance h from it, and the image point B' is at a transverse distance h', then B, B', and the centre of curvature of the surface, C, lie on a straight line called the auxiliary axis. Then, by simple proportion,

$$m = \frac{h'}{h} = \frac{l' - r}{l - r} = \frac{nu}{n'u'}.$$

Hence,

$$h'n'u' = hnu, \tag{7}$$

and the product (hnu) is invariant for all the spaces between the lens surfaces, including the object and image spaces, for any lens system of any degree of complexity. This theorem has been named after the French scientist Joseph-Louis Lagrange, although it is sometimes called the Smith-Helmholtz theorem, after Robert Smith, an English scientist, and Hermann Helmholtz, a German scientist; the product (hnu) is often known as the optical invariant. As it is easy to determine the quantities h, n, and u for the original object, it is only necessary to calculate u' by tracing a paraxial ray in order to find the image height h' for any lens. If the lens is used in air, as most lenses are, the refractive indices are both unity, and the magnification becomes merely $m = u/u'$.

THE GAUSS THEORY OF LENSES

In 1841 German mathematician Carl Friedrich Gauss published a now famous treatise on optics in which he demonstrated that, so far as paraxial rays are concerned, a lens of any degree of complexity can be replaced by two principal, or nodal, points and two focal points, the distances from the principal points to their respective focal points being the focal lengths of the lens, and, furthermore, that the two focal lengths are equal to one another when the refractive indices of object and image spaces are equal, as when a lens is used in air.

The principal and focal points may be defined by considering a lens system of any construction, with a bundle of rays entering from the left in a direction parallel to the lens axis. After refraction by the lens each ray will cross the axis at some point, and the entering and emerging portions of each ray are then extended until they intersect at a point such as Q. The locus of all the points Q is a surface of revolution about the lens axis known as the equivalent refracting locus of the lens. The point where this locus crosses the axis is called the principal point, P_2, and the central portion of the locus in the neighbourhood of the axis, which is virtually a plane perpendicular to the axis, is called the principal plane. The point where the emerging paraxial ray crosses the axis is called the focal point F_2, the distance from P_2 to F_2 being the (posterior) focal length f'. A similar situation exists for a parallel beam of light entering from the right, giving the anterior principal point P_1, the anterior

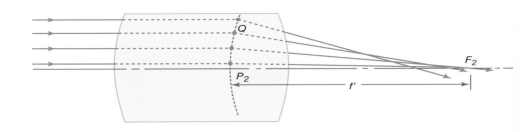

The Gauss theory. Encyclopædia Britannica, Inc.

focal point F_1, and the front focal length f. For a lens in air it can be shown that the two focal lengths are equal in magnitude but opposite in direction—i.e., if F_2 is to the right of P_2, then F_1 must lie to the left of P_1, as in the case of an ordinary positive lens (one that gives a real image). In a negative lens (one that gives a virtual image), F_2 lies to the left of P_2, and the posterior focal length f' is negative.

The relation between the distances of object and image from a lens can be easily stated if the positions of the two principal points and the two focal points are known. (In using these expressions, distances are considered positive or negative depending on whether they are measured to the right or to the left from their respective origins.) For a lens in air: (a) If the conjugate distances measured from the respective focal points are x and x', and if m is the image magnification (height of image divided by height of object), then $m = -x'/f' = f'/x$ and $xx' = -f'^2$. (b) If the conjugate distances measured from the respective principal points are p and p' and if m is the image magnification, then $m = p'/p$ and $1/p' = 1/p + 1/f'$. The Lagrange equation (7) requires modification for a distant object because in that case the object height h is infinite, and the slope angle u is zero. If the off-axis distance h is divided by the object distance L, and u is multiplied by L, equation (7) becomes $h' = (n/n')f\phi$, in which ϕ is the angle in radians subtended by the distant object at the lens. This formula provides a means for defining focal length and for measuring the focal length of an unknown lens.

THE THIN LENS

In a thin lens such as a spectacle, the two principal planes coincide within the lens, and then the conjugate distances p and p' in the formula above become the distances of object and image from the lens itself.

The focal length of a thin lens can be computed by applying the surface-conjugate formula (6)

$$\frac{n'}{l'} = \frac{n}{l} + \frac{n'-n}{r}.$$ (6)

to the two surfaces in succession, writing the l of the first surface as infinity and the l of the second surface equal to the l' of the first surface. When this is done, the lens power (P) becomes

$$P = \frac{1}{f'} = (n-1)\left(\frac{1}{r_1} - \frac{1}{r_2}\right).$$

Chromatic Aberration

Because the refractive index of glass varies with wavelength, every property of a lens that depends on its refractive index also varies with wavelength, including the focal length, the image distance, and the image magnification. The change of image distance with wavelength is known as chromatic aberration, and the variation of magnification with wavelength is known as chromatic difference of magnification, or lateral colour. Chromatic aberration can be eliminated by combining a strong lens of low-dispersion glass (crown) with a weaker lens made of high-dispersion (flint) glass. Such a combination is said to be achromatic. This method of removing chromatic aberration was discovered in 1729 by Chester Hall, an English inventor, and it was exploited vigorously in the late 18th century in numerous small telescopes. Chromatic variation of magnification can be eliminated by achromatizing all the components of a system or by making the system symmetrical about a central diaphragm. Both chromatic aberration and lateral colour are corrected in every high-grade optical system.

LONGITUDINAL MAGNIFICATION

If an object is moved through a short distance δp along the axis, then the corresponding image shift $\delta p'$ is related to the object movement by the longitudinal magnification (m with a bar over it, or m-bar). Succinctly,

$$\bar{m} = \delta p' / \delta p = m^2.$$

in which m is the lateral magnification. The fact that the longitudinal magnification is equal to the square of the transverse magnification means that m is always positive; hence, if the object is moved from left to right, the image must also move from left to right. Also, if m is large, then m-bar is very large, which explains why the depth of field (δp) of a microscope is extremely small. On the other hand, if m is small, less than one as in a camera, then m-bar is very small, and all objects within a considerable range of distances (δp) appear substantially in focus.

IMAGE OF A TILTED PLANE

If a lens is used to form an image of a plane object that is tilted relative to the lens axis, then the image will also be tilted in such a way that the plane of the object, the plane of the image, and the median plane of the lens all meet. This construction can be derived by the use of the lateral and longitudinal magnification relations just established above. With a tilted object the magnification at any point is given by the ratio of the distances of image and object from the lens at that point in the image, and, consequently, *m* varies progressively from one end of the image to the other. This arrangement is frequently used in view cameras equipped with "swings" to increase depth of field and in enlargers to rectify the convergence of parallel lines caused by tilting the camera, for example, in photographing tall buildings. The rule finds extensive application in photogrammetry and in the making of maps from aerial photographs.

Optical Systems

An optical system consists of a succession of elements, which may include lenses, mirrors, light sources, detectors, projection screens, reflecting prisms, dispersing devices, filters and thin films, and fibre-optic bundles.

Lenses

All optical systems have an aperture stop somewhere in the system to limit the diameter of the beams of light passing through the system from an object point. By analogy with the human eye, this limiting aperture stop is called the iris of the system, its images in the object and image spaces being called the entrance pupil and exit pupil, respectively. In most photographic lenses the iris is inside the objective, and it is often adjustable in diameter to control the image illumination and the depth of field. In telescope and microscope systems the cylindrical mount of the objective lens is generally the limiting aperture or iris of the system; its image, formed behind the eyepiece where the observer's eye must be located to see the whole area being observed, called the field, is then the exit pupil.

The pupils of a lens system can be regarded as the common bases of oblique beams passing through the system from all points in an extended object. In most systems, however, the mounts of some of the lens elements cut into the oblique beams and prevent the beams from being perfectly circular, and the pupils are then not fully filled with light. This effect is known as vignetting and leads to a reduction in illumination in the outer parts of the field of view.

A common feature of many optical systems is a relay lens, which may be introduced to invert an image or to extend the length of the system, as in a military periscope. An example of the use of a relay lens is found in the common rifle sight. Here the front lens *A* is the objective, forming an inverted image of the target on the cross wire or reticle at *B*. The light then proceeds to the relay lens *C*, which forms a second image, now erect, at *D*. Beyond this image is the eyepiece *E* to render the light parallel so that the image may be seen sharply by the observer. Unfortunately, the oblique beam from the objective will usually miss the relay lens, and so a field lens must be inserted at or near the first image *B* to bend the oblique beams around and redirect them toward the relay lens. The power of the field lens is chosen so that it will form an image of the objective lens aperture on the relay lens aperture. The iris and entrance pupil of this system coincide

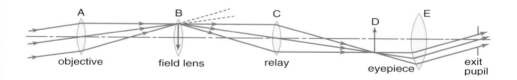

Operating principle of the telescopic rifle sight. Encyclopædia Britannica, Inc.

at the objective; there is an internal pupil at the relay lens, and the exit pupil lies beyond the eyepiece.

Mirrors

Mirrors are frequently used in optical systems. Plane mirrors may be employed to bend a beam of light in another direction, either for convenience or to yield an image reversed left for right if required. Curved mirrors, concave and convex, may be used in place of lenses as image-forming elements in reflecting telescopes. All of the world's largest telescopes and many small ones are of the reflecting type. Such telescopes use a concave mirror to produce the main image, a small secondary mirror often being added to magnify the image and to place it in a convenient position for observation or photography. Telescope mirrors are commonly made parabolic or hyperbolic in section to correct the aberrations of the image. Originally telescope mirrors were made from polished "speculum metal," an alloy of copper and tin, but in 1856 Justus von Liebig, a German chemist, invented a process for forming a mirror-like layer of silver on polished glass, which was applied to telescope mirrors by the German astronomer C.A. von Steinheil. Today most mirrors are made of glass, coated with either a chemically deposited silver layer or more often one made by depositing vaporized aluminum on the surface. The aluminum surface is as highly reflective as silver and does not tarnish as readily.

A large astronomical mirror presents many problems to the optical engineer, mainly because even a distortion of a few microns of the mirror under its own weight will cause an intolerable blurring of the image. Though many schemes for supporting a mirror without strain have been tried, including one to support it on a bag of compressed air, the problem of completely eliminating mirror distortion remains unsolved. A metal mirror, if well ribbed on the back, may be lighter than a glass mirror and therefore easier to handle, but most metals are slightly flexible and require just as careful support as glass mirrors. Since temperature changes can also cause serious distortion in a mirror, astronomers try to hold observatory temperatures as constant as possible.

Light Sources

Many types of optical instruments form images by natural light, but some, such as microscopes and projectors, require a source of artificial light. Tungsten filament lamps are the most common, but if a very bright source is required, a carbon or xenon arc is employed. For some applications, mercury or other gas discharge tubes are used; a laser beam is often employed in scientific applications. Laser light is brilliant, monochromatic, collimated (the rays are parallel), and coherent (the waves are all in step with each other), any or all of these properties being of value in particular cases.

Detectors

The image formed by an optical system is usually received by the eye, which is a remarkably adaptable and sensitive detector of radiation within the visible region of the electromagnetic spectrum. A photographic film, another widely used detector, has the advantage of yielding a permanent record of events. Since about 1925 many types of electrical detectors of radiation, both within the visible region and beyond it, have been developed. These include photoelectric cells of various kinds in which either a voltage or a resistance is modified by light falling on the device. Many new types of detectors are sensitive far into the infrared spectrum and are used to detect the heat radiated by a flame or other hot object. A number of image intensifiers and converters, particularly for X-ray or infra-red radiation, which have appeared since World War II, embody a radiation detector at one end of a vacuum tube and an electron lens inside the tube to relay the image on to a phosphor screen at the other end. This arrangement produces a visible picture that may be observed by eye or photographed to make a permanent record.

Television camera tubes detect real images by electronic scanning, the picture on the viewing tube being a replica of the image in the original camera. The combined application of electronics and optics has become common.

PROJECTION SCREENS

The simplest screen for the projection of slides or motion pictures is, of course, a matte white surface, which may be on a hard base as in outdoor theatres or on a stretched cloth indoors. A theatre screen is often perforated to transmit sound from loudspeakers placed behind it.

Improved screen materials have been developed to increase the brightness of the picture to suit the particular shape of the auditorium. A screen covered with tiny beads tends to send the light back in the general direction of the projector, and is suitable for use at one end of a long, narrow auditorium. Another type of screen is covered with fine embossed vertical grooves; this tends to distribute the light in a horizontal band across the audience with little or no vertical spread. A real advantage of these highly reflective screens is that they tend to reflect ambient room light away from the viewer as by a mirror, so that the pictures appear almost as bright and clear by day as in a darkened room.

REFLECTING PRISMS

Reflecting prisms are pieces of glass bounded by plane surfaces set at carefully specified angles. Some of these surfaces transmit light, some reflect light, while some serve both functions in succession. A prism is thus an assembly of plane reflectors at relatively fixed angles, which are traversed in succession by a beam of light.

The simplest prism is a triangular block of glass with two faces at right angles and one at an angle of 45°. The face at 45° deflects a beam of light through a right angle. The common Porro prism used in a pair of binoculars contains four 45° reflecting surfaces, two to reverse the beam direction in the vertical plane and two in the horizontal plane. These reflecting faces could be replaced by pieces of mirror mounted on a metal frame, but it is hard to hold mirrors rigidly and harder still to keep them clean. Some microscopes are equipped with a 45° deflection prism behind the eyepiece; this prism may provide two or three

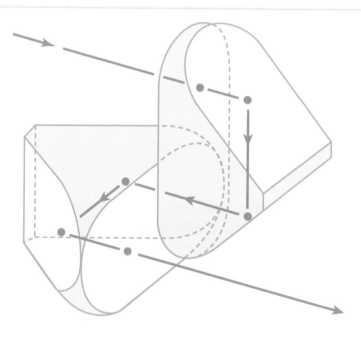

Porro prism. Encyclopædia Britannica, Inc.

reflections depending on the type of image inversion or left-for-right reversal required.

Prisms containing a semireflecting, semitransmitting surface are known as beam splitters and as such have many uses. An important application is found in some colour television cameras, in which the light from the lens is divided by two beam splitters in succession to form red, green, and blue images on the faces of three image tubes in the camera.

Dispersing Devices

There are two forms of dispersing element used to spread out the constituent colours of a beam of light into a "spectrum," namely a prism and a grating. The prism, known to Newton, is the older; it separates the colours of the spectrum because the refractive index of the glass is lowest for red light and progressively increases through the yellow and green to the blue, where it is highest. Prism spectroscopes and spectrographs are made in a variety of forms and sizes, but in all cases the blue end of the spectrum is greatly spread out while the red end is relatively compressed.

A diffraction grating is a ruled mirror or transparent plate of glass having many thousands of fine parallel grooves to the inch. It separates the colours of the spectrum by a process of diffraction. Each groove diffracts, or scatters, light in all directions, and in the case of light of one particular wavelength, there will be one direction in which the light wave from one groove lags behind the light wave from the next groove by precisely one or more whole wavelengths. This results in a strong beam of diffracted light in that direction and darkness in all other directions. Since each spectral colour corresponds to a different wavelength, the grating spreads out the spectrum into a fan where it can be observed or photographed. The red rays are bent most and the blue rays least, the opposite of the situation with a prism.

Although a prism or grating is the essential dispersing element in a spectrograph, a fine slit and additional lenses or focussing mirrors must be used to form a sharply defined spectrum. Prism spectroscopes are, of course, limited to those wavelengths for which the prism material is transparent; a reflecting grating can be used for any wavelength that the material will reflect.

FILTERS AND THIN FILMS

A colour filter is a sheet of transparent material that modifies a light beam by selective absorption of some colours in relation to others. A neutral filter absorbs all wavelengths equally and merely serves to reduce the intensity of a beam of light without changing its colour.

Filters may be made from sheets of coloured glass, plastic, or dyed gelatin, and in some cases glass cells filled with liquid have been used. Since World War II, another type of filter depending on the interference of light has been developed in which one or more metallic or other types of films of controlled thickness have been deposited on a glass plate, the layers being so thin as to cause selective interference of some wavelengths in relation to others and thus act as a nonabsorbing filter. In this case the rejected colours are reflected instead of being absorbed.

Polarizing filters have the property of transmitting light that vibrates in one direction while absorbing light that vibrates in a perpendicular direction. These filters are used extensively in scientific instruments. In sunglasses and when placed over a camera lens, polarizing filters reduce unwanted reflections from nonmetallic surfaces. Polarizing spectacles have been used to separate the left-eye and right-eye beams in the projection of stereo-scopic pictures or movies.

Fibre-Optic Bundles

As noted earlier, a thin rod or fibre of glass or other transparent material transmits light by repeated internal reflections, even when the rod is somewhat curved. An ordered bundle of rods or fibres is thus capable of taking an image projected upon one end of the bundle and reproducing it at the other end. A fibre-optic bundle can be fused together into a rigid channel, or it may be left flexible, only the ends being rigidly fastened together. Because a fibre bundle is exceedingly delicate, it must be handled with care; breaking a fibre would cause a black dot to appear in the reproduced image.

Nonclassical Imaging Systems

Besides the familiar optical systems cited above, there are many nonclassical optical elements that are used to a limited extent for special purposes. The most familiar of these is the aspheric (nonspherical) surface. Because plane and spherical surfaces are the easiest to generate accurately on glass, most lenses contain only such surfaces. It is occasionally necessary, however, to use some other axially symmetric surface on a lens or mirror, generally to correct a particular aberration. An example is the parabolic surface used for the primary mirror of a large astronomical telescope; another is the elliptic surface molded on the front of the little solid glass reflector units used on highway signs.

Another commonly used optical surface is the side of a cylinder. Such surfaces have power only in the meridian perpendicular to the cylinder axis. Cylindrical lenses are therefore used wherever it is desired to vary the magnification from one meridian to a perpendicular meridian. Cylindrical surfaces are employed in the anamorphic lenses used in some wide-screen motion-picture systems to compress the image horizontally in the camera and stretch it back to its original shape in the projected image.

To correct astigmatism in the eye, many spectacles are made with toric surfaces—i.e., with a stronger curvature in one meridian than in the perpendicular meridian, like the bowl of a teaspoon. These surfaces are generated and polished by special machines and are made by the million every year.

Another nonclassical optical system is the bifocal or trifocal spectacle lens. They are made either by forming two or three separate surfaces on a single piece of glass or obtaining additional power by fusing a piece of high-index glass on to the front of the main lens and then polishing a single spherical surface over both glasses.

Two French scientists, Georges-Louis Buffon and Augustin-Jean Fresnel, in the 18th century suggested forming a lens in concentric rings to save weight, each ring being a portion of what would normally be a continuous spherical surface but flattened out. On a large scale, Fresnel lenses have been used in lighthouses, floodlights, and traffic signals, and as cylindrical ship's lanterns. With fine steps a few thousandths of an inch wide, molded plastic Fresnel lenses are often used as condensers in overhead projectors and in cameras as a field lens in contact with a ground-glass viewing screen.

Lenses have occasionally been made with one surface taking the form of a flattened cone. Such lenses produce a long, linear image of a point source, lying along the lens axis; for this reason they are commonly referred to as axicons. They have been used to produce a straight line of light in space for aligning machines and shafting, but since about 1965 the beam from a gas laser has generally been used instead.

LENS ABERRATIONS

If a lens were perfect and the object were a single point of monochromatic light, then, as noted above, the light wave emerging from the lens would be a portion of a sphere centred about the ideal image point, lying in the paraxial image plane at a height above the axis given by the Lagrange theorem. In practice, however, this condition is most unlikely to occur; it is much more probable that the emerging wave will depart slightly from a perfect sphere, the departure varying from point to point over the lens aperture. This departure is extremely small, being of the order of the wavelength of light that is only half a micron, so it would be impossible to show this departure on a drawing.

SEIDEL SUMS

This departure can be represented mathematically, however, in the following way: The coordinates of a point in the exit-pupil aperture will be represented by x_o and y_o, the y_o coordinate lying in the meridian plane containing the object point and the lens axis. The departure of the wave from the ideal sphere is generally called OPD, meaning optical path difference. It can be shown that OPD is related to x_o and y_o by five constants S_1 through S_5, and the quantity h'_o,

$$\text{OPD} = S_1(x_0^2 + y_0^2)^2 + S_2\, y_0(x_0^2 + y_0^2)h'_0 +$$
$$+ S_3(x_0^2 + 3y_0^2)h'^2_0 + S_4(x_0^2 + y_0^2)h'^2_0 + S_5 y_0 h'^3_0.$$

Each of these five terms is considered to be a separate "aberration," the coefficients $S_1, \ldots S_5$, being called Seidel sums after the 19th-century German scientist L.P. Seidel, who identified the imperfections. These aberrations are respectively spherical, coma, astigmatism, Petzval field curvature, and distortion. The symbol h'_o refers to the height of the final image point above the lens axis, and hence it defines the obliquity of the beam.

The five Seidel sums can be calculated by tracing a paraxial ray from object to image through the lens and by tracing also a paraxial principal ray from the centre of the aperture stop outward in both directions toward the object and image, respectively. The angle of incidence i and the ray slope angle u of each of these paraxial rays at each surface are then listed and inserted into the following expressions for the five sums. The angle u'_o represents the final emerging slope of the paraxial ray.

The calculation starts by determining the radius A of the exit pupil by $A = \sqrt{x_o^2 + y_o^2}$ and also the quantity K at each surface by

$$K = \tfrac{1}{2} y n \left(\frac{n}{n'} - 1 \right) (i - u').$$

The corresponding K_{pr} for the paraxial principal ray is also determined at each surface. Then, the five aberrations may be written

$$S_1 = \frac{1}{4A_4} \sum K i^2 \qquad S_2 = \frac{1}{A^3 h'_0} \sum K i i_{pr}$$

$$S_3 = \frac{1}{2 A^2 h_0'^2} \sum K i_{pr}^{\ 2} \qquad S_4 = \frac{u_0'^2}{4 A^2} \sum \frac{n - n'}{n n' r}$$

$$S_5 = \frac{1}{A h_0'^3} \sum \left[K_{pr} i i_{pr} + \tfrac{1}{2} h_0' u_0' (u_{pr}'^2 - u_{pr}^2) \right].$$

To interpret these aberrations, the simplest procedure is to find the components x', y' of the displacement of a ray from the Lagrangian image point in the paraxial focal plane, by differentiating the OPD expression given above. The partial derivatives $\partial \text{OPD}/\partial x_o$ and $\partial \text{OPD}/\partial y_o$ represent respectively the components of the slope of the wave relative to the reference sphere at any particular point (x_o, y_o). Hence, because a ray is always perpendicular to the wave, the ray displacements in the focal plane can be found by

$$x' = f \frac{\partial \text{OPD}}{\partial x_0} \qquad \text{and} \qquad y' = f \frac{\partial \text{OPD}}{\partial y_0},$$

in which f is the focal length of the lens. The aggregation of rays striking the focal plane will indicate the kind of image that is characteristic of each aberration.

This procedure will be applied to each of the five aberration terms separately, assuming that all the other aberrations are absent. Obviously, in a perfect lens x' and y' are zero because OPD is zero. It must be remembered, however, that by using rays instead of waves, all fine-structure effects caused by diffraction will be lost, and only the macroscopic image structure will be retained.

Spherical Aberration

The first term in the OPD expression is OPD $= S_1(x_0^2 + y_0^2)^2$. Hence

$$x' = f\frac{\partial \text{OPD}}{\partial x_0} = 4fA^2S_1 \cdot x_0 \quad \text{and} \quad y' = f\frac{\partial \text{OPD}}{\partial y_0} = 4fA^2S_1 \cdot y_0.$$

These displacements can both be eliminated simultaneously by applying a longitudinal shift L to the focal plane. This changes x' by $-Lx_0/f$ and y' by $-Ly_0/f$; hence, if L is made equal to $4f^2A^2S_1$, both ray displacements vanish. The aberration, therefore, represents a condition in which each zone of the lens has a different focus along the axis, the shift of focus from the paraxial image being proportional to A^2. This is known as spherical aberration.

Coma

The S_2 term in the OPD expression represents the aberration called coma, in which the image of a point has the appearance of a comet. The x' and y' components are as follows:

$$x' = fh_0' S_2(2x_0y_0)$$
$$y' = fh_0' S_2(x_0^2 + 3y_0^2).$$

When this aberration is present, each circular zone of the lens forms a small ringlike image in the focal plane, the rings formed by successive concentric zones of the lens fitting into two straight envelope lines at 60° to each other.

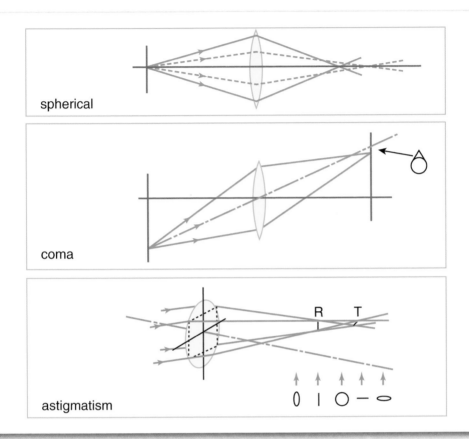

spherical

coma

astigmatism

Lens aberrations. Encyclopædia Britannica, Inc.

Because the brightness of this image is greatest at the tip, coma tends to form a one-sided haze on images in the outer parts of the field.

ASTIGMATISM

If only the S_3 term is present, then

$$x' = 2fh_0'^2 S_3(x_0)$$
$$y' = 2fh_0'^2 S_3(3y_0).$$

For any one zone of the lens, x' and y' describe a vertical ellipse with major axis three times the minor axis. The images formed by all the smaller zones of the lens fit into this ellipse and fill it out with a uniform intensity of light. If the image plane is moved along the axis by a distance L, as in focussing a camera, then, at $L = 2f^2h_0'^2S_3$, the ellipse shrinks to a radial focal line (R). Twice this displacement yields a circle; three times this L gives a tangential focal line (T), which is followed by an ellipse with its major axis in the x direction. The usual effect of astigmatism in an image is the appearance of radial or tangential blurring in the outer parts of the field.

PETZVAL CURVATURE

For the S_4 term taken alone,

$$x' = 2fh_0'^2S_4 \cdot x_0$$
$$y' = 2fh_0'^2S_4 \cdot y_0.$$

The image of a point is now a small circle that contracts to a point at a new focus situated at a longitudinal distance $L = 2f^2h_0'^2S_4$ from the paraxial image. As the longitudinal displacement of the focus is proportional to the square of the image height h_0', this aberration represents a pure field curvature without any accompanying loss of definition (all lines remain sharp). It is named after the Hungarian mathematician József Petzval, who studied its properties in the early 1840s. The effect of Petzval curvature can be somewhat offset by the deliberate introduction of sufficient overcorrected astigmatism, as was done in all the pre-anastigmat photographic objectives. This added astigmatism is, of course, undesirable, and in order to design an anastigmat lens having a flat field free from astigmatism, it is necessary to reduce the Petzval sum S_4 drastically.

For a succession of thin lenses (1, 2, 3, . . . etc.) in a system, the Petzval sum becomes simply $1/f_1 n_1 + 1/f_2 n_2 + 1/f_3 n_3 +$ . . . etc., in which f is the focal length of each element and n is its refractive index. Therefore, to reduce the sum and minimize this aberration, relatively strong negative elements of low-index glass can be combined with positive elements of high-index glass. The positive and negative elements must be axially separated to provide the lens with a useful amount of positive power. The introduction of high-index barium crown glass with a low dispersive power in the 1880s initiated the development of anastigmat lenses.

DISTORTION

For the S_5 aberration,

$$x' = 0$$
$$y' = f h_0'^3 S_5.$$

When this aberration is present, the entire image point is displaced toward or away from the axis by an amount proportional to the third power of the transverse distance h_0' of the image from the axis. This leads to the formation of an image of a square that is either a barrel-shaped or a cushion-shaped figure.

It is to be noted that the five Seidel aberrations represent the largest and most conspicuous defects that can arise in an uncorrected optical system. Even in the best lenses in which these five aberrations have been perfectly corrected for one zone of the lens and for one point in the field, however, there will exist small residuals of these aberrations and of many other higher-order aberrations also, which are significantly different from the classical types just described. Actually, it requires some magnification of a star image to render these appearances clearly visible. Nevertheless, they are important enough to require drastic reduction in high-quality lenses intended to make sharp negatives capable of considerable enlargement.

Image Brightness

All photometric concepts are based on the idea of a standard candle, lamps having accurately known candle power being obtainable from the various national standards laboratories. The ratio of the candle power of a source to its area is called the luminance of the source; luminances range from about 2,000 candles per square millimetre at the surface of the Sun down to about 3×10^{-6} candle per square centimetre (3×10^{-6} stilb) for the luminous paint on a watch dial. Ordinary outdoor scenes in daylight have an average luminance of several hundred candles per square foot. The quantity of light flux flowing out from a source is measured in lumens, the lumen being defined as the amount of flux radiated by a small "point" source of one candle power into a cone having a solid angle of one steradian. When light falls upon a surface it produces illumination (i.e., illuminance), the usual measure of illuminance being the foot-candle, which is one lumen falling on each square foot of receiving surface.

General Relations

It is often important to be able to calculate the brightness of an image formed by an optical system, because photographic emulsions and other light receptors cannot respond satisfactorily if the light level is too low. The problem is to relate the luminance of an object with the illuminance in the image, knowing the transmittance and aperture of the optical system. A small area A of a plane object having a luminance of B candles per square unit will have a normal intensity of AB candles. This source radiates light into a cone of semi-angle U, limited, for example, by the rim of a lens. The light flux (F) entering the cone can be found by integration to be

$$F = \pi A B \sin^2 U \text{ lumens.}$$

If the object luminance is expressed as B_L lamberts, the lambert being an alternative luminance unit equal to $1/\pi$ (i.e., 0.32) candle per unit area, the flux (F) is

$$F = A B_L \sin^2 U \text{ lumens,}$$

because there are π times as many lamberts in a given luminance as there are candles per unit area.

A fraction t of this flux finds its way to the image, t being the lens transmittance, generally about 0.8 or 0.9 but less if a mirror is involved. The area of the image is Am^2, in which m, the magnification, is given by

$$m = \frac{\sin U}{\sin U'}.$$

Hence, the image illuminance (E) is

$$E = (t\pi A B \sin^2 U) \div (A \sin^2 U / \sin^2 U') = t\pi B \sin^2 U' \quad (8)$$
$$\text{or } E = t B_L \sin^2 U'.$$

The image illuminance thus depends *only* on the luminance of the source and the cone angle of the beam proceeding from the lens to the image. This is a basic and most important relation underlying all calculations of image illuminance.

It is often more convenient to convert the angle U' into other better known quantities, such as the *f*-number of the lens and the image magnification. The relation here is

$$\sin U' = \frac{1}{2\,(f\text{-number})\,(1 + m/m_p)}.$$

(9)

The *f*-number of the lens is defined as the ratio of the focal length to the diameter of the entrance pupil; m is the image magnification; and m_p is the pupil magnification—i.e., the diameter of the exit pupil divided by the diameter of the entrance pupil. Combining equations (8) and (9) gives

$$\text{Image illuminance} = E = \frac{\pi t B}{4\,(f\text{-number})^2\,(1 + m/m_p)^2}.$$

As an example in the use of this relation, if it is supposed that an f/2 lens is being used to project an image of a cathode-ray tube at five times magnification, the tube luminance being 5,000 foot-lamberts (1.7 candles per square centimetre), the lens transmittance is 0.8, and the pupil magnification is unity. Then the image illuminance will be

$$E = \frac{0.8 \times 5,000}{4 \times 4 \times 36} = 6.9 \text{ foot-candles}.$$

The image is very much less bright than the object, a fact that becomes clear to anyone attempting to provide a bright projected image in a large auditorium.

DISTRIBUTION OF ILLUMINATION OVER AN IMAGE

So far only the illumination at the centre of an image has been considered, but the distribution of illumination over a wide field is often important. In the absence of any lens, the small plane source already considered radiates in a direction inclined at an angle ϕ to the axis with an intensity $AB \cos \phi$. This light has to travel farther than the axial light to reach a screen, and then it strikes the screen at another angle ϕ. The net result is that the oblique illumination on the screen is smaller than the axial illumination by the factor $\cos_4 \phi$.

The same law can be applied to determine the oblique illumination due to a lens, assuming a uniform extended diffusing source of light on the other side of the lens. In this case, however, the exit pupil will not in general be a perfect circle because of possible distortion of the iris by that part of the optical system lying between the iris and the image. Also, any mechanical vignetting in the lens will make the aperture noncircular and reduce still further the oblique illumination. In a camera this reduction in oblique illumination results in darkened corners of the picture, but, if the reduction in brightness is gradual, it is not likely to be detected because the eye adapts quickly to changing brightness as the eyes scan over the picture area. Indeed, a 50 percent drop in brightness between the centre and corners of an ordinary picture is scarcely detectable.

VISUAL BRIGHTNESS

The apparent brightness of things seen by the eye follows the same laws as any other imaging system, because the apparent brightness is measured by the illuminance in the image that is projected on the retina. The angle U' in equation (8)

$$E = (t\pi AB \sin^2 U) \div (A \sin^2 U / \sin^2 U') = t\pi B \sin^2 U'$$

$$\text{or } E = tB_L \sin^2 U'. \tag{8}$$

inside the eye is determined by the size of the pupil of the eye, which varies from about one millimetre to about eight millimetres, depending on the brightness of the environment. Apart from this variation, retinal illuminance is directly proportional to object luminance, and objects having the same luminance appear equally bright, no matter at what distance they are observed.

From this argument, it is clear that no visual instrument, such as a telescope, can possibly make anything appear brighter than when viewed directly. To be sure, a telescope having a large objective lens accepts more light from an object in proportion to the area of the lens aperture, but it magnifies the image area in the same proportion; so the increased light is spread over an increased area of the retina, and the illuminance remains unchanged. Actually, the telescopic view is always dimmer than the direct view because of light losses in the telescope due to glass absorption and surface reflections and because the exit pupil of the telescope may be smaller than the pupil of the eye, thus reducing the angle U'.

The case of a star being observed through a telescope is quite different, because no degree of magnification can possibly make a star appear as anything other than a point of light. Hence, star images appear brighter in proportion to the area of the telescope objective (assuming that the exit pupil is larger than the eye pupil), and the visibility of a star against the sky background is thus improved in proportion to the square of the diameter of the telescope objective lens.

OPTICS AND INFORMATION THEORY

A new era in optics commenced in the early 1950s, following the impact of certain branches of electrical engineering—most notably communication and information theory. This impetus was sustained by the development of the laser in the 1960s.

GENERAL OBSERVATIONS

The initial tie between optics and communication theory came because of the numerous analogies that exist between the two subjects and because of the similar mathematical techniques employed to formally describe the behaviour of electrical circuits and optical systems. A topic of considerable concern since the invention of the lens as an optical imaging device has always been the description of the optical system that forms the image; information about the object is relayed and presented as an image. Clearly, the optical system can be considered a communication channel and can be analyzed as such. There is a linear relationship (i.e., direct proportionality) between the intensity distribution in the image plane and that existing in the object, when the object is illuminated with incoherent light (e.g., sunlight or light from a large thermal source). Hence, the linear theory developed for the description of electronic systems can be applied to optical image-forming systems. For example, an electronic circuit can be characterized by its impulse response—that is, its output for a brief impulse input of current or voltage. Analogously, an optical system can be characterized by an impulse response that for an incoherent imaging system is the intensity distribution in the image of a point source of light; the optical impulse is a spatial rather than a temporal impulse—otherwise the concept is the same. Once the appropriate impulse response function is known, the output of that system for any object intensity distribution can be determined by a linear superposition of impulse responses suitably weighted by the value of the intensity at each point in the object. For a continuous object intensity distribution this sum becomes an integral. While this example has been given in terms of an optical imaging system, which is certainly the most common use of optical elements, the concept can be used independent of whether the receiving plane is an image plane or not. Hence, for example, an impulse response can be defined for an optical system that is deliberately defocussed or for systems used for the display of Fresnel or Fraunhofer diffraction patterns. (Fraunhofer diffraction occurs when the light source and diffraction patterns are effectively at infinite distances from the diffracting system, and Fresnel diffraction occurs when one or both of the distances are finite.)

Temporal Frequency Response

A fundamentally related but different method of describing the performance of an electronic circuit is by means of its temporal frequency response. A plot is made of the response for a series of input signals of a variety of frequencies. The response is measured as the ratio of the amplitude of the signal obtained out of the system to that put in. If there is no loss in the system, then the frequency response is unity (one) for that frequency; if a particular frequency fails to pass through the system, then the response is zero. Again, analogously the optical system may also be described by defining a spatial frequency response. The object, then, to be imaged by the optical system consists of a spatial distribution of intensity of a single spatial frequency—an object the intensity of which varies as ($1 + a$ cos ωx), in which x is the spatial coordinate, a is a constant called the contrast, and ω is a variable that determines the physical spacing of the peaks in the intensity distribution. The image is recorded for a fixed value of a and ω and the contrast in the image measured. The ratio of this contrast to a is the response for this particular spatial frequency defined by ω. Now if ω is varied and the measurement is repeated, a frequency response is then obtained.

NONLINEAR OPTICAL SYSTEMS

The analogies described above go even further. Many optical systems are nonlinear, just as many electronic systems are nonlinear. Photographic film is a nonlinear optical element in that equal increments of light energy reaching the film do not always produce equal increments of density on the film.

A different type of nonlinearity occurs in image formation. When an object such as two stars is imaged, the resultant intensity distribution in the image is determined by first finding the intensity distribution formed by each star. These distributions must then be added together in regions where they overlap to give the final intensity distribution that is the image. This example is typical of an incoherent imaging system—i.e., the light emanating from the two stars is completely uncorrelated. This occurs because there is no fixed phase relationship between the light emanating from the two stars over any finite time interval.

A similar nonlinearity arises in objects illuminated by light from the Sun or other thermal light source. Illumination of this kind, when there is no fixed relationship between the phase of the light at any pair of points in the incident beam, is said to be incoherent illumination. If the illumination of the object is coherent, however, then there is a fixed relationship between the phase of the light at all pairs of points in the incident beam. To determine the resultant image intensity under this condition for a two point object requires that the amplitude and phase of the light in the image of each point be determined. The resultant amplitude and phase is then found by summation in regions of overlap. The square of this resultant amplitude is the intensity distribution in the image. Such a system is nonlinear. The mathematics of nonlinear systems was developed as a branch of communication theory, but many of the results can be used to describe nonlinear optical systems.

This new description of optical systems was extremely important to, but would not alone account for, the resurgence of optical research and development. This new approach resulted in the development of whole new branches of study, including optical processing and holography. It also had an effect, together with the development of digital computers, on the concepts and versatility of lens design and testing. Finally, the invention of the laser, a device that produces coherent radiation, and the development and implementation of the theory of partially coherent light gave the added impetus necessary to change traditional optics into a radically new and exciting subject.

IMAGE FORMATION

An optical system that employs incoherent illumination of the object can usually be regarded as a linear system in intensity. A system is linear if the addition of inputs produces an addition of corresponding outputs. For ease of analysis, systems are often considered stationary (or invariant). This property implies that if the location of the input is changed, then the only effect is to change the location of the output but not its actual distribution.

IMPULSE RESPONSE

With these concepts it is then only necessary to find an expression for the image of a point input to develop a theory of image formation. The intensity distribution in the image of a point object can be determined by solving the equation relating to the diffraction of light as it propagates from the point object to the lens, through the lens, and then finally to the image plane. The result of this process is that the image intensity is the intensity in the Fraunhofer diffraction pattern of the lens aperture function (that is, the square of the Fourier transform of the lens aperture function; a Fourier transform is an integral equation involving periodic components). This intensity distribution is the intensity impulse response (sometimes called point spread function) of the optical system and fully characterizes that optical system.

With the knowledge of the impulse response, the image of a known object intensity distribution can be calculated. If the object consists of two points, then in the image plane the intensity impulse response function must be located at the image points and then a sum of these intensity distributions made. The sum is the final image intensity. If the two points are closer together than the half width of the impulse response, they will not be resolved. For an object consisting of an array of isolated points, a similar procedure is followed—each impulse response is, of course, multiplied by a constant equal to the value of the intensity of the appropriate point object. Normally, an object will consist of a continuous distribution of intensity, and, instead of a simple sum, a convolution integral results.

TRANSFER FUNCTION

The concept of the transfer function of an optical system can be approached in several ways. Formally and fundamentally it is the Fourier transform of the intensity impulse response. Because the impulse response is related to the lens aperture function, so is the transfer function. In particular, the transfer function can be obtained from a knowledge of the aperture function by taking the function and plotting the resultant overlapping areas as the aperture function is slid over itself (i.e., the autocorrelation of the aperture function).

Conceptually, however, the transfer function is best understood by considering the object intensity distribution to be a linear sum of cosine functions of the form ($1 + a \cos 2\pi\mu x$), in which a is the amplitude of each component of spatial frequency μ. The image of a cosine intensity distribution is a cosine of the same frequency; only the contrast and phase of the cosine can be affected by a linear system. The image of the above object intensity distribution can be represented by [$1 + b \cos (2\pi\mu x + \phi)$], in which b is the amplitude of the output cosine of frequency μ and ϕ is the phase shift. The transfer function, $\tau(\mu)$, for that frequency is then given by the ratio of the amplitudes:

$$\tau(u) = \frac{b}{a} e^{j\varphi(\mu)}.$$

If μ is now varied, the spatial frequency response of the system is measured by determining $\tau(\mu)$ for the various values of μ. It should be noted that $\tau(\mu)$ is in general complex (containing a term with $\sqrt{-1}$).

The transfer function, like the impulse response, fully characterizes the optical system. To make use of the transfer function to determine the image of a given object requires that the object be decomposed into a series of periodic components called its spatial frequency spectrum. Each term in this series must then be multiplied by the appropriate value of the transfer function to determine the individual components of the series that is the spatial frequency spectrum of the image—a transformation of this series will give the image intensity. Thus, any components in the object spectrum that have a frequency for which $\tau(\mu)$ is zero will be eliminated from the image.

PARTIALLY COHERENT LIGHT

Image formation is concerned above with incoherent object illumination, which results in an image formed by the addition of intensities. The study of diffraction and interference, on the other hand, requires coherent illumination of the diffracting object, the resulting diffracted optical field being determined by an addition of complex amplitudes of the wave disturbances. Thus, two different mechanisms exist for the addition of light beams, depending upon whether the beams are coherent or incoherent with respect to each other. Unfortunately, this is not the whole story; it is not sufficient to consider only the two situations of strictly coherent and strictly incoherent light. In fact, strictly incoherent fields are only approximately obtainable in practice. Furthermore, the possibility of intermediate states of coherence cannot be ignored; it is necessary to describe the result of mixing incoherent light with coherent light. It was to answer the question, How coherent is a beam of light? (or the equivalent one, How incoherent is a beam of light?) that the theory of partial coherence was developed.

DEVELOPMENT AND EXAMPLES OF THE THEORY

Marcel Verdet, a French physicist, realized in the 19th century that even sunlight is not completely incoherent, and two objects separated by distances of over approximately $\frac{1}{20}$ millimetre will produce interference effects. The eye, operating unaided in sunlight, does not resolve this separation distance and hence can be considered to be receiving an incoherent field. Two physicists, Armand Fizeau in France and Albert Michelson in the United States, were also aware that the optical field produced by a star is not completely incoherent, and hence they were able to design interferometers to measure the diameter of stars from a measurement of the partial coherence of the starlight. These early workers did not think in terms of partially coherent light, however, but derived their results by an integration over the source. At the other extreme, the output from a laser can produce a highly coherent field.

The concepts of partially coherent light can best be understood by means of some simple experiments. A circular uniform distant source produces illumination on the front of an opaque screen containing two small circular apertures, the separation of which can be varied. A lens is located behind this screen, and the resultant intensity distribution in its focal plane is obtained. With either aperture open alone, the intensity distribution observed is such that it is readily associated with the diffraction pattern of the aperture, and it may thus be concluded that the field is coherent over the dimensions of the aperture. When the two apertures are opened together and are at their closest separation, two-beam interference fringes are observed that are formed by the division of the incident wave front by the two apertures. As the separation of the apertures increases, the observed interference fringes get weaker and finally disappear, only to reappear faintly as the separation is further increased. As the separation of the apertures is increased, these results show that (1) the fringe spacing decreases; (2) the intensities of the fringe minima are never zero; (3) the relative intensity of the maxima above the minima steadily decreases; (4) the absolute value of the intensity of the maxima decreases and that of the minima increases; (5) eventually, the fringes disappear, at which point the resultant intensity is just twice the intensity observed with one aperture alone (essentially an incoherent addition); (6) the fringes reappear with a further increase in separation of the aperture, but the fringes contain a central minimum, not a central maximum.

If the intensities of the two apertures are equal, then the results (1) through (5) can be summarized by defining a quantity in terms of the maximum intensity (I_{max}) and the minimum intensity (I_{min}), called the visibility (V) of the fringes—i.e., $V = (I_{max} - I_{min})/(I_{max} + I_{min})$. The maximum value of the visibility is unity, for which the light passing through one aperture is coherent with respect to the light passing through the other aperture; when the visibility is zero, the light passing through one aperture is incoherent with respect to the light passing through the other aperture. For intermediate values of V the light is said to be partially coherent. The visibility is not a completely satisfactory description because it is, by definition, a positive quantity and cannot, therefore, include a description of item (6) above. Furthermore, it can be shown by a related experiment that the visibility of the fringes can be varied by adding an extra optical path between the two interfering beams.

THE MUTUAL COHERENCE FUNCTION

The key function in the theory of partially coherent light is the mutual coherence function $\Gamma_{12}(\tau) = \Gamma(x_1, x_2, \tau)$, a complex quantity, which is the time averaged value of the cross correlation function of the light at the two aperture points x_1 and x_2 with a time delay τ (relating to a path difference to the point of observation of the interference fringes). The function can be normalized (i.e., its absolute value set equal to unity at $\tau = 0$ and $x_1 = x_2$) by dividing by the square root of the product of the intensities at the points x_1 and x_2 to give the complex degree of coherence, hence

$$\gamma_{12}(\tau) = \frac{\Gamma_{12}(\tau)}{\sqrt{I(x_1)I(x_2)}}.$$

The modulus of $\gamma_{12}(\tau)$ has a maximum value of unity and a minimum value of zero. The visibility defined earlier is identical to the modulus of the complex degree of coherence if $I(x_1) = I(x_2)$.

Often the optical field can be considered to be quasimonochromatic (approximately monochromatic), and then the time delay can be set equal to zero in the above expression, thus defining the mutual intensity function. It is often convenient to describe an optical field in terms of its spatial and temporal coherence by artificially separating out the space- and time-dependent parts of the coherence function. Temporal coherence effects arise from the finite spectral width of the source radiation; a coherence time Δt can be defined as $1/\Delta v$, in which Δv is the frequency bandwidth. A related coherence length Δl can also be defined as $c/\Delta v = \lambda^2/\Delta\lambda^2$, in which c is the velocity of light, λ is the wavelength, and $\Delta\lambda$ the wavelength bandwidth. Providing that the path differences in the beams to be added are less than this characteristic length, the beams will interfere.

The term *spatial coherence* is used to describe partial coherence arising from the finite size of an incoherent source. Hence, for the equipath position for the addition of two beams, a coherence interval is defined as the separation of two points such that the absolute value $|\gamma_{12}(o)|$ is some prechosen value, usually zero.

The mutual coherence function is an observable quantity that can be related to the intensity of the field. The partially coherent field can be propagated by use of the mutual coherence function in a similar way to the solution of diffraction problems by propagation of the complex amplitude. The effects of partially coherent fields are clearly of importance in the description of normally coherent phenomena, such as diffraction and interference, but also in the analysis of normally incoherent phenomena, such as image formation. It is notable that image formation in coherent light is not linear in intensity but is linear in the complex amplitude of the field, and in partially coherent light the process is linear in the mutual coherence.

OPTICAL PROCESSING

Optical processing, information processing, signal processing, and pattern recognition are all names that relate to the process of spatial frequency filtering in a coherent imaging system—specifically, a method in which the Fraunhofer diffraction pattern (equivalently the spatial frequency spectrum or the Fourier transform) of a given input is produced optically and then operated upon to change the information content of the optical image of that input in a predetermined way.

COHERENT OPTICAL SYSTEMS

The idea of using coherent optical systems to allow for the manipulation of the information content of the image is not entirely new. The basic ideas are essentially included in German physicist Ernst Abbe's theory of vision in a microscope first published in 1873; the subsequent illustrative experiments of this theory, notably by Albert B. Porter in 1906, are certainly simple examples of optical processing.

Abbe's ideas can be interpreted as a realization that image formation in a microscope is more correctly described as a coherent image-forming process than as the more familiar incoherent process. Thus, the coherent light illuminating the object on the microscope stage would be diffracted by that object. To form an image, this diffracted light must be collected by the objective lens of the microscope, and the nature of the image and the resolution would be affected by how much of the diffracted light is collected. As an example, an object may be considered consisting of a periodic variation in amplitude transmittance—the light diffracted by this object will exist in a series of discrete directions (or orders of diffraction). This series of orders contains a zero order propagating along the optical axis and a symmetric set of orders on both sides of this zero order. Abbe correctly discerned what would happen as the microscope objective accepted different combinations of these orders. For example, if the zero order and one first order are collected, then the information obtained will be that the object consisted of a periodic distribution, but the spatial location of

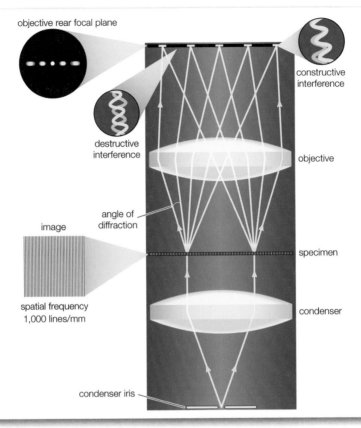

Image formation in a microscope, according to the Abbe theory. Specimens are illuminated by light from a condenser. This light is diffracted by the details in the object plane: the smaller the detailed structure of the object, the wider the angle of diffraction. The structure of the object can be represented as a sum of sinusoidal components. The rapidity of variation in space of the components is defined by the period of each component, or the distance between adjacent peaks in the sinusoidal function. The spatial frequency is the reciprocal of the period. The finer the details, the higher the required spatial frequency of the components that represent the object detail. Each spatial frequency component in the object produces diffraction at a specific angle dependent upon the wavelength of light. Here, for example, a specimen with structure that has a spatial frequency of 1,000 lines per millimetre produces diffraction with an angle of 33.6°. The microscope objective collects these diffracted waves and directs them to the focal plane, where interference between the diffracted waves produces an image of the object.
Encyclopædia Britannica, Inc.

the periodic structure is not correctly ascertained. If the other first order of diffracted light is included, the correct spatial location of the periodic structure is also obtained. As more orders are included, the image more closely resembles the object.

Coherent optical data processing became a serious subject for study in the 1950s, partly because of the work of a French physicist, Pierre-Michel Duffieux, on the Fourier integral and its application to optics, and the subsequent use of communication theory in optical research. The work was initiated in France by André Maréchal and Paul Croce, and today a variety of problems can be attempted by the technique. These include removal of raster lines (as in a TV picture) and halftone dots (as in newspaper illustration); contrast enhancement; edge sharpening; enhancement of a periodic or isolated signal in the presence of additive noise; aberration balancing in which a recorded aberrated image can be somewhat improved; spectrum analysis; cross correlation of data; matched and inverse filtering in which a bright spot of light in the image indicates the presence of a particular object.

Filtering

The basic system required for coherent optical processing consists of two lenses. A collimated beam of coherent light is used to transilluminate the object. The first lens produces the characteristic Fraunhofer diffraction pattern of the object, which is the spatial frequency distribution associated with the object. (Mathematically, it is the Fourier transform of the object amplitude distribution.) A filter that consists of amplitude (density) or phase (optical path) variations, or both, is placed in the plane of the diffraction pattern. The light passing through this filter is used to form an image, this step being accomplished by the second lens. The filter has the effect of changing the nature of the image by altering the spatial frequency spectrum in a controlled way so as to enhance certain aspects of the object information. Maréchal gave the descriptive title double diffraction to this type of two-lens system.

The filters can be conveniently grouped into a variety of types depending upon their action. Blocking filters have regions of complete transparency and other regions of complete opacity. The opaque areas completely remove certain portions of the spatial frequency spectrum of the object. The removal of raster lines and halftone dots is accomplished with this type of filter. The object can be considered as a periodic function the envelope of which is the scene or picture—or equivalently the periodic function samples the picture. The diffraction pattern consists of a periodic distribution with a periodicity reciprocally related to the raster periodicity. Centred at each of these

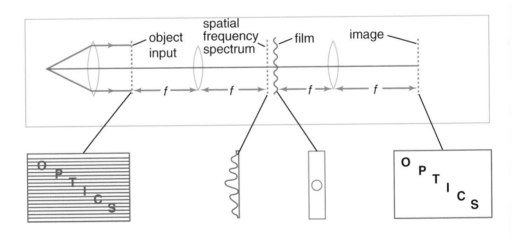

Two-lens coherent optical processing system, showing how the raster periodicity is removed but the scene information is retained. Encyclopædia Britannica, Inc.

periodic locations is the diffraction pattern of the scene. Hence, if the filter is an aperture centred at one of these locations so that only one of the periodic elements is allowed to pass, then the raster periodicity is removed, but the scene information is retained. The problem of the removal of halftone dots is the two-dimensional equivalent of the above process. Because the two-dimensional spatial frequency spectrum of an object is displayed in a coherent optical processing system, it is possible to separate out information by means of its orientation. Other applications of blocking filters include band-pass filters, which again have a direct relationship to the band-pass filters in electronic circuits.

A second type of filter is an amplitude filter that will consist of a continuous density variation. These filters can be produced to achieve the enhancement of contrast of the object input or the differentiation of the object. They are often constructed by controlled exposure of photographic film or evaporation of metal onto a transparent substrate.

Certain optical processing techniques require that the phase of the optical field be changed, and, hence, a filter with no absorption but varying optical thickness is required. Usually, both the amplitude and the phase have to be modified, however, thus requiring a complex filter. In simple cases the amplitude and phase portions can be made separately, the phase filter being manufactured by using an evaporated layer of transparent material, such as magnesium fluoride. Current practice is to fabricate the complex filter by an interferometric method in which the required complex amplitude function is recorded as a hologram.

The phase-contrast microscope can be considered to be an example of an optical processing system. Only the simplest form will be considered here. The spatial frequency spectrum of the phase object is formed and the phase of the central portion of that spectrum changed by $\pi/2$ or $3\pi/2$ to produce positive or negative phase contrast, respectively. To improve the contrast of the image an additional filter covering the same area as the phase filter is used that is partially absorbing (i.e., an amplitude filter). The restriction on this process is that the variations of the phase $\phi(x)$ are small so that $e^{i\phi(x)} \cong 1 + i\phi(x)$. With incoherent light, phase information is not visible, but many biological samples consist only of variations of refractive index, which results in optical path and hence phase, differences. The image in the phase-contrast microscope is such that the intensity in that image relates linearly to, and hence is a display of, the phase information in the object—e.g., $I(x) \propto 1 \pm 2\phi(x)$ for positive and negative phase contrast, respectively.

One of the important motivations for the study of optical processing methods is to achieve some correction of aberrated images. Considerable technological advantage can be gained if photographs taken with an aberrated optical system in incoherent light can be corrected by subsequent processing. Within definable limits this can be accomplished, but the impulse response or the transfer function of the aberrated system must be known. The recorded image intensity distribution is the convolution of the object intensity with the intensity impulse response of the aberrated system. This record is the input to the coherent optical processing system; the diffraction pattern formed in this system is the product of the spatial frequency spectrum of the object and the transfer function of the aberrated system. Conceptually, the filter has to be the inverse of the transfer function in order to balance out its effect. The final image would then ideally be an image of the object intensity distribution. It is critical, however, that the transfer function has a finite value over only a limited frequency range, and only those frequencies that are recorded by the original aberrated system can be present in the processed image. Hence, for these spatial frequencies that were recorded, some processing can be carried out to get a flatter effective transfer function; both the contrast and the phase of the spatial frequency spectrum may have to be changed because the transfer function is, in general, a complex function. Prime examples are for images aberrated by astigmatism, defocussing, or image motion.

HOLOGRAPHY

Holography is a two-step coherent image-forming process in which an intermediate record is made of the complex optical field associated with the object. The invention of the wave-front reconstruction process (now called holography) was first described in 1948 by Dennis Gabor, a Hungarian-born physicist, with a specific application in mind—to attempt to improve the resolution of images formed with electron beams. The technique has, however, had most of its success to date when light beams are employed particularly in the visible part of the spectrum. The first step in the process is to record (often on high-resolution film) the interference pattern produced by the interaction of the light diffracted by the object of interest and a coherent background or reference wave. In the second step, this record, which is the hologram, is illuminated coherently to form an image of the original object. In fact, two images are usually formed—a real image (often called the conjugate image) and a virtual image (often called the primary image).

THEORY

There are two basic concepts that underlie the holographic process: first, the addition of a coherent background (or reference) beam. Two optical fields may be considered, the complex amplitudes of which vary as the cosine of an angle proportional to the space coordinate and as the modulus (absolute magnitude) of the cosine of the angle, respectively. From a measurement of the intensity of these fields it is impossible to distinguish them because both vary as the cosine squared of the space coordinate. If a second coherent optical field is added to each of these two fields, however, then the resultant fields become $(1 + \cos x)$ and $(1 + |\cos x|)$, respectively. The measured intensities are now different, and the actual fields can be determined by taking the square root of the intensity. The amplitude transmittance of a photographic record is, in fact, the square root of the original intensity distribution that exposed the film. In a more general sense, an optical field of the form $a(x)$ $\exp [i\phi_1(x)]$, in which $a(x)$ is the amplitude and $\phi_1(x)$ is the phase, can be distinguished from a field $a(x) \exp [i\phi_2(x)]$ by adding a coherent background; the phases $\phi_1(x)$ and $\phi_2(x)$ are then contained as cosine variations of intensity in the resulting pattern. Hence, the problem of recording the phase information of the optical field is circumvented. When the hologram is illuminated, however, the optical field that originally existed in that plane is recreated. To apply the second basic concept—that of an image-forming property—it is necessary to determine what the hologram of a point object is; in actuality it is a sine-wave zone plate or zone lens. If a collimated beam of light is used to illuminate a zone lens, then two beams are produced; the first comes to a real focus, and the other is a divergent beam that appears to have come from a virtual focus. (By comparison, the more classical zone plate has a multitude of real and virtual focuses, and a real lens has but one.) When the object is other than a point, the zone lens is modified by the diffraction pattern of the object; i.e., each point on the object produces its own zone lens, and the resultant hologram is a summation of such zone lenses.

In Gabor's original system the hologram was a record of the interference between the light diffracted by the object and a collinear background. This automatically restricts the process to that class of objects that have considerable areas that are transparent. When the hologram is used to form an image, twin images are formed. The light associated with these images is propagating in the same direction, and hence in the plane of one image light from the other image appears as an out-of-focus component. This type of hologram is usually referred to as an in-line Fresnel hologram because it is the pattern of the object that interferes with the collinear coherent background. The deleterious effects of the second image can be minimized if the hologram is made in the far field of the object so that it is a Fraunhofer diffraction pattern of the object that is involved. This latter technique has found significant application in microscopy, particularly in the measurement of small particles, and in electron microscopy.

A more versatile method of recording the hologram is to add a second beam of light as a reference wave to produce the hologram. The hologram is now the record of the interference pattern produced by the light diffracted by the object and this separate reference wave. The reference wave is usually introduced at an angle to the diffracted beam, hence this method is often called off-axis (or sideband) holography. When the hologram is illuminated, the image-forming beams do not propagate in the same direction but are inclined to each other with an angle twice that between the diffracted beam and the original reference beam. Hence, the light associated with an image is completely separated from the other image.

A further technique that has some value and relates to the earlier discussion of optical processing is the production of the so-called generalized or Fourier transform hologram. Here the reference beam is added coherently to a Fraunhofer diffraction pattern of the object or formed by a lens.

The process described so far has been in terms of transmitted light through the object. The methods involving the separate reference beam can be used in reflected light, and the virtual (primary) image produced from the hologram has all the properties of an ordinary image in terms of three-dimensionality and parallax. Normally, a recorded image is only a two-dimensional representation of the object. Full-colour holograms can be recorded by essentially recording three holograms simultaneously—one in red light, one in blue, and one in green.

APPLICATIONS

The applications mentioned here are in three groups: image-forming applications, non-image-forming applications, and the hologram as an optical element. It is notable that all three groups relate to the basic use of the process rather than specific holographic techniques.

Image-Forming

The first group involves those applications using image formation when, for a variety of reasons, normal incoherent or coherent image formation is not satisfactory. It is not sufficient merely to replace a normal image process by a holographic technique unless there is some significant gain—i.e., the required record can be obtained more easily or more accurately. Applications that fall into this category are holographic microscopy; particle-size analysis; high-speed photography of various types, particularly of gas flows; data storage and retrieval, including displays; image formation through a random medium; and non-optical holography, particularly acoustic holography.

Non-Image-Forming

The second group of interest involves those applications that are not image-forming. One of the very real and exciting applications of holography is to the non-destructive testing of fabricated materials. An interesting example of this method is for the testing of tires for the detection of flaws (debonds) that exist between the plies of the tire. The realm of interferometry is thus extended to whole new classes of objects. In a similar but separate development, interference microscopy has been used successfully.

Optical Elements

The third and final group involves those applications that use the hologram as an optical element in its own right. This includes the building of accurate, specialized gratings and the application of holographic filters in coherent optical data processing.

Holography has been adapted to the conventional microscope, which is modified by the inclusion of a separate reference beam so that the light diffracted by the object in the microscope is made to interfere with the light from the reference beam. An increase in the depth of field available is achieved by this type of recording process. The image is produced when the hologram is illuminated again by a coherent beam.

The application of holography to particle-size analysis (e.g., to determine the size distribution of dust and liquid droplets) was really the first of the modern-day applications. In a sense this, too, can be thought of as microscopy. The principles of Fraunhofer holography were developed to solve this particular problem. Because the particles are in motion, a hologram must be made instantaneously. A pulsed-ruby laser technique is therefore used. The hologram is formed between the light diffracted by the particles or droplets and the coherent background light that passes directly through the sample. In reconstruction, a series of stationary images are formed that can be examined at leisure. Hence, a transient event has been transformed into a stationary image for evaluation.

Data storage and retrieval is perhaps one of the more important applications of holography, which is in the process of development and refinement. Because the information about the image is not localized, it cannot be affected by scratches or dust particles. Recent advances in materials, particularly those that might be erasable and reusable, have added further interest in holographic optical memories.

Among the non-image-forming applications are interferometry, interference microscopy, and optical processing. Holographic interferometry can be done in several ways. The basic technique involves recording a hologram of the object of interest and then interfering the image produced from this hologram with the coherently illuminated object itself. A variation on this technique would be to form two holograms at different times of the same object as it undergoes testing. The two holograms can then be used together to form two images, which would again interfere. The interference fringes seen would be related to the changes in the object between the two exposures. A third technique uses a time-average hologram, which is particularly applicable to the study of vibrating objects.

There are two applications that come under the heading holographic optical elements—the use of holographic gratings and the use of holographic filters for coherent optical data processing.

NONLINEAR OPTICS

Nonlinear effects in optics are now quite readily observable using the highly coherent and highly energetic laser beams. These effects occur when the output of a system is not linearly related to the input (e.g., a nonlinear electronic amplifier can be built with a gain that increases with signal intensity). The most important nonlinear effect is probably frequency doubling. Optical radiation of a given frequency is propagated through a crystalline material and interacts with that material to produce an output of a different frequency that is twice the input frequency. For example, the 10,600-angstrom infrared output of a neodymium laser can, under suitable conditions, be converted into green light at 5,300 angstroms in a crystal of barium strontium niobate.

CHAPTER 8
BIOGRAPHIES

Some of the lives of those who delved into the mysteries of sound and light are presented in this section. They had many different professions and interests: Sir George Biddell Airy and Christiann Huygens were astronomers; Erasmus Bartholin was a physician; and Thomas Young discovered the wave nature of light and helped decipher Egyptian hieroglyphics.

SIR GEORGE BIDDELL AIRY

(b. July 27, 1801, Alnwick, Northumberland, Eng.—d. Jan. 2, 1892, Greenwich, London)

English scientist Sir George Biddell Airy was astronomer royal from 1835 to 1881.

Airy graduated from Trinity College, Cambridge, in 1823. He became Lucasian professor of mathematics at Cambridge in 1826 and Plumian professor of astronomy and director of the Cambridge observatory in 1828. In 1835 he was appointed the seventh astronomer royal, i.e., director of the Royal Greenwich Observatory, a post he would hold for more than 45 years.

Airy completely reorganized the Greenwich observatory, installing new apparatus and rescuing thousands of lunar observations from oblivion. Most important, he modernized the observatory's system for making extremely precise observations of stellar positions. He wielded great power within the British scientific community, and he opposed government support of pure science, arguing that original research was best left to private individuals and institutions.

Airy was severely criticized for his part in the failure of British astronomers to search for a new planet (Neptune) whose existence and probable location were predicted in 1845 by British astronomer John Couch Adams on the basis of irregularities in the motion of Uranus. A similar calculation was made in the next year by the French astronomer Urbain-Jean-Joseph Le Verrier, which led almost immediately to the discovery of Neptune by German astronomer Johann Gottfried Galle and his student Heinrich Louis d'Arrest at the Berlin observatory. Modern scholars differ on how much blame to give Airy, and from today's perspective the one-year delay in the discovery of Neptune does not seem very important. However, at the time, it produced a stormy episode in British-French scientific relations.

Airy in 1827 made the first successful attempt to correct astigmatism in the human eye (his own) by use of a cylindrical eyeglass lens. He also contributed to the study of interference fringes, and the Airy disk, the central spot of light in the diffraction pattern of a point light source, is named for him. In 1854 he used a new method to determine the mean density of Earth. This involved swinging the same pendulum at the top and bottom of a deep mine to measure the change in the strength of gravity between the top and bottom of the mine. Airy was also the first to propose (c. 1855) the theory that mountain ranges must have root structures of lower density, proportional to their height, in order to maintain isostatic equilibrium. He was knighted in 1872.

ERASMUS BARTHOLIN

(b. Aug. 13, 1625, Roskilde, Den.—d. Nov. 4, 1698, Copenhagen)

Erasmus Bartholin was a Danish physician, mathematician, and physicist who discovered the optical phenomenon of double refraction.

While professor of medicine (1657–98) at the University of Copenhagen, Bartholin observed that images seen through Icelandic feldspar (calcite) were doubled and that, when the crystal was rotated, one image remained stationary while the other rotated with the crystal. Perceiving that light passing through calcite was split into two rays, he called the stationary image the "ordinary beam" and the moving image the "extraordinary beam." Although Bartholin himself was unable to explain double refraction, it was recognized as a serious contradiction to Isaac Newton's optical theories.

NIKOLAY G. BASOV

(b. Dec. 14, 1922, Usman, near Voronezh, Russia, U.S.S.R. — d. July 1, 2001, Moscow, Russia)

Soviet physicist Nikolay Gennadiyevich Basov was one of the founders of quantum electronics and a corecipient of the Nobel Prize for Physics in 1964, with Aleksandr Mikhaylovich Prokhorov of the Soviet Union and Charles H. Townes of the United States, for research leading to the development of both the maser and the laser.

Basov served in the military during World War II and in 1945 became a physics student at the Moscow Engineering Physics Institute. Upon graduation in 1950, he worked in Moscow at the P.N. Lebedev Physical Institute. In 1953 he received his doctorate (Russian *kandidat nauk*) degree from the Moscow Engineering Physics Institute. The higher degree of *doktor nauk* was awarded to him in 1956 for the theory and experimental realization of the maser.

In 1954, together with Prokhorov, Basov published a paper describing the possibility of a molecular generator of coherent microwave radiation. The idea was based on the effect of stimulated emission of radiation by atoms, which had been postulated by Albert Einstein in 1917. The device—subsequently named the maser—was also independently constructed in 1954 by Townes, James Gordon, and Herbert Zeiger at Columbia University in New York City. Basov continued to make further important contributions to the development of the maser and to the development of the laser, an analogous generator of coherent optical radiation. In addition to proposing the idea of a three-level laser in 1955 with Prokhorov, in 1959 Basov suggested constructing a semiconductor laser, which he built with collaborators in 1963. In 1962 Basov was elected a corresponding member, and in 1966 a full member, of the U.S.S.R. Academy of Sciences. He served as director of the P.N. Lebedev Physical Institute from 1973 to 1988.

SIR DAVID BREWSTER

(b. Dec. 11, 1781, Jedburgh, Roxburghshire, Scot.—d. Feb. 10, 1868, Allerby, Melrose, Roxburghshire)

Scottish physicist Sir David Brewster was noted for his experimental work in optics and polarized light—i.e., light in which all waves lie in the same plane. When light strikes a reflective surface at a certain angle (called the polarizing angle), the reflected light becomes completely polarized. Brewster discovered a simple mathematical relationship between the polarizing angle and the refractive index of the reflective substance. This law is useful in determining the refractive index of materials that are opaque or available only in small samples.

Brewster was educated for the ministry at the University of Edinburgh, but his interest in science deflected him from pursuing this profession. In 1799 he began his investigations of light. His most important studies involved polarization, metallic reflection, and light absorption. He was elected a fellow of the Royal Society in 1815, and he invented the kaleidoscope the following year. He was knighted in 1831. In the early 1840s he improved the stereoscope by utilizing lenses to combine the two dissimilar binocular pictures and produce the three-dimensional effect. Brewster was instrumental in persuading the British to adopt the lightweight, flat Fresnel lens for use in lighthouses. In 1838 he became principal of the United College of St. Salvator and St. Leonard of the University of St. Andrews and in 1859 became principal of the University of Edinburgh.

Of Brewster's numerous published works, his *Treatise on Optics* (1831) and *Memoirs of the Life, Writings and Discoveries of Sir Isaac Newton* (1855) are probably the most important.

ARTHUR HOLLY COMPTON

(b. Sept. 10, 1892, Wooster, Ohio, U.S.—d. March 15, 1962, Berkeley, Calif.)

American physicist Arthur Holly Compton was a joint winner, with C. T. R. Wilson of England, of the Nobel Prize for Physics in 1927 for his discovery and explanation of the change in the wavelength of X-rays when they collide with electrons in metals. This so-called Compton effect is caused by the transfer of energy from a photon to an electron. Its discovery in 1922 confirmed the dual nature of electromagnetic radiation as both a wave and a particle.

Compton, a younger brother of the physicist Karl T. Compton, received his doctorate from Princeton University in 1916 and became head of the department of physics at Washington University, St. Louis, in 1920. Compton's Nobel Prize–winning research focused on the strange phenomena that occur when beams of short-wavelength X-rays are aimed at elements of low atomic weight. He discovered that some of the X-rays scattered by the elements are of longer wavelength than they were before being scattered. This result is contrary to the laws of classical physics, which could not explain why the scattering of a wave should increase its wavelength. Compton initially theorized that the size and shape of electrons in the target atoms could account for the change in the X-rays' wavelength. In 1922, however, he concluded that Einstein's quantum theory, which argued that light consists of particles rather than waves, offered a better explanation of the effect. In his new model, Compton interpreted X-rays as consisting of particles, or "photons," as he called them. He argued that an X-ray photon can collide with an electron of a carbon atom; when this happens, the photon transfers some of its energy to the electron and then continues on with diminished energy and a longer wavelength than it had before. Compton's interpretation provided the first widely accepted experimental evidence that electromagnetic radiation can exhibit both particle and wave behaviour, and thus helped to establish the legitimacy of the still-radical quantum theory.

From 1923 to 1945 Compton was a professor of physics at the University of Chicago. In 1941 he was chairman of the committee of the National Academy of Sciences that studied the military potential of atomic energy. In this capacity he was instrumental, with the physicist Ernest O. Lawrence, in initiating the Manhattan Project, which created the first atomic bomb. From 1942 to 1945 he was director of the Metallurgical Laboratory at the University of Chicago, which developed the first self-sustaining atomic chain reaction and paved the way for controlled release of nuclear energy. He became chancellor of Washington University in 1945 and was professor of natural history there from 1953 until 1961.

CHRISTIAN DOPPLER

(b. Nov. 29, 1803, Salzburg, Austria—d. March 17, 1853, Venice, Italy)

Austrian physicist Christian Doppler first described how the observed frequency of light and sound waves is affected by the relative motion of the source and the detector. This phenomenon became known as the Doppler effect.

Educated at the Polytechnical Institute in Vienna, Doppler became director of the Physical Institute and professor of experimental physics of the University of Vienna in 1850. His earliest writings were on mathematics, but in 1842 he published *Über das farbige Licht der Doppelsterne* ("Concerning the Coloured Light of Double Stars"), which contained his first statement of the Doppler effect. He theorized that since the pitch of sound from a moving source varies for a stationary observer, the colour of the light from a star should alter, according to the star's velocity relative to Earth.

ARMAND-HIPPOLYTE-LOUIS FIZEAU

(b. Sept. 23, 1819, Paris, France—d. Sept. 18, 1896, Nanteuil-le-Haudouin)

Armand-Hippolyte-Louis Fizeau was a French physicist noted for his experimental determination of the speed of light.

Fizeau worked with Jean-Bernard-Léon Foucault on investigations of the infrared portion of the solar spectrum and made other observations of heat and light. Unaware of Christian Doppler's publication (1842), Fizeau in 1848 gave an explanation of the shift in wavelength in light coming from a star and showed how it could be used to measure the relative velocities of stars that lie in the same line of sight. In 1849 Fizeau found the first reasonably accurate value of the velocity of light obtained in a nonastronomical experiment.

Armand-Hippolyte-Louis Fizeau. © Photos.com/Jupiterimages

In 1851 he carried out a series of experiments in an attempt to detect the luminiferous ether—a hypothetical material that was thought to occupy all of space and to be necessary for carrying the vibrations of light waves. The experimental results failed to demonstrate the existence of the ether, but his work helped lead to the discarding of the ether theory in the early years of the 20th century.

Fizeau became a member of the French Academy in 1860 and was appointed superintendent of physics at the École Polytechnique, Paris, in 1863.

HARVEY FLETCHER

(b. Sept. 11, 1884, Provo, Utah, U.S.—d. July 23, 1981, Provo)

U.S. physicist Harvey Fletcher was a leading authority in the fields of psychoacoustics and acoustical engineering.

Fletcher graduated from Brigham Young University in Provo, Utah, in 1907 and received a Ph.D. in physics from the University of Chicago in 1911. In 1916 he joined the staff of Bell Telephone Laboratories, where he worked for 33 years, primarily in the fields of speech, music, and hearing. Much of his work on the fundamentals of psychoacoustics is described in his book *Speech and Hearing* (1922).

Fletcher's research group developed and demonstrated two separate but related methods for reproducing sound: binaural sound reproduction and stereophonic reproduction. He and his team gave the first public demonstration of stereophonic sound in 1934 in New York City. In 1949 he moved to Columbia University, where he established a department of acoustical engineering. In 1952 he was appointed director of research at Brigham Young University, becoming dean of the College of Physical Engineering Sciences (1954) and professor of physics (1958). In 1974 he became professor emeritus, continuing his research in acoustics until a few weeks before his death.

JEAN FOUCAULT

(b. Sept. 18, 1819, Paris, France—d. Feb. 11, 1868, Paris)

French physicist Jean-Bernard-Léon Foucault introduced and helped develop a technique of measuring the absolute velocity of light with extreme accuracy. He provided experimental proof that the Earth rotates on its axis.

Foucault was educated for the medical profession, but his interests turned to experimental physics. With Armand Fizeau, he began a series of investigations of light and heat. By 1850 he established that light travels slower in water than in air. In the same year he measured the velocity of light, finding a value that is within 1 percent of the true figure.

In 1851, by interpreting the motion of a heavy iron ball swinging from a wire 67 metres (220 feet) long, he proved that the Earth rotates about its axis. Such a "Foucault pendulum" always swings in the same vertical plane, but on a rotating Earth, this vertical plane slowly changes, at a rate and direction dependent on the geographic latitude of the pendulum. For this demonstration and a similar one utilizing a gyroscope, Foucault received in 1855 the Copley Medal of the Royal Society of London and was made physical assistant at the Imperial Observatory, Paris. He discovered the existence of eddy currents, or "Foucault currents," in a copper disk moving in a strong magnetic field; constructed an improved mirror for the reflecting telescope; and in 1859 invented a simple but extremely accurate method of testing telescope mirrors for surface defects.

AUGUSTIN-JEAN FRESNEL

(b. May 10, 1788, Broglie, France—d. July 14, 1827, Ville-d'Avray)

Augustin-Jean Fresnel was a French physicist who pioneered in optics and did much to establish the wave theory of light advanced by Thomas Young.

Augustin-Jean Fresnel, detail of an engraving by Ambroise Tardieu after a contemporary portrait, 1825. H. Roger-Viollet

Fresnel served as an engineer in various departments of France but lost his post temporarily during the period following Napoleon's return from Elba (1814). About that time he seems to have begun his researches in optics. He studied the aberration of light, created various devices for producing interference fringes, and, by applying mathematical analysis to his work, removed a number of objections to the wave theory.

With François Arago he studied the laws of the interference of polarized light. He obtained circularly polarized light and developed the use of compound lenses instead of mirrors for lighthouses. Although his work in optics received scant public recognition during his lifetime, Fresnel maintained that not even acclaim from distinguished colleagues could compare with the pleasure of discovering a theoretical truth or confirming a calculation experimentally.

DENNIS GABOR

(b. June 5, 1900, Budapest, Hung.—d. Feb. 8, 1979, London, Eng.)

Hungarian-born electrical engineer Dennis Gabor won the Nobel Prize for Physics in 1971 for his invention of holography, a system of lensless, three-dimensional photography that has many applications.

A research engineer for the firm of Siemens and Halske in Berlin from 1927, Gabor fled Nazi Germany in 1933 and worked with the Thomson-Houston Company in England, later becoming a British subject. In 1947 he conceived the idea of holography and, by employing conventional filtered-light sources, developed the basic technique. Because conventional light sources generally provided either too little light or light that was too diffuse, holography did not become commercially feasible until the demonstration, in 1960, of the laser, which amplifies the intensity of light waves.

In 1949 Gabor joined the faculty of the Imperial College of Science and Technology, London, where in 1958 he became professor of applied electron physics. His other work included research on high-speed oscilloscopes, communication theory, physical optics, and television. Gabor was awarded more than 100 patents.

HERMANN VON HELMHOLTZ

(b. Aug. 31, 1821, Potsdam, Prussia [Germany] — d. Sept. 8, 1894, Charlottenburg, Berlin, Ger.)

German scientist and philosopher Hermann von Helmholtz made fundamental contributions to physiology, optics, electrodynamics, mathematics, and meteorology. He is best known for his statement of the law of the conservation of energy.

Helmholtz in 1838 entered the Friedrich Wilhelm Medical Institute in Berlin, where he received a free medical education on the condition that he serve eight years as an army doctor. At the institute he did research under the greatest German physiologist of the day, Johannes Müller. He attended physics lectures, worked his way through the standard textbooks of higher mathematics, and learned to play the piano with a skill that later helped him in his work on the sensation of tone.

On graduation from medical school in 1843, Helmholtz was assigned to a regiment at Potsdam. Because his army duties were few, he did experiments in a makeshift laboratory he set up in the barracks. At that time he also married Olga von Velten, daughter of a military surgeon. Before long, Helmholtz's obvious scientific talents led to his release from military duties. In 1848 he was appointed assistant at the Anatomical Museum and lecturer at the Academy of Fine Arts in Berlin, moving the next year to Königsberg, in East Prussia (now Kaliningrad), to become assistant professor and director of the Physiological Institute. But Königsberg's harsh climate was injurious to his wife's health, and in 1855 he became professor of anatomy and physiology at the University of Bonn, moving in 1858 to Heidelberg. During these years his scientific interests progressed from physiology to physics. His growing scientific stature was further recognized in 1871 by the offer of the professorship of physics at the University of Berlin; in 1882, by his elevation to the nobility; and, in 1888, by his appointment as first director of the Physico-Technical Institute at Berlin, the post that he held for the rest of his life.

The variety of positions he held reflects his interests and competence but does not reflect the way in which his mind worked. He did not start out in medicine, move to physiology, then drift into mathematics and physics. Rather, he was able to coordinate the insights he had acquired from his experience in these disciplines and to apply them to every problem he examined. His greatest work, *Handbook of Physiological Optics* (1867), was characterized—like all of his scientific works—by a keen philosophical insight, molded by exact physiological investigations, and illustrated with mathematical precision and sound physical principles.

Among Helmholtz's most valuable inventions were the ophthalmoscope and the ophthalmometer (1851). While doing work on the eye, and incidentally showing that it was a rather imperfect piece of workmanship not at all consonant with the vitalistic idea of the divine mind at work, Helmholtz discovered that he could focus the light reflected from the retina to produce a sharp image of the tissue. The ophthalmoscope remains one of the most important instruments of the physician, who can use it to examine retinal blood vessels, from which clues to high blood pressure and to arterial disease may be observed. The ophthalmometer permits the measurement of the accommodation of the eye to changing optical circumstances, allowing, among other things, the proper prescription of eyeglasses.

Helmholtz's researches on the eye were incorporated in his *Handbook of Physiological Optics*, the first volume of which appeared in 1856. In the second volume (1867), Helmholtz further investigated optical appearances and, more importantly, came to grips with a philosophical problem that was to occupy him for some years—Kant's insistence that such basic concepts as time and space were not learned by experience but were provided by the mind to make sense of what the mind perceived. The problem had been greatly complicated by German physiologist Johannes Müller's statement of what he called the law of specific nerve energies. Müller discovered that sensory organs always "report" their own sense no matter how they are stimulated. Thus, for example, a blow to the eye, which has nothing whatsoever to do with optical phenomena, causes the recipient to "see stars." Obviously, the eye is not reporting accurately on the external world, for the reality is the blow, not the stars. How, then, is it possible to have confidence in what the senses report about the external world? Helmholtz examined this question exhaustively in both his work on optics and in his masterly *On the Sensation of Tone As a Physiological Basis for the Theory of Music* (1863). What he tried to do, without complete success, was to trace sensations through the sensory nerves and anatomical structures (such as the inner ear) to the brain in the hope of laying bare the complete mechanism of sensation. This task, it might be noted, has not been completed, and physiologists are still engaged in solving the mystery of how the mind knows anything about the outside world.

Helmholtz's detailed investigation of vision permitted him to refute Kant's theory of space by showing exactly how the sense of vision created the idea of space. Space, according to Helmholtz, was a learned, not an inherent, concept. Moreover, Helmholtz also attacked Kant's insistence that space was necessarily three-dimensional because that was how the mind had to conceive it. Using his considerable mathematical talents, he investigated the properties of non-Euclidean space and showed that these could be conceived and worked with as easily as the geometry of three dimensions.

Helmholtz's early work on sound and music had led him to the study of wave motion. His work on the conservation of energy familiarized him with the problems of energy transfer. These two areas coalesced in his later years in his studies of meteorology, but the phenomena were so complex that he could do little more than point the way to future areas of research.

Helmholtz's work was the end product of the development of classical mechanics. He pushed it as far as it could go. When Helmholtz died, the world of physics was poised on the brink of revolution. The discovery of X-rays, radioactivity, and relativity led to a new kind of physics in which Helmholtz's achievements, although impressive, had little to offer the new generation.

CHRISTIAAN HUYGENS

(b. April 14, 1629, The Hague, Neth.—d. July 8, 1695, The Hague)

Christiaan Huygens was a Dutch mathematician, astronomer, and physicist, who founded the wave theory of light, discovered the true shape of the rings of Saturn, and made

Christiaan Huygens, portrait by C. Netscher, 1671; in the Collection Haags Gemeentemuseum, The Hague. Courtesy of the Collection Haags Gemeentemuseum, The Hague

original contributions to the science of dynamics—the study of the action of forces on bodies.

Huygens was from a wealthy and distinguished middle-class family. His father, Constantijn Huygens, a diplomat, Latinist, and poet, was the friend and correspondent of many outstanding intellectual figures of the day, including the scientist and philosopher René Descartes. From an early age, Huygens showed a marked mechanical bent and a talent for drawing and mathematics. Some of his early efforts in geometry impressed Descartes, who was an occasional visitor to the Huygens' household. In 1645 Huygens entered the University of Leiden, where he studied mathematics and law. Two years later he entered the College of Breda, in the midst of a furious controversy over the philosophy of Descartes. Although Huygens later rejected certain of the Cartesian tenets including the identification of extension and body, he always affirmed that mechanical explanations were essential in science, a fact that later was to have an important influence on his mathematical interpretation of both light and gravitation.

In 1655 Huygens for the first time visited Paris, where his distinguished parentage, wealth, and affable disposition gave him entry to the highest intellectual and social circles. During his next visit to Paris in 1660, he met Blaise Pascal, with whom he had already been in correspondence on mathematical problems. Huygens had already acquired a European reputation by his publications in mathematics, especially his *De Circuli Magnitudine Inventa* of 1654, and by his discovery in 1659 of the true shape of the rings of Saturn—made possible by the improvements he had introduced in the construction of the telescope with his new method of grinding and polishing lenses. Using his improved telescope, he discovered a satellite of Saturn in March 1655 and distinguished the stellar components of the Orion nebula in 1656. His interest, as an astronomer, in the accurate measurement of time then led him to his discovery of the pendulum as a regulator of clocks, as described in his *Horologium* (1658).

In 1666 Huygens became one of the founding members of the French Academy of Sciences, which granted him a pension larger than that of any other member and an apartment in its building. Apart from occasional visits to Holland, he lived from 1666 to 1681 in Paris, where he made the acquaintance of the German mathematician and philosopher Gottfried Wilhelm Leibniz, with whom he remained on friendly terms for the rest of his life. The major event of Huygens's years in Paris was the publication in 1673 of his *Horologium Oscillatorium*. That brilliant work contained a theory on the mathematics of curvatures, as well as complete solutions to such problems of dynamics as the derivation of the formula for the time of oscillation of the simple pendulum, the oscillation of a body about a stationary axis, and the laws of centrifugal force for uniform circular motion. Some of the results were given without proof in an appendix, and Huygens's complete proofs were not published until after his death.

The treatment of rotating bodies was partly based on an ingenious application of the principle that in any system of bodies the centre of gravity could never rise of its own accord above its initial position. Earlier, Huygens had applied the same principle to the treatment of the problem of collisions, for which he had obtained a definitive solution in the case of perfectly elastic bodies as early as 1656, although his results remained unpublished until 1669.

The somewhat eulogistic dedication of the *Horologium Oscillatorium* to Louis XIV brought to a head murmurs against Huygens at a time when France was at war with Holland, but in spite of this he continued to reside in

Paris. Huygens's health was never good, and he suffered from recurrent illnesses, including one in 1670 which was so serious that for a time he despaired of his own life.

A serious illness in 1681 prompted him to return to Holland, where he intended to stay only temporarily. But the death in 1683 of his patron, Jean-Baptiste Colbert, who had been Louis XIV's chief adviser, and Louis's increasingly reactionary policy, which culminated in the revocation (1685) of the Edict of Nantes, which had granted certain liberties to Protestants, militated against his ever returning to Paris.

Huygens visited London in 1689 and met Isaac Newton and lectured on his own theory of gravitation before the Royal Society. Although he did not engage in public controversy with Newton directly, it is evident from Huygens' correspondence, especially that with Leibniz, that in spite of his generous admiration for the mathematical ingenuity of the *Principia*, he regarded a theory of gravity that was devoid of any mechanical explanation as fundamentally unacceptable. His own theory, published in 1690 in his *Discours de la cause de la pesanteur* ("Discourse on the Cause of Gravity"), though dating at least to 1669, included a mechanical explanation of gravity based on Cartesian vortices. Huygens's *Traité de la Lumière* (*Treatise on Light*), already largely completed by 1678, was also published in 1690. In it he again showed his need for ultimate mechanical explanations in his discussion of the nature of light. But his beautiful explanations of reflection and refraction—far superior to those of Newton—were entirely independent of mechanical explanations, being based solely on the so-called Huygens's principle of secondary wave fronts.

As a mathematician Huygens had great talent rather than genius of the first order. He sometimes found difficulty in following the innovations of Leibniz and others, but he was admired by Newton because of his love for the old synthetic methods. For almost the whole of the 18th century his work in both dynamics and light was overshadowed by that of Newton. In gravitation his theory was never taken seriously and remains today of historical interest only. But his work on rotating bodies and his contributions to the theory of light were of lasting importance. Forgotten until the early 19th century, these latter appear today as one of the most brilliant and original contributions to modern science and will always be remembered by the principle bearing his name.

The last five years of Huygens's life were marked by continued ill health and increasing feelings of loneliness and melancholy. He made the final corrections to his will in March 1695 and died after much suffering later that same year.

EDWIN HERBERT LAND

(b. May 7, 1909, Bridgeport, Conn., U.S.—d. March 1, 1991, Cambridge, Mass.)

Edwin Herbert Land was an American inventor and physicist whose one-step process for developing and printing photographs culminated in a revolution in photography unparalleled since the advent of roll film.

While a student at Harvard University, Land became interested in polarized light, i.e., light in which all rays are aligned in the same plane. He took a leave of absence, and, after intensive study and experimentation, succeeded (1932) in aligning submicroscopic crystals of iodoquinine sulfate and embedding them in a sheet of plastic. The resulting polarizer, for which he envisioned numerous uses and which he dubbed Polaroid J sheet, was a tremendous advance. It allowed the use of almost any size of polarizer and significantly reduced the cost.

With George Wheelwright III, a Harvard physics instructor, Land founded the Land-Wheelwright Laboratories, Boston, in 1932. He developed and, in 1936, began to use numerous types of Polaroid material in sunglasses and other optical devices. Polaroid was later used in camera filters and other optical equipment.

Land founded the Polaroid Corporation, Cambridge, Mass., in 1937. Four years later he developed a widely used, three-dimensional motion-picture process based on polarized light. During World War II he applied the polarizing principle to various types of military equipment.

Land began work on an instantaneous developing film after the war. In 1947 he demonstrated a camera (known as the Polaroid Land Camera) that produced a finished print in 60 seconds. The Land photographic process soon found numerous commercial, military, and scientific applications. Many innovations were made in the following years, including the development of a colour process. Land's Polaroid Land cameras, which were able to produce developed photographs within one minute after the exposure, became some of the most popular cameras in the world.

Land's interest in light and colour resulted in a new theory of colour perception. In a series of experiments he revealed certain conflicts in the classical theory of colour perception. He found that the colour perceived is not dependent on the relative amounts of blue, green, and red light entering the eye; he proposed that at least three independent image-forming mechanisms, which he called retinexes, are sensitive to different colours and work in conjunction to indicate the colour seen.

Land received more than 500 patents for his innovations in light and plastics. In 1980 he retired as chief executive officer of Polaroid but remained active in the field of light and colour research by working with the Rowland Institute of Science, a nonprofit centre supported by the Rowland

Foundation, Inc., a corporation that Land founded in 1960. Under Land's direction, Rowland researchers discovered that perception of light and colour is regulated essentially by the brain, rather than through a spectrum system in the retina of the eye, as was previously believed.

HANS LIPPERSHEY

(b. *c.* 1570, Wesel, Ger.—d. *c.* 1619, Middelburg, Neth.),

Hans Lippershey was a spectacle maker from the United Netherlands, traditionally credited with inventing the telescope (1608).

Lippershey applied to the States General of the Netherlands for a 30-year patent for his instrument, which he called a *kijker* ("looker"), or else an annual pension, in exchange for which he offered not to sell telescopes to foreign kings. Two other claimants to the invention came forward, Jacob Metius and Sacharias Jansen. The States General ruled that no patent should be granted because so many people knew about it and the device was so easy to copy. However, the States General granted Lippershey 900 florins for the instrument but required its modification into a binocular device. His telescopes were made available to Henry IV of France and others before the end of 1608. The potential importance of the instrument in astronomy was recognized by, among others, Jacques Bovedere of Paris; he reported the invention to Galileo, who promptly built his own telescope.

THEODORE H. MAIMAN

(b. July 11, 1927, Los Angeles, Calif., U.S.—d. May 5, 2007, Vancouver, B.C., Can.),

American physicist Theodore Harold Maiman constructed the first laser, a device that produces monochromatic coherent light, or light in which the rays are all of the same wavelength and phase. The laser has found numerous practical uses, ranging from delicate surgery to measuring the distance between Earth and the Moon.

After receiving a Ph.D. from Stanford University in 1955, Maiman accepted a position with the Hughes Research Laboratories (now HRL Laboratories, LLC), where he became interested in a device developed and built by Charles H. Townes and colleagues and known as a maser (acronym for "microwave [or molecular] amplification by stimulated emission of radiation"). Maiman made design innovations that greatly increased the practicability of the solid-state maser. He then set out to develop an optical maser, or laser, which is based on the maser principle but produces visible light rather than microwaves. He operated the first successful laser in 1960 and two years later established Korad Corporation for research, development, and manufacture of lasers. Maiman later sold Korad and worked as a consultant at TRW, a technology corporation. His autobiography, *The Laser Odyssey*, was published in 2000.

ÉTIENNE-LOUIS MALUS

(b. June 23, 1775, Paris, France—d. Feb. 23, 1812, Paris)

French physicist Étienne-Louis Malus discovered that light, when reflected, becomes partially plane polarized; i.e., its rays vibrate in the same plane. His observation led to a better understanding of the propagation of light.

A member of the corps of engineers, Malus accompanied Napoleon's invasion of Egypt in 1798 and remained in the Near East until 1801. After he returned, he held official posts at Antwerp, Strasbourg, and Paris and did research in optics. He published a paper in 1809 on his discovery of the polarization of light by reflection and a memoir in

Malus, engraving by A. Tardieu after a painting. Courtesy of the trustees of the British Museum; photograph, J.R. Freeman & Co. Ltd.

1810 on the theory of double refraction (bending) of light in crystals.

A.A. MICHELSON

(b. Dec. 19, 1852, Strelno, Prussia [now Strzelno, Pol.]—d. May 9, 1931, Pasadena, Calif., U.S.)

German-born American physicist Albert Abraham Michelson established the speed of light as a fundamental constant and pursued other spectroscopic and metrological investigations. He received the 1907 Nobel Prize for Physics.

Michelson came to the United States with his parents when he was two years old. From New York City, the family made its way to Virginia City, Nev., and San Francisco, where the elder Michelson prospered as a merchant. At 17, Michelson entered the United States Naval Academy at Annapolis, Md., where he did well in science but was rather below average in seamanship. He graduated in 1873, then served as science instructor at the academy from 1875 until 1879.

In 1878 Michelson began work on what was to be the passion of his life, the accurate measurement of the speed of light. He was able to obtain useful values with home-made apparatuses. Feeling the need to study optics before he could be qualified to make real progress, he traveled to Europe in 1880 and spent two years in Berlin, Heidelberg, and Paris, resigning from the U.S. Navy in 1881. Upon his return to the United States, he determined the velocity of light to be 299,853 km (186,329 miles) per second, a value that remained the best for a generation, until Michelson bettered it.

While in Europe, Michelson began constructing an interferometer, a device designed to split a beam of light in two, send the parts along perpendicular paths, then bring them back together. If the light waves had, in the interim, fallen out of step, interference fringes of alternating light and dark bands would be obtained. From the width and number of those fringes, unprecedentedly delicate measurements could be made, comparing the velocity of light rays traveling at right angles to each other.

It was Michelson's intention to use the interferometer to measure the Earth's velocity against the "ether" that was then thought to make up the basic substratum of the universe. If the Earth were traveling through the light-conducting ether, then the speed of the light traveling in the same direction would be expected to be equal to the velocity of light plus the velocity of the Earth, whereas the speed of light traveling at right angles to the Earth's path would be expected to travel only at the velocity of light. His earliest experiments in Berlin showed no interference fringes, however, which seemed to signify that there was no difference in the speed of the light rays and, therefore, no Earth motion relative to the ether.

In 1883 he accepted a position as professor of physics at the Case School of Applied Science in Cleveland and there concentrated his efforts on improving the delicacy of his interferometer experiment. By 1887, with the help of his colleague, American chemist Edward Williams Morley, he was ready to announce the results of what has since come to be called the Michelson-Morley experiment. Those results were still negative; there were no interference fringes and apparently no motion of the Earth relative to the ether.

It was perhaps the most significant negative experiment in the history of science. In terms of classical Newtonian physics, the results were paradoxical. Evidently, the speed of light plus any other added velocity was still equal only to the speed of light. To explain the result of the Michelson-Morley experiment, physics had to be recast on a new and more refined foundation, something that resulted, eventually, in Albert Einstein's formulation of the theory of relativity in 1905.

In 1892 Michelson, after serving as professor of physics at Clark University at Worcester, Mass., from 1889, was appointed professor and the first head of the department of physics at the newly organized University of Chicago, a position he held until his retirement in 1929. From 1923 to 1927 he served as president of the National Academy of Sciences. In 1907 he became the first American ever to receive a Nobel Prize in the sciences, for his spectroscopic and metrological investigations, the first of many honours he was to receive.

Michelson advocated using some particular wavelength of light as a standard of distance (a suggestion generally accepted in 1960) and, in 1893, measured the standard metre in terms of the red light emitted by heated cadmium. His interferometer made it possible for him to determine the width of heavenly objects by matching the light rays from the two sides and noting the interference fringes that resulted. In 1920, using a 6-metre (20-foot) interferometer attached to a 254-cm (100-inch) telescope, he succeeded in measuring the diameter of the star Betelgeuse (Alpha Orionis) as 386,160,000 km (239,948,699 miles; 300 times the diameter of the Sun). This was the first substantially accurate determination of the size of a star.

In 1923 Michelson returned to the problem of the accurate measurement of the velocity of light. In the California mountains he surveyed a 35-km (21.7-mile) pathway between two mountain peaks, determining the distance to an accuracy of less than 2.5 cm (.98 inch). He made use of a special eight-sided revolving mirror and obtained a value of 299,798 km/sec for the velocity of light. To refine matters further, he made use of a long, evacuated tube through which a light beam was reflected back and forth until it had traveled 16 km (9.9 miles) through a vacuum. Michelson died before the results of his final tests could be evaluated, but in 1933 the final figure was announced as 299,774 km/sec, a value less than 20 km/sec higher than the currently accepted value.

SIR ISAAC NEWTON

(b. Dec. 25, 1642 [Jan. 4, 1643, New Style], Woolsthorpe, Lincolnshire, Eng.—d. March 20 [March 31], 1727, London)

English physicist and mathematician Sir Isaac Newton was the culminating figure of the scientific revolution of the 17th century. In optics, his discovery of the composition of white light integrated the phenomena of colours into the science of light and laid the foundation for modern physical optics.

Born in the hamlet of Woolsthorpe, Newton was the only son of a local yeoman, also Isaac Newton, who had died three months before, and of Hannah Ayscough. A tiny and weak baby, Newton was not expected to survive his first day of life, much less 84 years. Deprived of a father before birth, within two years she married a second time.

After his mother was widowed a second time, she determined that her first-born son should manage her now considerable property. It quickly became apparent, however, that this would be a disaster, both for the estate and for Newton. Fortunately, the mistake was recognized, and Newton was sent back to the grammar school in Grantham to prepare for the university. At the school he apparently gained a firm command of Latin but probably received no more than a smattering of arithmetic. By June 1661, he was ready to matriculate at Trinity College, Cambridge.

When Newton arrived in Cambridge in 1661, the movement now known as the scientific revolution was well advanced, and many of the works basic to modern science had appeared. Astronomers from Copernicus to Kepler had elaborated the heliocentric system of the universe. Galileo had proposed the foundations of a new mechanics built on the principle of inertia. Led by Descartes, philosophers had begun to formulate a new conception of nature as an intricate, impersonal, and inert machine.

When Newton received the bachelor's degree in April 1665, on his own, without formal guidance, he had sought out the new philosophy and the new mathematics and made them his own, but he had confined the progress of his studies to his notebooks. Then, in 1665, the plague closed the university, and for most of the following two years he was forced to stay at his home, contemplating at leisure what he had learned. During the plague years Newton laid the foundations of the calculus and extended an earlier insight into an essay, "Of Colours," which contains most of the ideas elaborated in his *Opticks*.

Newton was elected to a fellowship in Trinity College in 1667, after the university reopened. Two years later, Isaac Barrow, Lucasian professor of mathematics, who had transmitted Newton's *De Analysi* to John Collins in London, resigned the chair to devote himself to divinity and recommended Newton to succeed him. He chose the work he had done in optics as the initial topic; during the following three years (1670–72), his lectures developed the essay "Of Colours" into a form which was later revised to become Book One of his *Opticks*.

Beginning with Kepler's *Paralipomena* in 1604, the study of optics had been a central activity of the scientific revolution. Descartes's statement of the sine law of refraction, relating the angles of incidence and emergence at interfaces of the media through which light passes, had added a new mathematical regularity to the science of light, supporting the conviction that the universe is constructed according to mathematical regularities. Descartes had also made light central to the mechanical philosophy of nature;

the reality of light, he argued, consists of motion transmitted through a material medium. Newton fully accepted the mechanical nature of light, although he chose the atomistic alternative and held that light consists of material corpuscles in motion. The corpuscular conception of light was always a speculative theory on the periphery of his optics, however. The core of Newton's contribution had to do with colours. An ancient theory extending back at least to Aristotle held that a certain class of colour phenomena, such as the rainbow, arises from the modification of light, which appears white in its pristine form. Descartes had generalized this theory for all colours and translated it into mechanical imagery. Through a series of experiments performed in 1665 and 1666, in which the spectrum of a narrow beam was projected onto the wall of a darkened chamber, Newton denied the concept of modification and replaced it with that of analysis. Basically, he denied that light is simple and homogeneous—stating instead that it is complex and heterogeneous and that the phenomena of colours arise from the analysis of the heterogeneous mixture into its simple components. The ultimate source of Newton's conviction that light is corpuscular was his recognition that individual rays of light have immutable properties; in his view, such properties imply immutable particles of matter. He held that individual rays (that is, particles of given size) excite sensations of individual colours when they strike the retina of the eye. He also concluded that rays refract at distinct angles— hence, the prismatic spectrum, a beam of heterogeneous rays, i.e., a like incident on one face of a prism, separated or analyzed by the refraction into its component parts— and that phenomena such as the rainbow are produced by refractive analysis. Because he believed that chromatic aberration could never be eliminated from lenses, Newton turned to reflecting telescopes; he constructed the first ever built. The heterogeneity of light has been the foundation of physical optics since his time.

There is no evidence that the theory of colours, fully described by Newton in his inaugural lectures at Cambridge, made any impression, just as there is no evidence that aspects of his mathematics and the content of the *Principia*, also pronounced from the podium, made any impression. Rather, the theory of colours, like his later work, was transmitted to the world through the Royal Society of London, which had been organized in 1660. When Newton was appointed Lucasian professor, his name was probably unknown in the Royal Society; in 1671, however, they heard of his reflecting telescope and asked to see it. Pleased by their enthusiastic reception of the telescope and by his election to the society, Newton volunteered a paper on light and colours early in 1672. On the whole, the paper was also well received, although a few questions and some dissent were heard.

Among the most important dissenters to Newton's paper was Robert Hooke, one of the leaders of the Royal Society who considered himself the master in optics and hence he wrote a condescending critique of the unknown parvenu. One can understand how the critique would have annoyed a normal man. The flaming rage it provoked, with the desire to humiliate Hooke publicly, however, bespoke the abnormal. Newton was unable to confront criticism rationally. Less than a year after submitting the paper, he was so unsettled by the give-and-take of honest discussion that he began to cut his ties, and he withdrew into virtual isolation.

In 1675, during a visit to London, Newton thought he heard Hooke accept his theory of colours. He was emboldened to bring forth a second paper, an examination of the colour phenomena in thin films, which was identical to most of Book Two as it later appeared in the *Opticks*. The purpose of the paper was to explain the colours of solid bodies by showing how light can be analyzed into its components by reflection as well as refraction. His explanation of the colours of bodies has not survived, but the paper was significant in demonstrating for the first time the existence of periodic optical phenomena. He discovered the concentric coloured rings in the thin film of air between a lens and a flat sheet of glass; the distance between these concentric rings (Newton's rings) depends on the increasing thickness of the film of air. In 1704 Newton combined a revision of his optical lectures with the paper of 1675 and a small amount of additional material in his *Opticks*.

A second piece, which Newton had sent with the paper of 1675, provoked new controversy. Entitled "An Hypothesis Explaining the Properties of Light," it was in fact a general system of nature. Hooke apparently claimed that Newton had stolen its content from him, and Newton boiled over again. The issue was quickly controlled, however, by an exchange of formal, excessively polite letters that fail to conceal the complete lack of warmth between the men.

During his final years Newton brought out further editions of his central works. After the first edition of the *Opticks* in 1704, which merely published work done 30 years before, he published a Latin edition in 1706 and a second English edition in 1717–18. In both, the central text was scarcely touched, but he did expand the "Queries" at the end into the final statement of his speculations on the nature of the universe.

ALEKSANDR MIKHAYLOVICH PROKHOROV

(b. July 11, 1916, Atherton, Queensland, Austl. — d. Jan. 8, 2002, Moscow, Russia)

Soviet physicist Aleksandr Mikhaylovich Prokhorov, with Nikolay G. Basov and Charles H. Townes, won the Nobel

Prize for Physics in 1964 for fundamental research in quantum electronics that led to the development of the maser and laser.

Prokhorov's father was involved in revolutionary activities that eventually forced the family to leave Russia. In 1911 they settled in Australia, where Prokhorov was born. Following the overthrow of the tsar (1917), the family returned to Russia in 1923. In 1951 Prokhorov received a doctorate from Leningrad State University and later joined the P.N. Lebedev Physical Institute, Moscow, as a senior associate. In 1952 he and Basov jointly suggested the maser principle of amplifying and emitting parallel electromagnetic waves that are all in phase and all of the same wavelength. By the time they published their suggestion in 1954, Townes had built the first working maser.

In 1954 Prokhorov became head of the institute's Oscillation Laboratory and later professor at Moscow M.V. Lomonosov State University. He wrote a number of fundamental works on the construction of infrared and visible-light lasers and on nonlinear optics. From 1969 to 1978 he served as editor in chief of the *Bolshaya Sovetskaya Entsiklopediya* (*Great Soviet Encyclopedia*). Prokhorov received the Lenin Prize (1959) and two Orders of Lenin as well as various medals.

JOHN WILLIAM STRUTT, 3RD LORD RAYLEIGH

(b. Nov. 12, 1842, Langford Grove, Maldon, Essex, Eng.—d. June 30, 1919, Terling Place, Witham, Essex)

English physical scientist John William Strutt, 3rd Lord Rayleigh, made fundamental discoveries in the fields of acoustics and optics that are basic to the theory of wave propagation in fluids. He received the Nobel Prize for

Lord Rayleigh, engraving by R. Cottot. Courtesy of the International Telecommunication Union, Geneva

Physics in 1904 for his successful isolation of argon, an inert atmospheric gas.

Strutt suffered from poor health throughout his childhood and youth, and it was necessary for him to be withdrawn from both Eton and Harrow. In 1857 he began four years of private study under a tutor. In 1861 Strutt entered Trinity College, Cambridge, from which he was graduated with a B.A. in 1865. He early developed an absorbing interest in both the experimental and mathematical sides of physical science, and in 1868 he purchased an outfit of scientific apparatus for independent research. In his first paper, published in 1869, he gave a lucid exposition of some aspects of the electromagnetic theory of James Clerk Maxwell, the Scottish physicist, in terms of analogies that the average man would understand.

An attack of rheumatic fever shortly after his marriage in 1871 threatened his life for a time. A recuperative trip to Egypt was suggested, and Strutt took his bride, Evelyn Balfour, the sister of Arthur James Balfour, on a houseboat journey up the Nile for an extended winter holiday. On this excursion he began work on his great book, *The Theory of Sound*, in which he examined questions of vibrations and the resonance of elastic solids and gases. The first volume appeared in 1877, followed by a second in 1878, concentrating on acoustical propagation in material media. After some revision during his lifetime and successive reprintings after his death, the work has remained the foremost monument of acoustical literature.

Shortly after returning to England he succeeded to the title of Lord Rayleigh in 1873, on the death of his father. Rayleigh then took up residence at Terling Place, where he built a laboratory adjacent to the manor house. His early papers deal with such subjects as electromagnetism, colour, acoustics, and diffraction gratings. Perhaps his most significant early work was his theory explaining the blue colour of the sky as the result of scattering of sunlight by small particles in the atmosphere. The Rayleigh scattering law, which evolved from this theory, has since become classic in the study of all kinds of wave propagation.

Rayleigh's one excursion into academic life came in the period 1879–84, when he agreed to serve as the second Cavendish professor of experimental physics at Cambridge, in succession to James Clerk Maxwell. There Rayleigh carried out a vigorous research program on the precision determination of electrical standards. A classical series of papers, published by the Royal Society, resulted from this ambitious work. After a tenure of five years he returned to his laboratory at Terling Place, where he carried out practically all his scientific investigations.

A few months after resigning from Cambridge, Rayleigh became secretary of the Royal Society, an administrative post that, during the next 11 years, allowed considerable freedom for research.

Rayleigh's greatest single contribution to science is generally considered to have been his discovery and isolation of argon, one of the rare gases of the atmosphere. Precision measurements of the density of gases conducted by him in the 1880s led to the interesting discovery that the density of nitrogen obtained from the atmosphere is greater by a small though definite amount than is the density of nitrogen obtained from one of its chemical compounds, such as ammonia. Excited by this anomaly and stimulated by some earlier observations of the ingenious but eccentric 18th-century scientist Henry Cavendish on the oxidation of atmospheric nitrogen, Rayleigh decided to explore the possibility that the discrepancy he had discovered resulted from the presence in the atmosphere of a hitherto undetected constituent. After a long and arduous experimental program, he finally succeeded in 1895 in isolating the gas, which was appropriately named argon, from the Greek word meaning "inactive." Rayleigh shared the priority of the discovery with the chemist William Ramsay, who also isolated the new gas, though he began his work after Rayleigh's publication of the original density discrepancy. Shortly before winning the Nobel Prize, Rayleigh wrote the entry on argon for the 10th edition (1902) of the *Encyclopædia Britannica*. In 1904 Rayleigh was awarded the Nobel Prize for Physics; Ramsay received the award in chemistry for his work on argon and other inert elements. The next year Rayleigh was elected president of the Royal Society.

In his later years, when he was the foremost leader in British physics, Rayleigh served in influential advisory capacities in education and government. In 1908 he accepted the post of chancellor of the University of Cambridge, retaining this position until his death. He was also associated with the National Physical Laboratory and government committees on aviation and the treasury. Retaining his mental powers until the end, he worked on scientific papers until five days before his death, on June 30, 1919.

OLE RØMER

(b. Sept. 25, 1644, Århus, Jutland, Den.—d. Sept. 23, 1710, Copenhagen)

Danish astronomer Ole Christensen Rømer demonstrated conclusively that light travels at a finite speed.

Rømer went to Paris in 1672, where he spent nine years working at the Royal Observatory. The observatory's director, Italian-born French astronomer Gian Domenico Cassini, was engaged with a problem that had been studied long before by Galileo: how to use the periodic eclipses of the moons of Jupiter as a universal clock that would be an aid to navigation. (As a satellite goes behind Jupiter, it passes into the shadow of the planet and disappears.) Cassini and his coworkers discovered that the times between successive eclipses of the same satellite (e.g., Io) show an irregularity that is connected with the location of Earth on its own orbit. The time elapsed between successive eclipses of Io becomes shorter as Earth moves closer to Jupiter and becomes longer as Earth and Jupiter draw farther apart. Cassini had considered but then rejected the idea that this might be due to a finite propagation speed for light. In 1676, Rømer announced that the eclipse of Io scheduled for November 9 would be 10 minutes later than the time deduced on the basis of earlier eclipses of the same satellite. When events transpired as he had predicted, Rømer explained that the speed of light was such that it takes light 22 minutes to cross the diameter of Earth's orbit. (Seventeen minutes would be more accurate.) Dutch mathematician Christiaan Huygens, in his *Traité de la lumière* (1690; "Treatise on Light"), used Rømer's ideas to give an actual numerical value for the speed of light that was reasonably close to the value accepted today—though somewhat inaccurate due to an overestimate of the time delay and some error in the then-accepted figure for the diameter of Earth's orbit.

In 1679 Rømer went on a scientific mission to England, where he met Isaac Newton and the astronomers John Flamsteed and Edmond Halley. Upon his return to Denmark in 1681, he was appointed royal mathematician and professor of astronomy at the University of Copenhagen. At the university observatory he set up an instrument with altitude and azimuth circles and a telescope, which accurately measured the position of celestial objects. He also held several public offices, including that of mayor of Copenhagen in 1705.

WILHELM RÖNTGEN

(b. March 27, 1845, Lennep, Prussia [now Remscheid, Ger.]—d. Feb. 10, 1923, Munich, Ger.),

German physicist Wilhelm Conrad Röntgen was a recipient of the first Nobel Prize for Physics, in 1901, for his discovery of X-rays, which heralded the age of modern physics and revolutionized diagnostic medicine.

Röntgen studied at the Polytechnic in Zürich and then was professor of physics at the universities of Strasbourg (1876–79), Giessen (1879–88), Würzburg (1888–1900), and Munich (1900–20). His research also included work on elasticity, capillary action of fluids, specific heats of gases, conduction of heat in crystals, absorption of heat by gases, and piezoelectricity.

In 1895, while experimenting with electric current flow in a partially evacuated glass tube (cathode-ray tube), Röntgen observed that a nearby piece of barium platinocyanide gave off light when the tube was in operation. He theorized that when the cathode rays (electrons) struck the glass wall of the tube, some unknown radiation was formed that traveled across the room, struck the chemical, and caused the fluorescence. Further investigation revealed that paper, wood, and aluminum, among other materials, are transparent to this new form of radiation. He found that it affected photographic plates, and, since it did not noticeably exhibit any properties of light, such as reflection or refraction, he mistakenly thought the rays were unrelated to light. In view of its uncertain nature, he called the phenomenon X-radiation, though it also became known as Röntgen radiation. He took the first X-ray photographs,

Wilhelm Conrad Röntgen. Historia-Photo

of the interiors of metal objects and of the bones in his wife's hand.

ARTHUR L. SCHAWLOW

(b. May 5, 1921, Mount Vernon, N.Y., U.S.—d. April 28, 1999, Palo Alto, Calif.)

American physicist Arthur Leonard Schawlow was a core-cipient, with Nicolaas Bloembergen of the United States and Kai Manne Börje Siegbahn of Sweden, of the 1981 Nobel Prize for Physics for his work in developing the laser and in laser spectroscopy.

As a child, Schawlow moved with his family to Canada. He attended the University of Toronto, receiving his Ph.D. in 1949. In that year he went to Columbia University, where he began collaborating with Charles Townes on the development of the maser (a device that produces and amplifies electromagnetic radiation mainly in the microwave region of the spectrum), the laser (a device similar to the maser that produces an intense beam of light of a single colour), and laser spectroscopy. Schawlow worked on the project that led to the construction of the first working maser in 1953 (for which Townes received a share of the 1964 Nobel Prize for Physics). Schawlow was a research physicist at Bell Telephone Laboratories from 1951 to 1961. In 1958 he and Townes published a paper in which they outlined the working principles of the laser, though the first such working device was built by another American physicist, Theodore Maiman, in 1960. In 1961 Schawlow became a professor at Stanford University. He became a world authority on laser spectroscopy, and he and Bloembergen earned their share of the 1981 Nobel Prize by using lasers to study the interactions of electromagnetic radiation with matter. His works include *Infrared and Optical Masers* (1958) and *Lasers and Their Uses* (1983).

WILLEBRORD VAN ROIJEN SNELL

(b. 1591, Leiden, Neth.—d. Oct. 30, 1626, Leiden)

Dutch astronomer and mathematician Willebrord van Roijen Snell discovered the law of refraction, which relates the degree of the bending of light to the properties of the refractive material. This law is basic to modern geometrical optics.

In 1613 he succeeded his father, Rudolph Snell (1546–1613), as professor of mathematics in the University of Leiden. His *Eratosthenes Batavus* (1617; "Batavian Eratosthenes") contains the account of his method of measuring the Earth. The account of Snell's law of refraction (1621) went unpublished, capturing attention only when the Dutch physicist Christiaan Huygens related Snell's finding in *Dioptrica* (1703).

CHARLES TOWNES

(b. July 28, 1915, Greenville, S.C., U.S.)

American physicist Charles Hard Townes was a joint winner with the Soviet physicists Aleksandr M. Prokhorov and Nikolay G. Basov of the Nobel Prize for Physics in 1964 for his role in the invention of the maser and the laser.

Townes studied at Furman University (B.A., B.S., 1935), Duke University (M.A., 1937), and the California Institute of Technology (Ph.D., 1939). In 1939 he joined the technical staff of Bell Telephone Laboratories, Inc., where he worked until 1948, when he joined the faculty of Columbia University. Three years later he conceived the idea of using ammonia molecules to amplify microwave radiation. Townes and two students completed the first such device in December 1953 and gave it the name *maser*, an acronym for "microwave amplification by stimulated emission of radiation." In 1958 Townes and A.L. Schawlow showed that it was possible to construct a similar device using light—i.e., a laser.

From 1959 to 1961 Townes served as vice president and director of research of the Institute for Defense Analyses, Washington, D.C. He then was appointed provost and professor of physics at Massachusetts Institute of Technology, Cambridge. In 1967 he became a professor at the University of California, Berkeley, where he initiated a program of radio and infrared astronomy leading to the discovery of complex molecules (ammonia and water) in the interstellar medium. He became professor emeritus in 1986.

THOMAS YOUNG

(b. June 13, 1773, Milverton, Somerset, Eng.—d. May 10, 1829, London)

English physician and physicist Thomas Young established the principle of interference of light and thus resurrected the century-old wave theory of light. He was also an Egyptologist who helped decipher the Rosetta Stone.

In 1799 Young set up a medical practice in London. His primary interest was in sense perception, and, while still a medical student, he discovered the way in which the lens of the eye changes shape to focus on objects at differing distances. He discovered the cause of astigmatism in 1801, the same year he turned to the study of light.

By allowing light to pass through two closely set pinholes onto a screen, Young found that the light beams spread apart and overlapped, and, in the area of overlap, bands of bright light alternated with bands of darkness. With this demonstration of the interference of light, Young definitely established the wave nature of light. He used his new wave theory of light to explain the colours of thin films (such as soap bubbles), and, relating colour to wavelength, he calculated the approximate wavelengths of the seven colours recognized by Newton. In 1817 he proposed that light waves were transverse (vibrating at right angles to the direction of travel), rather than longitudinal (vibrating in the direction of travel) as had long been assumed, and thus explained polarization, the alignment of light waves to vibrate in the same plane.

Young's work was disparaged by most English scientists: any opposition to a theory of Newton's was unthinkable. It was only with the work of the French physicists Augustin J. Fresnel and François Arago that Young's wave theory finally achieved acceptance in Europe.

Young also studied the problem of colour perception and proposed that there is no need for a separate mechanism in the eye for every colour, it being sufficient to have three—one each for blue, green, and red. Developed later by the German physicist Hermann von Helmholtz, this theory is known as the Young–Helmholtz three-colour theory.

Having become interested in Egyptology, Young began studying the texts of the Rosetta Stone in 1814. After obtaining additional hieroglyphic writings from other sources, he succeeded in providing a nearly accurate translation within a few years and thus contributed heavily to deciphering the ancient Egyptian language.

Young also did work on measuring the size of molecules, surface tension in liquids, and on elasticity. He was the first to give the word *energy* its scientific significance, and Young's modulus, a constant in the mathematical equation describing elasticity, was named in his honour.

CONCLUSION

The two main subjects of this book, sound and light, are waves. Sound is a longitudinal wave that alternately compresses and expands the material through which it passes. Like waves in other media, sound can diffract when it passes through a small opening. Sound is refracted when it passes from one type of material to another and is reflected when it bounces off an object.

We experience sound in many different ways. Music is often sound that arises in an air column or from a standing wave on a string. Resonances inside the vocal tubes give rise to harmonic peaks called formants, which are key parts of speech.

The ear is capable of experiencing sounds with a range of a factor of one thousand in frequency and with a range of a factor of one trillion in intensity. What the ear hears is mediated by the environment in which the sound happens. The studies of these environmental effects is part of the science of acoustics, which studies sound. Although how sound is transmitted and absorbed in a room was a consideration of architectural design for millennia, it was only in the 20th century, with the discovery of the concept of reverberation time, that acoustics in the built environment was truly understood.

The second subject of this book was light, which is usually defined as electromagnetic waves that can be seen by the human eye. However, the totality of the electromagnetic spectrum stretches from the longest radio waves, which have wavelengths of hundreds of metres, to the shortest gamma rays, which have wavelengths of less than one-hundreth of one-billionth of a metre.

The nature of light was a long-contested subject in physics. In the 17th century Isaac Newton promulgated a theory in which light was made of small particles. However, in 1801, Thomas Young was able to show that light was a wave by producing constructive and destructive interference in light that passed through two slits. In the 1860s, in one of the great achievements of physics, James Clerk Maxwell presented four equations that described electric and magnetic fields. These equations had solutions that were waves that traveled at the speed of light.

Just as the science of acoustics is concerned with sound, the science of optics is concerned with light. Optics has led to the fibre-optic bundles that carry most of the world's information, the mirrors in telescopes that study galaxies at the edge of the universe, and the holograms that can form a three-dimensional image of an object.

GLOSSARY

acoustic Of or relating to sound.

amplitude The maximum displacement of a point on a wave from its rest position.

aperture The opening of a lens, such as that of a camera or the eye.

decibel A measurement of the intensity of sound.

diffraction The apparent bending of waves around small obstacles and the spreading out of waves past small openings.

Doppler effect A change in the frequency of sound or light waves due to a change in the position of the source or destination of the wave.

electromagnetism A fundamental physical force that is responsible for interactions between charged particles.

frequency Number of oscillations per second of a wave.

harmonic A wave with a frequency that is a multiple of that of another wave.

interference The meeting of two waves, causing changes in wave amplitude.

laser A beam of concentrated electromagnetic radiation.

light Electromagnetic radiation that is visible to the human eye.

linear Of or relating to a straight line.

medium The substance through which a wave travels.

microwave Electromagnetic radiation with a wavelength between 1 millimetre and 1 metre.

optics The scientific study of light.

perpendicular Two lines or planes (or a line and a plane) are considered perpendicular (or orthogonal) to each other if they are at right angles to each other.

pitch The frequency of a sound relative to other sounds.

polarization A property of electromagnetic radiation in which the electric field is confined to a specific direction or rotates about the direction of travel.

radiation The emission of energy.

reflection The act of a wave bouncing off a surface in a linear direction.

refraction Change in a wave's direction caused by its passage through a different medium and the resultant change in the wave's velocity.

sonic boom The sound made when a shockwave—created from an object going from supersonic to subsonic speed—reaches the ground.

sound Longitudinal waves of compressions and rarefactions that propagate through an elastic medium.

superposition The addition of two waves.

wave An oscillating pattern in which energy travels.

wavelength The distance between crests of a wave.

BIBLIOGRAPHY

SOUND

An enormous amount of physical data on such topics as the velocity of sound and the elastic properties of materials, as well as surveys of important theories in the field, are found in the following reference books: Herbert L. Anderson (ed.), *A Physicist's Desk Reference* (1989); and Rita G. Lerner and George L. Trigg (eds.), *Encyclopedia of Physics*, 2nd ed. (1991). For biographies of scientists who worked in the field of acoustics, see Charles Coulston Gillispie (ed.), *Dictionary of Scientific Biography*, 16 vol. (1970–80).

A most important modern work on the physiology of hearing is Georg von Békésy, *Experiments in Hearing* (1960, reprinted 1980). An excellent survey of psychoacoustics is provided in Brian C.J. Moore, *An Introduction to the Psychology of Hearing*, 3rd ed. (1989).

ACOUSTICS

Comprehensive discussions of the propagation and perception of sound, many containing sections on the ear, on sound recording and reproduction, and on architectural acoustics, are offered in the following books, which require almost no mathematical background: John R. Pierce, *The Science of Musical Sound*, rev. ed. (1992); Michael J. Moravcsik, *Musical Sound: An Introduction to the Physics of Music* (1987); and Ian Johnston, *Measured Tones: The Interplay of Physics and Music* (1989). A somewhat higher level of mathematics is needed for the comprehensive Arthur H. Benade, *Fundamentals of Musical Acoustics* (1976, reissued

1990), a relatively sophisticated classic in the field; and Thomas D. Rossing, *The Science of Sound*, 2nd ed. (1990), covering virtually every area of acoustics.

Important advanced texts include the following classics: Leo L. Beranek, *Acoustics* (1954, reissued 1986). More recent advanced comprehensive studies are Allan D. Pierce, *Acoustics: An Introduction to Its Physical Principles and Applications* (1981, reissued 1989); Donald E. Hall, *Basic Acoustics* (1987); and S.N. Sen, *Acoustics, Waves and Oscillations* (1990).

Leo L. Beranek (ed.), *Noise and Vibration Control*, rev. ed. (1988), contains excellent sections applying to concert halls; and 87 concert halls are surveyed in the illustrated work by Richard H. Talaske, Ewart A. Wetherill, and William J. Cavanaugh (eds.), *Halls for Music Performance: Two Decades of Experience, 1962–1982* (1982).

LIGHT

An excellent general science book on the nature of light and special visual effects is David K. Lynch and William Livingston, *Color and Light in Nature*, 2nd ed. (2001). Three excellent histories of the study of light and its role in human experience are David Park, *The Fire Within the Eye* (1997); Sidney Perkowitz, *Empire of Light: A History of Discovery in Science and Art* (1998); and Arthur Zajonc, *Catching the Light* (1995).

A textbook aimed at nonscience majors and requiring minimal mathematics is Thomas Rossing and Christopher Chiaverina, *Light Science: Physics and the Visual Arts* (1999). Technical presentations of the science of optics can be found in the comprehensive treatise by Eugene Hecht, *Optics*, 4th ed. (2001). An introduction to the quantum mechanical nature of light is Richard Feynman, *QED: The Strange Theory of Light and Matter* (1986).

ELECTROMAGNETIC RADIATION

Accounts of the historical development of electromagnetic theories may be found in I. Bernard Cohen, *Revolution in Science* (1985); and Thomas S. Kuhn, *Black-Body Theory and the Quantum Discontinuity, 1894–1912* (1978, reprinted 1987). Ivan Tolstoy, *James Clerk Maxwell* (1981), recounts the life of this pivotal figure, as well as his theory and its ramifications. Wave–particle dualism is addressed by S. Diner et al. (eds.), *The Wave–Particle Dualism* (1984). Quantum electrodynamics is discussed in Paul Davies (ed.), *The New Physics* (1989).

LASERS

James P. Harbison and Robert E. Nahory, *Lasers: Harnessing the Atom's Light* (1998, reissued 2001), contains a nontechnical explanation of laser principles, a bit of history, and some applications. Jeff Hecht, *Understanding Lasers: An Entry-Level Guide*, 2nd ed. (1994), is particularly suitable for hobbyists. C. Breck Hitz, J.J. Ewing, and Jeff Hecht (eds.), *Introduction to Laser Technology*, 3rd ed. (2001), is an excellent introductory textbook.

Joan Lisa Bromberg, *The Laser in America, 1950–1970* (1991), shows the wide-ranging academic, industrial, and government research that led to the development of the laser and its applications and also presents an evenhanded account of the dispute over conceptual credit for the invention of the laser. Theodore H. Maiman, *The Laser Odyssey* (2000), is a firsthand account by the builder of the first laser. Charles H. Townes, *How the Laser Happened: Adventures of a Scientist* (1999, reissued 2002), presents the author's claims to have invented the laser in addition to the maser. Nick Taylor, *Laser: The Inventor, the*

Nobel Laureate, and the Thirty-Year Patent War (2000), takes Gordon Gould's side in the dispute over the invention of the laser.

OPTICS

There are many journals and hundreds of books covering the general field of optics; some of the more familiar books include Max Born and Emil Wolf, *Principles of Optics*, 6th ed. (1980, reissued 1993); and Eugene Hecht and Alfred Zajac, *Optics*, 2nd ed. (1987). Walter T. Welford, *Useful Optics* (1991), is a succinct review of principles basic to implementing optical tools.

Recommended books on the subject of information theory are Ajoy Ghatak and K. Thyagarajan, *Optical Electronics* (1989); and Robert Jones and Catherine Wykes, *Holographic and Speckle Interferometry*, 2nd ed. (1989).

INDEX

A

Abbe, Ernst Karl, 226, 274
acoustics, 57–68
  amplifying, recording, and
    reproducing, 63
  architectural, 15, 57, 63–68
  definition of, 57
  early experimentation, 57–60
  modern advances, 60–62
acoustic shadows, 17, 68
Airy, George Biddell, 228, 287–288
Airy disk, 228, 229, 288
Alembert, Jean Le Rond d', 60
Ampère, André-Marie, 114
Arago, François, 108, 298, 331
architectural acoustics, 15, 57,
  63–68
  acoustic criteria, 65–67
  acoustic problems, 67–68
  reverberation time, 64–65
Aristotle, 58, 317
Ashkin, Arthur, 221
astigmatism, 255–256, 288, 330
attenuation of sound, 13–15

B

Bacon, Roger, 84
Barkla, Charles Glover, 186
Bartholin, Erasmus, 125, 287,
  288–289
Basov, Nikolay Gennadiyevich,
  199–200, 289–290, 319,
  320, 329

Békésy, Georg von, 62
"bell-in-vacuum" experiment,
  59–60, 63
Berliner, Emil, 63
Bernoulli, Daniel, 60
blackbody radiation, 136–137,
  154, 155, 165
Bloembergen, Nicolaas, 221, 328
Boethius, 58
Bohr atomic model, 143–144, 187
Bohr, Niels, 143–144, 187
Boyle, Robert, 59
Bragg, William Henry, 187
Bragg, William Lawrence, 187
Brewster, David, 130, 290–291
Brewster's law, 129–130
Broglie, Louis de, 140
Buffon, Georges-Louis, 250

C

Cassini, Gian Domenico,
  324–325
cavitation, 71, 74
Chladni, Ernst, 37, 61
chromatic aberration, 239–240
circular and spherical waves, 11–27
  attenuation, 13–15
  diffraction, 15–17
  Doppler effect, 25–26
  impedance, 20–23
  interference, 23–25
  reflection, 19–20
  refraction, 17–19
  sonic booms, 26–27

photons and, 137–139
quantum mechanics and,
  139–143

R

radio waves, 117, 168–173, 223
rainbow, formation of, 97,
  110–112
Rayleigh, Baron (John William
  Strutt), 21, 62, 71, 109, 130,
  134, 226, 229, 320–324
Rayleigh limit, 229
Rayleigh scattering, 130, 323
ray theories in ancient world,
  83–84
ray-tracing methods, 229–234
  graphical, 230–231
  trigonometrical, 231–234
reflecting prisms, 245–247
reflection, law of, 89–90
reflection and refraction of light,
  89–94
reflection of sound, 19–20
refraction, law of, 90–92, 329
refraction of sound, 17–19
resolution and the Airy disk,
  228–229
Reynolds, Osborne, 71
Ritter, Johann Wilhelm, 181
Rømer, Ole, 85, 119, 324–326
Ronchi, Vasco, 225
Röntgen, Wilhelm, 185, 186, 195,
  326–328
Rutherford, Ernest, 196

S

Sabine, Wallace, 62, 64
Sauveur, Joseph, 59

Savart, Félix, 58
Savart's disk, 58–59
scattering, 159–160
Schawlow, Arthur L., 200, 201,
  221, 328, 329–330
Seidel, L.P., 252
Seidel sums, 251–254
Seurat, Georges, 109–110
Smith, Robert, 236
Snell, Willebrord van Roijen, 85,
  230, 329
Snell's law, 85, 90–92
Snitzer, Elias, 208
solids, speed of sound in, 10–11
sonar, 72, 76
sonic booms, 26–27
sound, 1–56
  definition of, 1–2
  speed of, 1–11
sound absorption, 14–15
sound spectrograph, the, 42–43
sounds waves, types of, 1–2
spherical aberration, 254
standing waves, 27–41, 61
  in air columns, 33–37
  measuring techniques, 36–37
  in nonharmonic systems, 38–41
  in solid rods, 37
  in stretched strings, 28–33
steady-state waves and spectral
  analysis, 41–47
  generation by musical
    instruments, 43–45
  human vice, 45–46
  noise, 46–47
  sound spectrograph, 42–43
Steinheil, C.A. von, 243
superposition, principle of, 12,
  100, 103